Savoring Mexico

WILLIAMS-SONOMA

Savoring Mexico

Recipes and Reflections on Mexican Cooking

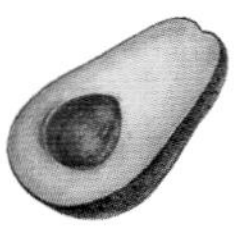

Recipes and Text
MARILYN TAUSEND

General Editor
CHUCK WILLIAMS

Recipe Photography
NOEL BARNHURST

Travel Photography
STEVEN ROTHFELD
IGNACIO URQUIZA

Illustrator
MARLENE McLOUGHLIN

Contents

MONTERREY
TAMAULIPAS
TAMPICO
VERACRUZ
VERACRUZ
QUERÉTARO
HIDALGO
CIUDAD DE MÉXICO
D.F.
TLAXCALA
MÉXICO
MORELOS
PUEBLA
GUERRERO
OAXACA
OAXACA
TABASCO
CHIAPAS
CAMPECHE
YUCATÁN
CHICHÉN ITZÁ
CANCÚN
QUINTANA ROO
BELIZE
GUATEMALA
GOLFO
DE TEHUANTEPEC
100°
98°
96°
94°
92°
90°
88°
31°
29°
27°
25°
23°
21°
19°
17°
15°
13°

INTRODUCCION

The Mexican Table

A TREE-SHROUDED COASTAL VILLAGE alongside a sluggish, swollen river, La Antigua drowses contentedly all week, then on Sunday comes to life as dozens of large families from nearby communities arrive to celebrate this day of rest with food, drink, and music. It was here, almost five centuries ago, that Hernán Cortés and his 508 fighting men, 100 sailors, and 4 priests came ashore. With a conscripted labor force made up of local Totonac Indians, they constructed a church, their first homes, and the seat of government, naming it all Villa Rica de la Vera Cruz (Rich Town of the True Cross). Today, after savoring a bowl of tiny blue crabs in a chile-enlivened broth at a riverside restaurant and listening to traditional refrains plucked on the harps of native troubadours, I take a walk to a roofless brick ruin held together by soft mosses and tangled vines—the only remnants of that historic site.

Just as Cortés started his conquest of the New World in what is now the state of Veracruz, it is my starting place as I take you on a culinary journey. As did he and his followers, we will travel across this land of towering peaks, fertile plains, pine forests, impenetrable marshlands, dense jungles, and barren wastelands. His was a journey that conquered a highly sophisticated civilization and, in doing so, transformed the culinary history, first of Mexico and then of the world. On my explorations, the reverse has been, and continues to

Left: The interior of the eighteenth-century Templo de San Francisco, in the town of Acatepec, is covered with images of celestial onlookers. **Above top:** The rich legacy of Maya civilization and culture is evident all over the Yucatán peninsula, from the sprawling archaeological sites at Chichén Itzá and Uxmal to the colorful embroidery that edges the traditional *huipiles* worn by the local women. **Above:** Slender, shiny, scarlet árbol chiles, found in nearly every *mercado,* contribute their smoky, searing, tart-sweet heat primarily to table sauces.

be, true. The people, their culture, and their food have conquered me. It is that experience I want to share with you.

Not far south of Veracruz, the Olmecs, oldest of Mexico's ancient civilizations, first forged a pattern of culture that has endured for over twenty-five hundred years. All that remains visible of their accomplishments are massive basalt heads left behind in the jungle, but their more important legacy was the cultivation of life-giving maize (corn), a knowledge that has proved integral to every succeeding civilization in Mexico. Early on, the indigenous people practiced a process of softening the kernels in water with lime or wood ashes that not only made the maize easier to grind but also enhanced the protein value, to produce a truly sustaining food.

This was an agricultural culture based on maize and beans, a combination that provided an almost perfect protein diet. When squash, tomatoes, and fiery chiles were added, along with wild greens and tropical fruits, eating was both nourishing and a pleasure. One of the joys of Mexico is its diverse and delicious fruits, from the more commonplace papaya and pineapple to the lesser-known *pitaya,* mamey, *zapote,* and *guanábana.* To supply themselves with animal food, the Aztecs, Mayas, and other native groups had domesticated the turkey, the Muscovy duck, and a now-extinct species of dog and looked to the abundance of wild deer, birds, peccary, iguana, and armadillo, as well as seafood and numerous insects and larvae.

Throughout my years of poking around in more remote areas of the country, I have sampled many of these indigenous ingredients, and although a few I could do without, many

Right: During a procession for El Día de la Candelaria, a priest sings, prays, and tosses handfuls of long-stemmed white flowers into the Rio Papaloapan below. **Below:** Rows of blue agave are cultivated for tequila production.

I truly enjoy. I admit that just one bite of a taco filled with live, wiggling *jumiles,* small, greenish triangular-shaped insects, a delicacy in the highlands of Guerrero, was enough. But a cooked tomato sauce using toasted, ground beetles for flavor was quite tasty. In a Hidalgo restaurant, the specialty on the menu was fat, well-salted, fried *gusanos de maguey,* the larvae of an insect that tunnels into the heart of the maguey plant. Another time, I found the sweet *escamoles,* or eggs, of a certain species of ant on the menu. Everyone who walks through Oaxaca's markets has seen the rows of village women sitting in the doorways calling out, *"chapulines, chapulines,"* referring to the baskets of tiny grasshoppers caught in the fields, fried with chiles, and sold to be eaten in tacos. Once the means of survival during times when crops failed, these unusual foods are now considered delicacies and are served in upscale restaurants.

Mexican cuisine as it is known today began with the advent of the Spaniards, who brought with them twenty-eight generations of Moorish domination. Livestock and poultry, rice and wheat, onions and garlic, citrus fruits, sugarcane, and spices from the Far East, when merged with the foodstuffs of the conquered land, forever changed the diet of the indigenous peoples and Spanish settlers alike. Of special importance was the role of the convent, where the nuns used their talents to transform

Above top: Mexico City is a lively metropolis with cutting-edge modern buildings, colonial architecture, peerless museums, and over 23 million inhabitants. **Above:** Large commercial producers turn out tens of thousands of corn tortillas daily, but the daily bread of Mexico is at its earthy best when made by hand and cooked on a blistering-hot *comal.* **Right:** White cotton clothing helps keep workers cool under the hot Yucatán sun.

these ingredients into exotic offerings to please visiting dignitaries. Complex dishes from moles to desserts soon found their way onto the tables of aristocratic Spanish families and now are served in homes and restaurants in every part of the country, but especially in Puebla and Oaxaca, where the influence of the church was greatest.

As I crisscrossed this country of diverse topography and cultures, I became aware of the considerable regional distinctions in cooking methods and ingredients. At a roadside *barbacoa* stand in Tlaxcala or Puebla, the fare is likely pieces of lamb coated with a chile-rich *adobo,* marinated with pulque, wrapped in the thin outer membrane of giant maguey leaves, and buried in hot coals. In the cattle country of Coahuila, the *barbacoa* is the whole head of a steer, while in Oaxaca, it is young goat or lamb anointed with *mezcal* and wrapped in banana leaves, and in Yucatán, pork flavored with a garlicky mixture of *achiote,* spices, and the juice of bitter oranges.

Modern transportation and refrigeration have broken down most of the natural barriers

Above top: The grand seventeenth-century cathedral at Morelia is a visual feast of pink stone walls, baroque twin towers, and cupolas covered with Talavera tiles. **Above:** Crisp, cooling radishes not only garnish plates of *flautas, frijoles refritos,* and spicy meat-filled tacos but also are at the heart of a lively Christmastime festival in Oaxaca known as La Noche de Rábanos (Night of the Radishes).

that created these regional dishes. Television, newspapers, and magazines tell of other ways of cooking. Markets in the larger cities carry ingredients from throughout the country, and regional restaurants thrive far from their roots. Cooks take traditional ingredients and use them in new ways, transforming generations-old recipes into contemporary classics.

Still, the cyclic nature of food persists. What is placed on the table is based on the seasons of the year. The local produce dictates the menu: wild greens in the spring, fresh corn tamales and mushroom dishes in the rainy season, *chiles en nogada* in early autumn when walnuts are fresh and pomegranates ripe.

Just as dependable an influence is the religious calendar. Food has always played an important part in the ceremonial practices of the Mexican people, and the numerous Catholic holy days give additional reasons for celebrations, each with its own special dishes. Lent is distinguished by meatless creations: soups of dried shrimp, vegetable fritters, cheese-stuffed chiles, and, for one special day, the raisin-and-nut-filled bread pudding, *capirotada,* for a sweet ending. The most Mexican of all holidays is the Day of the Dead, when the spirits of family members who have died return to celebrate with the living. They are welcomed home to feast at an altar bedecked with tamales and other favorite foods.

At Christmas, families serve the classic *bacalao,* a festive dish of chiles, olives, tomatoes, and little boiled potatoes combined with salt cod in a superbly flavored stew. Relatives come together to make tamales. Classic moles appear, as well as a version of *ensalada de Noche Buena,* a colorful Christmas salad with beets, jicama, pomegranate seeds, and other fruits. On Twelfth Night, January 6, the ring-shaped *rosca de reyes,* or king's cake, is shared, accompanied with hot chocolate or flavored *atoles.*

Every village and town has its own saint's day, which usually means an extended fiesta. In Xico, which stands at the center of the highland coffee-growing region of Veracruz, the villagers revel in observing the feast day of their patron saint, Mary Magdalene. With candles to light their way, gaily dressed celebrants stream from their homes and gather in great numbers in front of the ocher-tinted church. At midnight on July 22, when the feast day begins, "Las Mañanitas" is sung to their beloved lady. The festivities continue during the day, with people thronging the colorfully festooned streets, listening to music, dancing, and, of course, eating. The mole is sweetened with prunes, and dishes are made with *longaniza* sausage.

The highlight of the day comes when the ancient aerial dance of the Totonacs is performed on a towering pole that rises permanently in front of the church. Not until the last haunting notes of the flute music float away and the four brilliantly feathered dancers have completed the circular descent from the top of the pole, revolving as birds might fly, does the incongruity of a pagan ritual being performed for a Christian saint come briefly to mind. Somehow, here it fits.

This is a journey without end, for the cuisine of Mexico is ever changing. The one constant you will find is the important relation between food and family and friends. A meal is not just nourishment but a celebration of being alive—a celebration to be shared.

Below: A whimsical bronze sculpture by renowned Mexican artist Adolfo Riestra receives a daily dusting in the lemony light of early morning in Acapulco. From the earliest Olmec carvings to the vivid paintings of Frida Kahlo, Mexico's artistic heritage is justifiably celebrated and preserved—Mexico City alone offers visitors and residents no fewer than seventy museums.

ANTOJITOS, BOTANAS, Y ENTRADAS

These are small creations—the foods of the street, the marketplace, the beginning of the meal.

Preceding pages: Mexico produces a variety of fresh and aged cheeses, encased in woven or wooden boxes, knotted into milky rounds, or carved into crumbly chunks. **Above top:** Potent *mezcal* matures inside colorful hand-painted barrels. **Above:** In the small Jaliscan town of Tequila, famous for producing the powerful libation of the same name, testing a *tequila añejo* for the proper smooth, mellow character is serious business. **Right:** The *piña,* the heart of the maguey plant, will be steam-cooked, crushed, fermented, and distilled twice before being bottled and sold as tequila.

MY HUSBAND, FREDRIC, and I were on our way to Jalapa, the capital of Veracruz. About ten miles (17 km) from our goal, steam began billowing out from under the hood of our car, and that ominous warning light came on. At the very least we were out of water, and we didn't even have mineral water with us. Fredric, reacting instantly, thumbed a lift into the nearest town, leaving me on the side of the narrow two-lane highway.

It was a startlingly beautiful place to be stranded. As I stood looking about, the low drifting fog vanished. The suddenly bright sun spotlighted Mount Orizaba, at 18,500 feet (6,150 m) Mexico's highest peak, a cobalt-white tower against a blue background sky. A solitary barefoot woman walked by me, smiling shyly, with an empty flat basket balanced on her head. In about an hour she returned, laden with market goods and clearly concerned about me. Undaunted by my limited ability to explain my predicament, she just shook her head, laughing when finally she understood that my husband had gone to town for water for the car, and pointed to a

Below: On the streets of La Paz, capital of Baja California Sur and a lively commercial port, a vendor serves up a stack of *tacos de salpicón de pescado* loaded with crunchy cabbage, tomato slices, and freshly grilled fish. **Below bottom:** The paddles of the nopal cactus lend a pleasing texture to salads, salsas, and bean dishes. **Right:** Grinding corn the old-fashioned way—on a large, rectangular slab of basalt called a *metate*—for making tortillas is still a daily ritual in many parts of Mexico.

bubbly creek just down the bank. María, as she told me her name was, then opened a smaller basket lined with a cheerfully embroidered cloth and shared with me two of the most delicious *gorditas de frijol* I have ever had—thick and chewy, the *masa* made with black beans, savory with onions and epazote, and accented with jalapeño chile. She then handed me one of her sweet avocados to finish off my meal and was off down the road to her home in a nearby village. We could understand only a few of each other's words, but she knew I was distressed and she comforted me in the way she knew best—by sharing her meal.

Gorditas are just one of a multitude of *antojitos,* those little corn *masa* creations that the Mexican people eat whenever the hankering is upon them. They are the foods of the street, the foods of the marketplace, and the foods that start many a meal in the *fondas* and restaurants of the country.

For over five thousand years, maize (corn) has been central to Mexican cuisine. The whole culture is related to its growth, harvest, and consumption, and then the eternal cycle starts again with the planting of a cache of kernels reserved for ensuring the next crop.

It was from the very wet, very hot womb of what are now Veracruz and Tabasco that Mesoamerica's first civilization, the Olmecs, emerged. The success of the Olmec and the Maya cultures that followed is explained by their ability to grow corn. Indeed, whenever I am traveling in one of the daily torrential downpours that mark every summer rainy season, I see the farmers cultivating their hillside milpas (corn plots) in the same time-honored, back-wrenching method of their ancestors. In the early spring, they plant their fields. Using a pointed stick, they make a hole in the ground and drop in seeds, one by one. Some of the corn is picked while still tender, but most is allowed to mature and dry. In late November, I see young boys and their fathers collecting the ears to be stored until made into *masa* or *pozole,* with enough kernels left to plant and start the cycle once more.

Masa is the basis of most *antojitos:* the dried kernels of corn are boiled with slaked lime (the mineral, not the fruit) to remove the skins and enrich the grain. The processed corn is then ground and ready to make into a seemingly endless list of dishes.

Perhaps the most important role for *masa* is in the making of the tortilla, both the bread of

Left: Large bundles of leafy green cilantro (fresh coriander), harvested from fertile soil near the historic city of Puebla, will end up in the region's famous salsas, soups, tacos, and other specialties. **Below:** Jewel-like kernels of dried corn are sold both loose and still on the cob. **Below bottom:** Countless crates of smooth white melons await transportation to the nearest marketplace.

Above top: Cinco de Mayo celebrations are especially festive in Puebla, where vividly costumed participants on stilts reenact the failed French invasion of 1862. **Above:** Elaborate inlaid stonework and stylized figures, the latter believed to represent Chac, the all-important rain god, cover the ruins at Uxmal, once a major Maya center of astrology, architecture, and engineering. **Right top:** A Porfidio tequila packaging plant in Puerto Vallarta exports its 100 percent blue agave tequila in bottles containing miniature glass cacti. **Right bottom:** The cafés of Morelia, capital of Michoacán and a bustling university town, are perfect places to enjoy a cold beer and conversation.

Mexico and the primary utensil. Pressed into a circular shape and quickly cooked on a *comal,* the tortilla is used to scoop beans, stews, and moles from the plate to the mouth. If fried crisp, it becomes the plate itself—a tostada. In Baja California it may be topped with ceviche, while in Campeche it is spread with a black bean paste and pickled red onions. If the tortilla is folded over cheese with a pungent leaf of epazote for added flavor, it is the classic quesadilla, or it may have a more exotic filling. If the tortilla is rolled or folded around almost anything edible, it becomes a soft taco.

At Camineros, a *taquería* near my hotel in Mexico City, I order *tacos de bistec y queso* from one of the cooks behind the counter, along with a generous portion of *cebolla asada.* Thin slices of beef are seared, cheese is softened on top, and it is all piled on top of a stack of small hot tortillas, so you can make your own tacos. I add salsa, fold in some of the grilled smoky-sweet knob (spring) onions, complete with green stalks, and have one of the most delectable foods imaginable. If a taco is stuffed and fried, it becomes a *taco dorado;* if it is rolled first, it is a *flauta.*

A whole other world of *antojitos* is made by fashioning *masa* into a variety of free-form shapes and serving them with different toppings. Every region has its own specialty, and they go by a confusing array of names. The tiny dish-shaped *sopes* from Colima, filled with shredded beef in a fiery cumin-flavored salsa, may have little resemblance to similarly named ones from Jalisco. *Panuchos* may be stuffed with succulent shark and vinegar-soused red onions in Campeche, but in nearby Yucatán they carry only black beans. There are *chalupas, molotes,* and *memelas, huaraches, tlacoyas,* and *polkanes.* Different sizes and different shapes—and all are wonderful tastes to explore.

The *antojitos* of northern Mexico differ from those of their southern neighbors. This land had no early culinary traditions to draw on, as only bands of nomadic tribes moved about hunting, fishing, and gathering plants and fruits for survival. When the conquering Spanish moved north, they brought wheat with them and the beginning of today's vast cattle herds. It is only in these northern states that flour tortillas replace those of corn. The beef, thinly sliced and dried to become *carne seca, cecina,* or the shredded *machaca,* is, along with cheese, the base for most regional *antojitos.* Chihuahua cheese cut from enormous wheels made by the local Mennonite communities is a favorite for stuffing quesadillas. Such simple foods reflect the life of the range.

Then there are *tortas,* a tasty layering of meats, cheeses, and vegetables, all served up on a crusty roll. Ceviche or seafood cocktails, small portions of meats, and fanciful vegetable dishes are among the most common *entradas,* or appetizers, served to start a meal. And not to be overlooked are *botanas*—those tidbits that invite one to sit and snack for hours while drinking and talking to friends. Among them are bowls of salted nuts and seeds, various dips to scoop up with *totopos,* and fiery pickled chiles and vegetables that soon become addictive.

All of these dishes are foods that can be eaten casually any time of the day or night—foods designed for instant gratification.

Jalisco

Flautas de Pollo Deshebrado

crispy tortilla flutes stuffed with shredded chicken

The secret to making these long rolled tacos is the raspadas, *tortillas that have had the top layer literally rasped off and discarded, before they are wrapped around a tasty filling and fried until crisp. If you do not want to spend the effort to make them extra thin, you can still prepare delicious* flautas *using whole tortillas.*

FILLING

2 chicken breast halves

4 cups (32 fl oz/1 l) water

¼ white onion

1 tablespoon safflower or canola oil

½ cup (2 oz/60 g) chopped white onion

3 serrano chiles, chopped

1 clove garlic, minced

1 large, ripe tomato, finely chopped, or 1 can (7 oz/220 g) diced tomatoes, drained

sea salt to taste

TORTILLAS

12 purchased thin corn tortillas, 6–7 inches (15–18 cm) in diameter

peanut or safflower oil for frying

ACCOMPANIMENTS

2 cups (6 oz/185 g) thinly shredded cabbage seasoned, if desired, with juice of 1 lime (optional)

Avocado Salsa (page 190)

1 cup (8 fl oz/250 ml) crema *(page 248)*

12 radishes, sliced or cut into flowers (optional)

Pasilla and Arbol Chile Salsa (page 178)

To make the filling, place the chicken in a large saucepan and add the water and onion piece. Bring to a boil, reduce the heat to medium, cover, and simmer until the chicken is cooked through, 15–20 minutes. Remove the chicken and set aside to cool, reserving the broth for another use. Remove the skin from the chicken and discard. Shred the meat, discarding the bones.

In a frying pan over medium heat, warm the oil. Add the chopped onion, chiles, and garlic and sauté just until softened, about 3 minutes. Raise the heat to medium-high, add the tomato, and cook, stirring occasionally, until the color of the tomato deepens and the excess moisture is absorbed, several minutes longer. Remove from the heat and stir in the shredded chicken and salt. Set aside to cool.

If making the *raspadas* (see note), heat a hot, dry *comal,* griddle, or large, heavy frying pan over low heat. Place a tortilla on it and allow it to just dry out. It should take 3–5 minutes; do not allow it to brown. Remove from the pan and immediately use a table knife to scrape and then pull off the top layer of the tortilla, which, with luck, will have puffed up to make it easier. Repeat with the remaining tortillas.

Just before filling the tortillas, pour about 3 tablespoons oil into a deep, heavy frying pan over medium-high heat. When the oil is hot but not smoking, pass each tortilla briefly through it, turning once. Transfer to absorbent paper to drain.

To form each *flauta,* put a large spoonful of the shredded chicken mixture along the center of a tortilla, roll it up tightly, and secure with a wooden toothpick placed almost horizontally.

Add oil to a depth of ¾ inch (2 cm) into the same frying pan and place over medium-high heat until hot. Working in batches, add the *flautas* to the oil and fry, turning several times to cook evenly, until lightly browned and crisp, about 2 minutes. Using tongs, lift the *flautas* out of the oil, allowing any excess oil to run off, and lean them against a pan on absorbent paper so they can completely drain. Keep warm in a low oven while frying the rest of the *flautas.*

The *flautas* should be served immediately. Place on individual plates atop some shredded cabbage and drizzle with the Avocado Salsa and *crema.* Garnish with the radishes, if using, and serve the chile salsa on the side. Or arrange the *flautas* on a cabbage-lined platter, garnish with the radishes, and let everyone choose their own accompaniments.

serves 6

Local farmers cultivate their milpas in the time-honored way of their ancestors.

Oaxaca

Verduras en Escabeche

pickled mixed vegetables

Bowls of these brightly colored, chunky vegetables—a perfect condiment to serve with antojitos*—are set out on the counters of market* fondas *all over Mexico. I especially like this Oaxacan version.*

½ cup (4 fl oz/125 ml) safflower or canola oil

4 heads garlic, outside papery skin removed and top sliced off

6 carrots, peeled and cut into slices ¼ inch (6 mm) thick

6 jalapeño chiles, cut into slices ½ inch (12 mm) thick

1 white onion, cut vertically into slices ½ inch (12 mm) thick

4 cups (32 fl oz/1 l) mild white vinegar

2 cups (16 fl oz/500 ml) water

2 tablespoons dried oregano, preferably Mexican

3 bay leaves

2 teaspoons peppercorns

3 whole cloves

about 2 teaspoons sea salt

2 cups (6 oz/185 g) small cauliflower florets

20 green beans, ends trimmed and cut into 1½-inch (4-cm) lengths

6–8 very small potatoes, unpeeled, boiled until barely tender

In a large, deep frying pan over medium heat, warm the oil. Add the garlic heads and sauté, stirring often, until the skin begins to crisp, about 5 minutes. Add the carrots and cook for an additional 2 minutes, then stir in the chiles and onion. Continue to cook and stir for another 2 minutes. The vegetables should still be crisp.

Add the vinegar, water, oregano, bay leaves, peppercorns, cloves, and salt, and bring to a boil. Drop in the cauliflower and green beans and simmer until just tender, no more than 3–5 minutes. Add the potatoes and heat through.

Ladle the vegetables and liquid into 2 clean, sterilized jars and let cool. Seal tightly and store in the refrigerator overnight. Bring to room temperature before serving.

makes about 2 qt (2 l)

Jalisco

Jícama, Pepinos, y Piña con Cacahuates

tangy jicama, cucumber, and pineapple sticks with peanuts

Every few blocks in Guadalajara, mobile stands are strategically placed outside the most important buildings. Each is manned by a smiling vendor selling paper cups of colorful fruit and vegetables: always cucumber, with jicama in the winter when it is the crispest and usually mango or pineapple. In Jalisco, this combination, an irresistible botana *anytime of the day or night, is commonly known as* pico de gallo, *or "rooster's beak." The only trick to making this crunchy medley is to create pieces of equal size, from three very differently shaped items.*

2 cucumbers, peeled, halved, and seeded

1 small pineapple, peeled, halved, and cored

1 jicama, peeled

juice of 6 limes

1 teaspoon sea salt

1 cup (5 oz/155 g) raw peanuts, skins removed

4 árbol chiles, toasted (page 247)

Cut the cucumbers, pineapple, and jicama into sticks measuring about 3 inches (7.5 cm) long and ⅓ inch (9 mm) thick. Arrange the sticks in a single layer in a shallow glass dish. Sprinkle the sticks with the lime juice and salt. Cover and refrigerate, turning the pieces occasionally.

In a dry frying pan over medium heat, toast the peanuts, stirring often, until they are toasty gold, about 15 minutes. Remove from the heat and pour into a small bowl. Crumble the chiles over the nuts. Working in small batches, coarsely grind the peanut mixture in a spice grinder.

Sprinkle the ground nut mixture over the upper two-thirds of the sticks. To serve, slip the ends into a widemouthed container so that the sticks stand upright, or lay the sticks flat on a platter.

serves 6–8

Cinco de Mayo

It's 7:00 A.M. on a spring day so clear that the gently steaming volcano, Popocatépetl, slowly being topped with a crown of white-fringed, purple-bellied plumes, seems framed against the blue of the sky. As she has every morning for a dozen years, Emelia López, joined by her young daughter, has created an instant kitchen on the street outside Puebla's busiest market.

As the first customer appears, the daughter scoops out blue corn *masa* with two small cupped hands, forms it into a ball, and gives it to her mother. Emelia pats the *masa* into a large, thick oval tortilla and deftly slips it into hot melted lard, where it is instantly surrounded by softly popping bubbles. She flips the tortilla, frying the other side, takes it out, spreads on black beans, adds pungent epazote and other toppings, and presents the finished *memela* to the waiting man.

This is not just any day. It is Cinco de Mayo, a day of special significance in Puebla. For here, over three hundred years ago, on the fifth of May, a ragtag group of Mexican ex-guerrillas drove off a powerful army of six thousand French invaders. Never mind that the city was eventually conquered, resulting in the Viennese prince, Maximillian, being installed by Napoleon as emperor of Mexico. This holiday represents the Mexican spirit to survive.

By midday the downtown streets will be filled with school marching bands and legions of exuberant workers. The central plaza, transformed into an outdoor eatery, will draw Emelia and her mobile kitchen to sell her special regional *masa* snacks to the festive throngs. On a nearby hilltop, at the site of the Fort of Loreto, one of the main defense points during the victorious battle, a mammoth fair draws its share of fun seekers. High-spirited families and friends gather to celebrate with games, cockfights, and, of course, food.

In other parts of Mexico, Cinco de Mayo is a legal holiday, though the festivities are rather muted. But here in Puebla, where the struggle took place, it is a full-blown celebration.

Veracruz

Gorditas de Frijol

fat black bean tortillas

In the bustling port of Veracruz, Sr. Atenogenes Machorro operates a small restaurant where his busy staff prepare these puffy fried tortillas.

1 cup (7 oz/220 g) Pot Beans (page 201) made with black beans, with some liquid if needed

1 avocado leaf (optional), toasted (page 246) and crumbled

1 clove garlic, unpeeled, roasted (page 248)

1 lb (500 g) freshly prepared tortilla masa *or 1¾ cups (9 oz/280 g)* masa harina *for tortillas prepared as for corn tortillas (page 251)*

½ cup (4 fl oz/125 ml) crema *(page 248)*

sea salt to taste

2 tablespoons all-purpose (plain) flour, if needed

peanut or safflower oil for frying

Chipotle Chile Salsa (page 174)

In a food processor, combine the beans and avocado leaf, if using. Peel the garlic and add it. Process to form a smooth, thick paste, adding the bean liquid as needed.

In a bowl, mix the puréed beans, *masa, crema,* and salt until very smooth and the consistency of cookie dough. If it is too damp, knead in the flour. Form into about 20 balls and cover with plastic wrap. Pour oil to a depth of at least ½ inch (12 mm) into a heavy frying pan and place over medium-high heat. Adjust the heat to maintain a temperature of 375°F (190°C) on a deep-frying thermometer.

Press each ball of *masa* between sheets of heavy plastic in a tortilla press (page 251) into a round a little less than 4 inches (10 cm) across and about ¼ inch (6 mm) thick. Carefully slide the uncooked *gordita* into the hot oil. When it rises to the surface, spoon on some of the bubbling oil to help it puff. Fry until the bottom is golden and the *gordita* is puffy, about 1 minute. Turn and count to 15 before removing the *gordita* and draining on absorbent paper.

Serve immediately with the salsa on the side.

makes about 20 gorditas; *serves 10*

Puebla

Buñuelos de Flor de Calabaza

cheese-stuffed squash blossoms

I derive an intense pleasure from eating these delightfully light squash blossom fritters that Mónica Mastretta likes to stuff with goat cheese. Even with the abundance of goats everywhere in Mexico, cooking with goat cheese is, surprisingly, rare. In the countryside near the city where she lives, however, there is a home for abandoned young boys where goats are raised and an excellent cheese is made from their milk. Serve the fritters with Guacamole (page 43).

20 good-sized squash blossoms

1½ lb (750 g) fresh goat cheese

20 fresh epazote or cilantro (fresh coriander) leaves

5 eggs, separated

sea salt and freshly ground pepper to taste

safflower or canola oil for frying

3 tablespoons all-purpose (plain) flour

Remove the pistils from the squash blossoms. Rinse the blossoms carefully by dunking them in a bowl of water. Dry on paper towels, stem end up.

Cut the goat cheese into 20 pieces, each about ¾ inch (2 cm) square and 1 inch (2.5 cm) long. Place a piece of goat cheese and an epazote or cilantro leaf in each blossom and lightly twist the tops of the petals together.

In a bowl, beat the egg whites with a whisk until soft peaks form. Add the egg yolks one at a time, whisking after each addition. Add a pinch of salt and a liberal grinding of pepper.

Pour oil to a depth of at least 1 inch (2.5 cm) into a deep, heavy frying pan or a wok and place over medium heat until the oil starts to smoke.

While the oil is heating, spread the flour in a shallow dish. Lightly coat the stuffed flowers with the flour. Working in batches, dip each blossom into the egg batter and place in the hot oil. Fry, turning occasionally, until golden, about 3 minutes. Using a slotted spatula, transfer to absorbent paper to drain.

Arrange on a platter and serve immediately.

serves 4–6

Chihuahua

Chile con Queso

chiles with melted cheese

Northern Mexico is ranch country, and dishes made with an abundance of dairy products, like this one from Elba Valencia de Salcido, typify the cooking of the region. Scoop up the cheese and chiles with totopos *(page 251), or wrap in hot flour tortillas (page 251) for a more substantial snack.*

2 tablespoons unsalted butter or safflower oil

2 small white onions, finely chopped

4 jalapeño chiles, seeded and cut into strips

15 Anaheim chiles, roasted, peeled, seeded, and deveined (page 247), then cut into long, narrow strips

2 ripe tomatoes, chopped

1 cup (8 fl oz/250 ml) heavy (double) cream

¼ cup (2 fl oz/60 ml) warm water

sea salt to taste

1 lb (500 g) queso asadero, *Monterey jack, or other melting cheese, shredded*

In a large frying pan over medium heat, melt the butter or warm the oil. Add the onions and jalapeño chiles and sauté until the onions are limp and golden, about 5 minutes. Stir in the Anaheim chiles and tomatoes and cook until all the chiles are soft, about 5 minutes longer. Pour in the cream and warm water, season with salt, and simmer for several minutes.

Stir the cheese into the chiles, cover, and remove from the heat. When the cheese has melted, pour the chiles into a heated serving bowl. Serve while it is still bubbling hot, as the cheese will separate and become tough and stringy if allowed to cool.

serves 10–12 as a dip, or serves 6 as a filling for tortillas

Chihuahua is known for its cattle ranches and for having sheltered the great popular hero Pancho Villa.

Veracruz

Ceviche Rojo de Camarón y Sierra

seafood cocktail in spicy red sauce

This is a particularly refreshing example of ceviche, the centuries-old dish in which seafood is cooked by contact with acidic citrus juice instead of heat. Ricardo Muñoz Zurita, who grew up in Tabasco and Veracruz, likes to use sierra, the colorful Spanish mackerel from the Gulf of Mexico, but I find substituting black sea bass, rockfish, or red snapper equally satisfying. Serve this cooling treat along with glasses of Iced Spicy Beer (page 243).

½ lb (250 g) lean white-fleshed fish fillet (see note), cubed

½ cup (4 fl oz/125 ml) fresh lime juice

½ lb (250 g) bay shrimp

½ cup (2½ oz/75 g) minced white onion

2 teaspoons minced garlic

2 teaspoons sea salt

½ teaspoon freshly ground pepper

¼ cup (⅓ oz/10 g) finely chopped fresh cilantro (fresh coriander)

1 cup (8 fl oz/250 ml) tomato ketchup

1 tablespoon sauce from chiles chipotles en adobo

totopos *(page 251)*

1 avocado, preferably Haas, pitted, peeled, and sliced

♛ Place the fish in a shallow glass dish. Add the lime juice, cover, and marinate for up to 2 hours at room temperature, or until opaque. (The fish will not "cook" as quickly if refrigerated.)

♛ Stir in the shrimp, onion, garlic, salt, and pepper. Cover again and refrigerate for 30 minutes or so.

♛ Drain the fish mixture to remove the excess lime juice. Add the chopped cilantro, ketchup, and *adobo* sauce. Mix well.

♛ Spoon into glass dishes. Accompany with the *totopos* and garnish with the avocado slices.

serves 6

Colima

Ceviche de Callo de Hacha con Aguacate

scallop ceviche with avocado balls

Almost every indentation of Mexico's Pacific shoreline that includes sandy beaches will also have its contingent of palm-thatched palapas, *where the local seafood specialties such as ceviche are served. Each cook has her or his own version, and I was served this unusual one, made with scallops, while relaxing on the isolated gray sand beach at Boca de Pascuales, in the tiny, hot, and humid state of Colima.*

1 lb (500 g) bay scallops

½ cup (4 fl oz/125 ml) fresh lime juice, plus extra if needed

3 avocados, preferably Haas

1 ripe tomato, diced

1 tablespoon finely chopped fresh cilantro (fresh coriander)

1 serrano chile, minced

⅓ cup (3 fl oz/80 ml) extra-virgin olive oil

sea salt to taste

Put the scallops in a glass bowl and toss with the ½ cup (4 fl oz/125 ml) lime juice. Cover and let marinate at room temperature for 10–15 minutes.

Halve the avocados and remove the pits. With a small melon baller, spoon out balls of the avocado flesh, or make ½-inch (12-mm) hatched cuts through the flesh and scoop out the small cubes. Drain the scallops and stir in the tomato, cilantro, chile, and oil. When well mixed, add the avocado and gently toss together. Sprinkle in the salt and, if needed, add more lime juice.

Serve in tall wineglasses, small clear glass bowls, or the beautiful fluted shells of the scallops.

serves 6

Puebla

Guacamole con Totopos

guacamole with corn chips

This is simplicity itself: a rustic botana *that owes its flavor to the quality of the avocados. After all, the Nahuatl word* guacamole *means avocado mixture, and that is what it should be. I usually omit the garnishes, as they are apt to unbalance the flavor, but many cooks prefer to sprinkle on one or two. Use avocados that are firm, but soft to the touch.*

- *1 ripe tomato, finely chopped*
- *2 tablespoons finely minced white onion*
- *3 serrano chiles, finely chopped*
- *½ teaspoon sea salt, or to taste*
- *3 large avocados, preferably Haas*
- *2 tablespoons finely minced fresh cilantro (fresh coriander)*

GARNISH

- *1 tablespoon small fresh cilantro (fresh coriander) leaves (optional)*
- *1 tablespoon finely chopped white onion (optional)*
- *1 tablespoon finely chopped ripe tomato (optional)*

totopos *(page 251), warmed*

Put the tomato, onion, chiles, and ½ teaspoon salt in a *molcajete* or small bowl, and smash with a pestle or fork to a coarse paste. Cut the avocados in half, remove the pits, and scoop the flesh into the tomato mixture. Add the minced cilantro and mix and mash, leaving some lumps. Taste and adjust with more salt.

If you want, sprinkle the guacamole with any or all of the garnishes and serve at once, if possible. To keep at room temperature for up to 1 hour, cover with plastic wrap, pressing it directly onto the surface. To keep for up to no longer than 3 hours, do not add the cilantro until just before serving, and cover and store in the refrigerator.

Pass the warmed *totopos* in a basket at the table.

makes about 2 cups (1 lb/500 g)

Aguacates

One of my favorite swaths of Mexico lies en route to Michoacán's hot lands, an area called just that, *tierra caliente.* As you descend from the pine-cloaked highlands through the deeply folded slopes of a volcanic mountain range, the climate becomes delightfully temperate. The Cupatitzio River wanders through the region, brought to life from time to time by a long spill down a waterfall, and the hillsides are canopied by dark green *aguacate* (avocado) trees. My destination is always Uruapan, an agricultural community whose name means "Forever Springtime" in the Purépecha language.

Once in town, I can relax in a wondrous setting, enjoy the local foods, and visit with my longtime friend Enrique Bautista, whose family is one of Mexico's leading avocado growers. We wander the plantation and investigate the many varieties, besides the familiar Haas, that are grown. The most interesting to me is the tiny, round *criollo,* or now-cultivated "wild" avocado. The skins are so tender that you can eat the whole avocado, spitting out the small pit, and the leaves are what give an anise-flavored undercurrent to so many of the regional dishes.

Oaxaca

Tostadas de Chileajo con Verduras

tostadas of cold vegetables in chile-garlic sauce

One day in Oaxaca, I was served this riotous mixture of spicy cooked vegetables. It was piled on half of a crusty bread roll, partially scooped out to hold what I soon learned was called chileajo, *after the pungent chile-and-garlic sauce that coats the vegetables. I have found similar ones at* fondas *in Oaxaca's Abastos market, but served on a crispy tostada. The variety of vegetables seems to change, so feel free to create your own mixture. Only the potato remains a constant.*

SAUCE

6 guajillo chiles, seeded and toasted (page 247)

boiling water to cover

6 tablespoons (3 fl oz/90 ml) mild white vinegar

6 cloves garlic, unpeeled, roasted (page 248)

1 whole clove

1 allspice berry

1 tablespoon dried oregano, preferably Mexican

1 teaspoon sea salt

VEGETABLES

4 cups (32 fl oz/1 l) water

1 rounded teaspoon sea salt, plus salt to taste

½ lb (250 g) new potatoes, peeled and diced

¼ lb (125 g) green beans, ends trimmed and cut into ½-inch (12-mm) lengths

¼ lb (125 g) carrots, peeled, halved lengthwise, and cut into slices ½ inch (12 mm) thick

2 cups (6 oz/185 g) small cauliflower florets, coarsely chopped

¼ lb (125 g) zucchini (courgettes), diced

TOSTADAS

1 cup (7 oz/220 g) Well-Fried Beans (page 182) made with black beans

12 small corn tostadas (page 251)

1 cup (3½ oz/105 g) thinly sliced small white onion, separated into rings

½ lb (250 g) queso fresco, *crumbled*

To make the sauce, in a bowl, combine the toasted chiles with boiling water to cover and let soak for 15 minutes. The chiles should be quite soft. Drain the chiles, reserving the soaking water, and place in a blender with the vinegar, garlic, clove, allspice berry, and about 1 cup (8 fl oz/250 ml) of the soaking water. Process until a smooth purée forms, adding more water if necessary to facilitate blending. Pass the purée through a fine-mesh sieve placed over a bowl, pressing down with the back of a spoon. Stir in the oregano and salt and set aside.

To prepare the vegetables, in a saucepan, bring the water to a boil and add the 1 teaspoon salt. Drop in the potatoes and cook until just tender, about 5 minutes. Using a slotted spoon, transfer the potatoes to a bowl filled with very cold water to stop the cooking. Repeat the process with each of the vegetables. The beans and carrots should take about 4 minutes, and the cauliflower and zucchini about 3 minutes. The vegetables should be soft but still have a bite.

When all of the vegetables are cooked and cooled, remove them from the water and drain on a kitchen towel. Gently stir the vegetables into the chile sauce. Taste and adjust the seasoning with salt, if needed. Cover and refrigerate for at least several hours.

Spread a thin layer of black beans over a tostada and spoon on the vegetables and sauce. Top with a few onion rings and the crumbled cheese. Serve at once.

makes 12 tostadas; serves 6

Chihuahua

Burritos con Frijoles y Queso

bean and cheese burritos

Halfway between Chihuahua and Ciudad Juárez, on the Texas border, vendors congregate at a wide spot on the highway. Some of the burritos they sell are made with a type of queso asadero *that is formed into a thin round just like a tortilla. It fits perfectly inside a flour tortilla for the simplest burrito yet.*

1 tablespoon safflower or canola oil

1 cup (4 oz/125 g) chopped white onion

2 jalapeño chiles, chopped

4 cups (1¾ lb/875 kg) Well-Fried Beans (page 182) made with pinto beans

½ teaspoon sea salt, or to taste

6 large, thin flour tortillas, 7–8 inches (18–20 cm) in diameter, homemade (page 251) or purchased

2 cups (8 oz/250 g) shredded queso asadero, *Monterey jack, or other melting cheese*

shredded lettuce and chopped tomatoes

Fresh Tomato and Chile Salsa (page 173)

In a frying pan over medium heat, warm the oil. Add the onion and chiles and sauté until the onion is golden brown, about 8 minutes. Stir in the beans and cook until heated through. Season with salt.

Place a *comal,* griddle, or heavy frying pan over medium-high heat. Place a tortilla on the hot surface and heat briefly, turning once. Transfer to a plate and spread with the beans, leaving a ½-inch (12-mm) margin around the edges. Sprinkle with several spoonfuls of cheese. The amount of filling will depend on the size of the tortillas. Add some lettuce and tomatoes and fold the bottom of the tortilla over the filling, then fold in the two sides. Finish by rolling up the tortilla until completely closed. Serve at once with the salsa on the side.

makes 6 burritos; serves 6

Veracruz

Tacos de Salpicón de Pescado

fish tacos

Up and down the long coastline of Veracruz are weather-ravaged, palm-thatched stands selling tacos made of shredded fish, as well as all kinds of seafood cocktails. Frosty bottles of Mexican beer are set up on the counter along with guacamole and a pile of totopos *(page 43), and everyone forgets their troubles, relaxes, and enjoys the day.*

1½ lb (750 g) red snapper or other firm white-fleshed fish fillets

1 teaspoon sea salt

freshly ground pepper to taste

¾ cup (4 oz/125 g) all-purpose (plain) flour

¼ cup (2 oz/60 ml) corn or safflower oil

2 cups (16 fl oz/500 ml) Fresh Tomato and Chile Salsa (page 173)

10 corn tortillas, homemade (page 251) or purchased, warmed

1 cup (3 oz/90 g) chopped cabbage

2 limes, quartered

♛ Season both sides of each fish fillet with the salt and a generous amount of pepper. Spread the flour on a plate and dip the fish in it, coating evenly and shaking off any excess.

♛ In a large frying pan over medium-high heat, warm the oil until it is rippling hot but not smoking. Add the fish fillets and fry, turning once, until golden on both sides, just over 1 minute total. Using a slotted spatula, transfer the fillets to absorbent paper to drain briefly. While the fillets are still hot, shred them with a fork. Put the salsa in a bowl and stir in the fish.

♛ To assemble the tacos, place some fish into each tortilla and add a bit of the crunchy cabbage. Serve the limes on the side.

makes 10 tacos; serves 4

Chorizo

Over the years, I have searched many markets throughout Mexico for the best chorizo, old-fashioned pork sausage made using the ingredients and methods perfected by family traditions. In Zacatecas, I found that the meat is always heavily seasoned with cumin; in the northern states, it is finely ground, with barely a whisper of spices. I especially like chorizo's long, skinny cousin, *longaniza,* made in Yucatán, where it is flavored with *achiote* and allspice, then smoked.

A particular favorite is one I discovered in Tepatitlán, Jalisco, an area once well known for its chorizo, which is now made by only one man. I found the legendary butcher at his stall just finishing the preparation of his renowned sausage. The pork was lean, with just enough fat. The ancho chile was mixed with a blend of spices, and the final product was studded with almonds and carried a hint of chocolate. It was perfection. Unfortunately, he wouldn't share his recipe—not even with his best friend, he said.

Chorizo is the star of Toluca's Mercado Juárez. It may be links of *chorizo rojo* or a more contemporary green version made with fresh chiles and herbs. Here, I always indulge myself with a chewy roll stuffed with the spicy sausage, shredded cabbage, sliced avocado, pickled jalapeños, and chopped onions, or a taco of chorizo and potatoes.

Oaxaca

Molotes

masa fritters stuffed with chorizo and potatoes

On the days before Christmas, the side streets radiating from Oaxaca's central plaza, or zócalo, *are closed to traffic and crammed with rows of food stalls. Some vendors sell these unusual spindle-shaped* molotes *filled with potatoes and chorizo, topped with a sauce of black beans and lots of condiments, and served on a leaf of lettuce.*

SAUCE

¾ cup (6 oz/185 g) Pot Beans (page 201) made with black beans, with some liquid

½ árbol chile, toasted (page 247) and crumbled

1 small avocado leaf, toasted (page 246) and crumbled (optional)

2 teaspoons safflower or canola oil

1 tablespoon finely chopped white onion

sea salt to taste

MOLOTES

1 guajillo chile, toasted (page 247)

½ cup (4 fl oz/125 ml) boiling water

1 teaspoon safflower or canola oil

2 oz (60 g) good-quality chorizo, homemade (page 248) or purchased, crumbled

2 tablespoons finely chopped white onion

2 cloves garlic, finely chopped

2 small new potatoes, cubed, boiled, and coarsely mashed

sea salt and freshly ground pepper to taste

1 cup (8 oz/250 g) freshly prepared tortilla masa *or 1 scant cup (5 oz/155 g)* masa harina *for tortillas prepared as for corn tortillas (page 251)*

peanut or safflower oil for frying

GARNISHES

12 inner leaves of romaine (cos) lettuce, plus 1 cup (2 oz/60 g) shredded

Avocado Salsa (page 190)

⅓ cup (2 oz/60 g) crumbled queso fresco *or* queso ranchero

To make the sauce, put the beans and lots of their broth, the árbol chile, and the avocado leaf, if using, in a blender and process until a smooth, thin purée

forms. In a frying pan over medium heat, warm the oil. Add the onion and sauté until golden, 4 minutes. Pour in the bean purée and simmer, stirring occasionally, 5 minutes. Season with salt and keep warm.

Meanwhile, prepare the *molotes:* In a bowl, combine the guajillo chile and boiling water and let stand until the chile is soft, about 10 minutes. In a small frying pan over low heat, warm the oil. Add the chorizo and fry until it just starts to become crisp and brown, 3–5 minutes. Drain the chile and grind or mash it into a paste. Pour off any excess oil from the chorizo, add the onion, and cook, stirring in the chile and garlic after several minutes, until the onion is translucent, about 8 minutes. Spoon the potatoes into the chorizo mixture, stirring and mashing to combine. Season with salt and pepper. Raise the heat, cook for 1 more minute, remove from the heat, and set aside.

If necessary, add a few sprinkles of water to the *masa* to make a soft dough. I suggest adding a small pinch of salt as well. Roll the *masa* into 12 balls, each about 1 inch (2.5 cm) in diameter. Cover them with a damp kitchen towel or plastic wrap so they do not dry out. Press out each ball of *masa* between sheets of heavy plastic in a tortilla press (page 251) into a round about 5 inches (13 cm) in diameter and ⅛ inch (3 mm) thick. Remove the top sheet of plastic and spread a small spoonful of the chorizo-potato filling in the center of the *masa* round. Using the bottom sheet of plastic, fold the round over the filling. Transfer the *molote* to a flat surface. Lightly oil your hands and form the dough into a tapered oblong shape with pointed ends and a bulging middle. Place under the damp kitchen towel or plastic wrap. Repeat until all the *molotes* are formed.

In a heavy frying pan over medium-high heat, pour in oil to a depth of 1 inch (2.5 cm) and heat until it is rippling hot. Add the *molotes* a few at a time and fry until they turn a deep golden brown, about 5 minutes. Using a slotted spoon or spatula, transfer to absorbent paper to drain. Keep warm in a low oven until all of the *molotes* are cooked.

Place a *molote* on top of each lettuce leaf. Spread with a spoonful of the bean sauce, sprinkle with shredded lettuce, and drizzle with the salsa. Top with cheese and serve immediately.

---

makes 12 molotes; *serves 4–6*

Jalisco

Tortas Ahogadas

pork sandwiches drowned with two salsas

My friend Carlos insisted that my first torta ahogada *be the best that Guadalajara had to offer. To find these crusty sandwiches, which are filled with pork and half-drowned in both a mild sauce and a fiery sauce of árbol chiles, we had to drive through the back streets of one of the local neighborhoods to his favorite street stand. It was thronged with customers, some waiting to be served and others standing around chewing on these incendiary comestibles. He was right—I still have not found any better. These* tortas *are made with Mexico's classic roll, the* bolillo. *Similar to a French roll, it has a hard crust and a soft and flaky interior.*

1 rib-end pork loin, bone-in, about 3 lb (1.5 kg)

4 cloves garlic

1 teaspoon dried oregano, preferably Mexican

1 teaspoon sea salt

½ teaspoon freshly ground pepper

SWEET SALSA

3 ripe tomatoes, quartered, or 1½ cups (9 oz/280 g) drained canned diced tomatoes

3 tablespoons chopped white onion

2 cloves garlic, coarsely chopped

2 pinches of ground cumin

2 pinches of dried marjoram

½ teaspoon sea salt, or more to taste

1 tablespoon safflower or canola oil

PICANTE SALSA

3 ripe tomatoes, quartered, or 1½ cups (9 oz/280 g) drained canned diced tomatoes

15 árbol chiles, toasted (page 247)

¼ small white onion, chopped

2 cloves garlic, coarsely chopped

1 cup (8 fl oz/250 ml) water

½ cup (4 fl oz/125 ml) mild white vinegar

2 pinches of ground cumin

½ teaspoon sea salt, or to taste

8 bolillos *or small French rolls*

2 cups (14 oz/440 g) Well-Fried Beans (page 182) made with pinto or other pink or tan beans, heated

2 large, ripe tomatoes, sliced

2 avocados, preferably Haas, pitted, peeled, and sliced

¼ head lettuce, shredded

2 limes, quartered

Preheat an oven to 350°F (180°C).

Using a sharp knife, prick small holes over the surface of the meat. Smash the garlic with the oregano, salt, and pepper, and massage the mixture into the pork. Put the pork in a baking dish a little larger than the piece of meat. Add water to a depth of ½ inch (12 mm). Cover with aluminum foil and roast until an instant-read thermometer inserted in the thickest part of the loin away from the bone registers 150°F (65°C). Remove the foil and roast until browned on top and the internal temperature reaches 155°F (68°C). Let the meat rest for 10 minutes, then coarsely chop into bite-sized pieces, discarding the bones.

Meanwhile, prepare the salsas. For the sweet salsa, put the tomatoes, onion, garlic, cumin, marjoram, and salt in a blender or food processor. Purée until smooth. In a heavy saucepan over medium-high heat, warm the oil. Add the purée and let it bubble and sputter, stirring occasionally, until the flavors are well blended, about 5 minutes. Let cool slightly and pass through a medium-mesh sieve. This sauce can be served warm or at room temperature.

To make the *picante* salsa, in a saucepan, bring the tomatoes, chiles, onion, garlic, water, vinegar, cumin, and salt to a boil over medium heat, reduce the heat to low, and cook until thick and well seasoned, 20–25 minutes. Let cool slightly and pour into a blender or food processor. Process until a smooth purée forms. Pass the purée through a medium-mesh sieve. Pour into a bowl and serve at room temperature.

Slice each *bolillo* or French roll in half lengthwise. Pick out some of the doughy crumbs, making a shallow nest. Spread the bottom half with the warm beans, pile on some pork, and top with tomato, avocado, and some shredded lettuce. Since a *torta* is usually eaten out of hand, many cooks cover only half of it with the sweet salsa so it can be held with a minimum of mess, and the hotter sauce is set out in a bowl to be used very sparingly. Others cover the whole *torta* with lots of sweet salsa and just a drop or two of the liquid fire. Then there are the reckless people who drench the *torta* in the *picante* salsa and suffer happily. Squirt on some lime juice to accent the flavors. Serve with lots of napkins.

serves 8

Tabasco

Plátanos Machucos

plantain tostadas

Hot and humid Tabasco, the Mexican state named after the Nahuatl word for "flooded land," is the region with the greatest variety of ways to prepare plantains. My friend Doña Gloria Bulnes introduced me to this typical regional snack. Although she employs a very capable cook, Gloria insists on preparing the daily afternoon comida *for her family, and they come home looking for these crispy plantains. I warn you, they're addictive.*

1 tablespoon sea salt

2 tablespoons water

safflower or canola oil for frying

2 plantains, just beginning to ripen

salsa of choice

In a bowl, dissolve the salt in the water; set aside.

Pour oil to a depth of 1½ inches (4 cm) in a deep, heavy frying pan or a wok and place over medium high heat. While the oil is heating, peel the plantains and cut them into 2-inch (5-cm) pieces.

Working in batches, add the plantain pieces to the hot oil and fry, turning frequently, until just lightly golden, 1–2 minutes. Using a slotted spoon, transfer to absorbent paper to drain. Reduce the heat to low.

While the plantain pieces are still hot, press each one lightly with absorbent paper to remove excess oil, then flatten it with the palm of your hand. Line a tortilla press with 2 sheets of heavy plastic cut from a plastic storage bag. Place a flattened piece of plantain on the tortilla press and press lightly. The plantain may have to be turned several times so that it is flattened evenly and is quite thin. Remove from the press and sprinkle lightly with the salt water. Repeat until all of the plantain pieces are flattened.

Raise the heat under the oil to medium-high. When hot, one at a time carefully lay the plantain "tortillas" in the oil and fry until crisp and brown, 1–2 minutes. Using a slotted spatula, transfer to absorbent paper to drain. Keep warm in a low oven while you cook the remaining tostadas.

Arrange the tostadas, overlapping them, in a basket or on a plate. Serve immediately with salsa.

makes 10–12 tostadas; serves 6

Quintana Roo

Tostaditas con Queso y Mariscos

tiny tostadas with melted cheese, crab, and shrimp

With its streets of sand and laid-back atmosphere, Isla Mujeres—the Island of Women—is a serene respite from the glitz of nearby Cancún. There is little to do but stretch out on the white sand and eat seafood. This casual snack, almost like the nachos of the north, is easy to make and even easier to eat.

10 purchased thin corn tortillas, 6 inches (15 cm) in diameter

1 tablespoon unsalted butter

1 tablespoon safflower or canola oil

½ lb (250 g) shrimp (prawns), peeled, deveined, and coarsely chopped

½ lb (250 g) good-quality fresh-cooked crabmeat, picked over for shell fragments and flaked

1 cup (8 fl oz/250 ml) sour cream

½ teaspoon cumin seeds, toasted

sea salt to taste

3 cups (12 oz/375 g) shredded Manchego, Monterey jack, or other good melting cheese

10 pickled jalapeño chiles, sliced

Chipotle Chile Salsa (page 174)

Avocado Salsa (page 190)

Stack the tortillas in 2 equal piles. Cut into 4 triangular wedges, then fry (page 251). Set aside.

Preheat an oven to 500°F (260°C).

In a frying pan over medium heat, melt the butter with the oil. Add the shrimp and sauté until barely pink, about 3 minutes. Scoop out with a slotted spoon and put into a bowl. Stir in the crabmeat and sour cream. Put the cumin seeds between 2 sheets of waxed paper and crush with a rolling pin. Mix with the shrimp and crab and season with salt.

Place about 1 tablespoon of the seafood mixture on each tortilla piece and sprinkle with the shredded cheese. Arrange in a large, shallow baking pan. Bake until the cheese melts, about 30 seconds.

Arrange the *tostaditas* on a platter and top each with a chile slice. Serve immediately with bowls of the salsas for dipping.

serves 4–6

Oaxaca

Tacos con Cecina a la Parrilla

tacos of grilled chile-coated pork

If you were to order cecina *in most other parts of Mexico, it would be thinly sliced beef, but in Oaxaca, it is long, thin strips of chile-marinated pork.*

PORK

5 guajillo chiles, seeded and toasted (page 247)

4 ancho chiles, seeded and toasted (page 247)

boiling water to cover

6 cloves garlic, unpeeled, roasted (page 248)

¼ cup (2 fl oz/60 ml) mild white vinegar

½ teaspoon dried oregano, preferably Mexican

10 peppercorns or ¼ teaspoon freshly ground pepper

½-inch (12-mm) piece true cinnamon bark or ½ teaspoon ground cinnamon

1 whole clove or pinch of ground cloves

1 generous teaspoon sea salt, or to taste

1 pork tenderloin, about 1 lb (500 g), trimmed of excess fat

ACCOMPANIMENTS

12 large green (spring) onions, root ends trimmed

12 small Anaheim chiles

2–3 tablespoons safflower or canola oil

4 limes, halved

2 avocados, pitted, peeled, and sliced

Avocado Salsa (page 190)

Fresh Tomato and Chile Salsa (page 173)

12 small radishes with leaves attached

12 corn tortillas, homemade (page 251) or purchased, warmed

Place the chiles in a bowl, add boiling water to cover, and let stand until soft, about 20 minutes. Drain, reserving the soaking water, tear into small pieces, and place in a blender. Peel the garlic and add with the vinegar and oregano. If using whole spices, put in a spice grinder and pulverize. Add the spices and the salt to the blender and pulse to form a thick *adobo,* or sauce. If necessary, add a few drops or so of the chile soaking water.

Using a very sharp knife, accordion-cut the meat: Lay the pork horizontally in front of you. Pushing down firmly with one hand, begin making a slice ⅛ inch (3 mm) thick along the surface, from one end to about ⅛ inch (3 mm) from the opposite end. Do not cut through. Turn the meat 180 degrees. Still pushing down with one hand, slice back to the other side. Unfold the wide ribbon of meat as you complete a slice, and continue slicing back and forth until the entire piece is stretched out. Rub the *adobo* on both sides, fold the meat back into the original shape, and spread the outside with any remaining *adobo.* Seal in plastic wrap and refrigerate for at least 2 hours or as long as 12 hours.

Prepare a fire in a charcoal grill. When the coals are hot, lay a double thickness of heavy aluminum foil on the hottest coals. Rub the green onions and chiles with oil and place on the foil, with the white part of the onions over the coals. Grill, turning frequently, until browned, about 10 minutes. Place in a shallow bowl and toss with a squirt of lime juice. Cut the meat across the folds into long slices and lay on the grill rack. Brush with oil and grill, turning once, until browned, 2–3 minutes on each side.

Place the green onions, chiles, limes, avocados, salsas, and radishes in separate bowls. Serve each guest a portion of meat and 2 or 3 tortillas, and let everyone add their own fixings.

serves 4–6

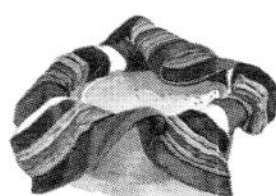

Tacos en Oaxaca

Just across the street from Oaxaca's busy Mercado Benito Juárez, smoke drifts through the narrow corridor of the large brick building that houses many *fondas.* Packed with hungry snackers at all hours, it attracts locals who come for their favorite tacos of grilled meats.

As you enter the long hall, you see long, flat market tables crammed with various salsas, avocados, radishes, green onions, and the feisty regional *chiles de agua.* One of the women at these tables hands you a large, flat wicker basket, into which you are to place your choice of the chiles and onions that you will want to have grilled for your taco.

To continue your taco making, you must then choose from a variety of hanging meats: links of chorizo, fresh *tasajo* (thinly sliced beef), salted and aged *tasajo,* wide ribbons of intestines, and spicy *cecina* (air-dried strips of pork). The vendor puts your selection on the grill along with the chiles and onions from your basket. Now you pay, but just for the meat, and you wait for the grilled food to be returned to your basket. Then you make your way back through the crowds to that first woman, who will offer salsas and other condiments. A third woman will appear with a basket of large tortillas with which to wrap the meat and accompaniments.

Your taco is complete, so you look for a seat, joining your fellow diners on an upside-down Pepsi crate in front of a nearby low concrete slab. Order a can of soda and you are ready to enjoy the taco. Sometimes, a blind violinist led by his small grandson will be there to play a scratchy but cheerful melody to eat by. Eventually, just as you start to leave, someone—usually a young boy—will stick a piece of paper in your hand stating the amount of pesos needed to finish paying for the meal.

Oaxaca

Empanadas de Maíz con Hongos

mushroom quesadillas

Although the aisle leading into the entrance of the neighborhood Mercado Merced in Oaxaca is quite wide, it is always packed with customers waiting to feast on Olivia Castro's scrumptious breakfast empanadas, which are like oversized quesadillas. It is hard for me to make my choice from among the many different mixtures that she prepares to stuff these unique creations. Some of my favorites are tinga *(page 158); a mix of squash blossoms, epazote, and Oaxacan cheese; the corn fungus* huitlacoche*; or this garlicky filling of mushrooms.*

What is different about Olivia's empanadas? The filling is piled onto a large tortilla that has first been lightly cooked on an earthenware comal *over a brazier filled with red-hot coals. She adds your choice of filling, folds the tortilla, presses the edges together, then puts it back on the* comal *to brown. The next step is to put it in an ovenlike space under the* comal*, where it finishes cooking, then back on top for a final browning. It is hard to duplicate her method, but these smaller empanadas are awfully good served with your favorite red or green salsa.*

MUSHROOMS

2 tablespoons unsalted butter or safflower oil

1 white onion, finely chopped

1 serrano chile, finely chopped

6 cloves garlic, minced

¾ lb (375 g) fresh mushrooms, preferably portobello, porcini, or other flavorful variety, brushed clean and coarsely chopped

2 tablespoons finely chopped fresh epazote (optional)

about ½ teaspoon sea salt

½ teaspoon freshly ground pepper

EMPANADAS

1 lb (500 g) freshly prepared tortilla masa *or 1¾ cups* masa harina *for tortillas prepared as for corn tortillas (page 251)*

1½ cups (6 oz/185 g) shredded quesillo de Oaxaca, *Muenster, or mozzarella cheese (optional)*

1 cup (8 fl oz/250 ml) Fresh Tomatillo Salsa (page 178) or other salsa

To prepare the mushrooms, in a frying pan, melt the butter or warm the oil over high heat. Add the onion and chile and sauté until the onion is translucent, about 30 seconds. Add the garlic and continue to sauté for just a few seconds. Toss in the mushrooms and cook for about 4 minutes, tossing every minute or so. They will give off a heady, earthy aroma. When the mushrooms just begin to give off a liquid, stir in the epazote (if using), salt, and pepper and immediately remove from the heat. Let cool.

If necessary, add a few sprinkles of water to the *masa* to make a soft dough. Roll the *masa* into balls 1½ inches (4 cm) in diameter. Cover with plastic wrap or a damp kitchen towel so they do not dry out. Make the tortillas one at a time (page 251), pressing hard so that they will be about 6–7 inches (15–18 cm) in diameter. It helps to rotate the *masa* on the plastic so that all sides are of equal thickness.

Remove the top piece of plastic and place 1 tablespoon of the shredded cheese, if using, in the center of the lower half of each tortilla, keeping the edges free. Spoon on some mushrooms. Fold the other half of the tortilla over the filling and press the edges together. Lift up the bottom piece of plastic and turn the quesadilla over to remove it.

Heat a *comal,* griddle, or large, heavy frying pan over medium-high heat. When hot, gently lay the quesadilla on the hot surface and cook until it starts to brown, 1 minute. Turn the quesadilla and move it to the side to continue cooking, while starting the next one. Repeat the process, and when the quesadillas are well cooked and brown on each side, carefully remove to a low oven to keep warm.

Serve the quesadillas at once, if possible, with the salsa on the side.

serves 4–6

For over five thousand years, maize has been central to the cuisine of Mexico.

Veracruz

Camarones Rellenos Envueltos con Tocino

cheese-stuffed shrimp wrapped in bacon

For years, one of my favorite seafood restaurants in Veracruz was El Lugar, which served these bacon-wrapped shrimp with an explosive chipotle mayonnaise.

1½ cups (12 fl oz/375 ml) mayonnaise

3 chiles chipotles en adobo, *finely chopped, with 1 teaspoon* adobo *sauce*

1 clove garlic, minced

1 tablespoon fresh lime juice

1 tablespoon minced lime zest

12 medium-thick slices lean bacon, cut in half crosswise

24 large shrimp (prawns), peeled, deveined, and butterflied, with tails attached

freshly ground pepper to taste

1½ cups (6 oz/185 g) shredded Manchego, Monterey jack, or other good melting cheese

about 4 tablespoons (2 fl oz/60 ml) olive oil

In a bowl or a food processor, combine the mayonnaise, chiles and *adobo* sauce, garlic, lime juice, and lime zest and stir or process to mix well. Cover and refrigerate until ready to use.

Lay as many bacon slices as will fit in a single layer in a large, heavy frying pan and cook over medium-low heat until opaque but still soft, about 5 minutes. Press down with a spatula to keep the bacon flat. Transfer to absorbent paper to drain. Wipe out the pan and repeat to cook the remaining bacon.

Dry the shrimp with paper towels. Sprinkle with pepper and stuff with the cheese. Push the sides together and wrap with a cooked bacon slice, covering all of the cheese so that it will not melt out. If necessary, secure with a toothpick. In the same frying pan over medium heat, warm 2 tablespoons of the oil. Add a few of the bacon-wrapped shrimp and fry, turning frequently and adding more oil as needed to prevent sticking, until the bacon is browned and the shrimp are pink, about 10 minutes. Transfer to absorbent paper. Repeat until all shrimp are fried.

Serve the shrimp on plates and accompany with the chipotle mayonnaise.

serves 6–8

Puebla

Rollo de Queso y Aguacate

avocado and cream cheese roll

I had forgotten how good it was: the slightly acrid smell, the salt white color, the soft texture, and the ripe sour taste of my grandmother's kitchen-made cream cheese. But here it was again: freshly ripened cream cheese served up in a basket woven from the reeds that border Lake Pátzcuaro, in Michoacán. Since then, I have discovered many other cheese makers throughout the country. Look for similar cottage-made cream cheese in specialty shops to make this party dish created by Ana Elena Martinez, a caterer in Puebla.

½ lb (250 g) cream cheese (see note), at room temperature

1 avocado, preferably Haas

2 tablespoons chopped fresh cilantro (fresh coriander)

1 tablespoon finely chopped white onion

1 serrano chile, finely chopped

¼ teaspoon fresh lime juice

sea salt to taste

2 cups (2 oz/60 g) crumbled chicharrones *(page 246) or 2 cups (6 oz/185 g) sesame seeds, toasted*

totopos *(page 251) or small crackers*

Place the cream cheese between 2 sheets of parchment paper. Using a rolling pin, roll to form a rectangle about 6 inches (15 cm) by 8 inches (20 cm) and ½ inch (12 mm) thick. Remove the top sheet.

Cut the avocado in half, remove the pit, and scoop the flesh into a bowl. Mash until it is rather smooth, leaving some small chunks to add texture. Stir in the cilantro, onion, chile, lime juice, and salt. Spread the avocado mixture evenly over the cream cheese. Using the bottom sheet of paper, roll up the cream cheese to form a log.

Coat the roll completely with the crushed *chicharrones* or sesame seeds. Cover lightly with plastic wrap and chill in the refrigerator for 15 minutes before serving. The roll can be made in advance and refrigerated for 6–8 hours, then set out at room temperature for 30 minutes before serving.

Unwrap the roll and place on a serving platter or tray. Serve with *totopos* or crackers.

serves 6–8

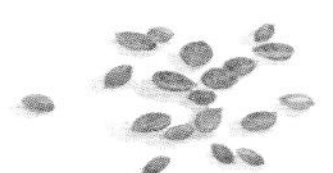

Pepitas

Think twice before you discard those scooped-out pumpkin seeds. They have been used by Mexican cooks since pre-Columbian times. Whether fat or skinny, raw or roasted, hulled or not, tasty *pepitas* are an essential ingredient in many sweets, snacks, and savory dishes.

Pipianes, green moles thickened with ground pumpkin seeds, are, in one form or another, the regional specialties of many states. In Guerrero, I had a *mole verde* so thick and coarse that a *totopo* could remain upright in it. In Puebla, a smooth, elegant pale green sauce napped chicken breasts, and in Tamaulipas, the *pipián,* mixed with cream, was spooned over fish.

Yucatán, however, boasts more different dishes using *pepitas* than any other state. A tamale with the tongue-twisting name of *dzotobichay* has a filling of chopped eggs and ground pumpkin seeds. Doña Lupita, a Maya cook, taught me to mix pumpkin seeds with tender white beans to stuff *polkanes,* a *masa* snack that resembles a snake head. To make *papadzules,* tortillas are dipped in a pumpkin-seed sauce, rolled around crumbled hard-boiled eggs, and then blanketed with a bright red tomato sauce beaded with shiny oil squeezed from the seeds. And ground pumpkin seeds, chiles, and tomatoes are combined to make one of the best dips ever—*zicil-p'ak.*

Coahuila

Nueces y Pepitas Picantes

spicy nuts and seeds

Pecans are native to Mexico, as are a great variety of pumpkin seeds. Peanuts, actually a legume rather than a nut, are native to Africa, but are plentiful here as well. They are a popular snack food wherever beer and other drinks are served, especially if they have been sprinkled with chile, garlic, and lime juice. This fiery trio makes for even better nibbling.

1 tablespoon peanut oil

10 small cloves garlic

1½ cups (7½ oz/235 g) raw peanuts, skins removed

1½ cups (7½ oz/235 g) raw hulled green pumpkin seeds

1 cup (4 oz/125 g) pecan halves

about 1 teaspoon sea salt

about 1 teaspoon ground dried árbol or cayenne chile

Preheat an oven to 275°F (135°C).

In a frying pan over medium-low heat, warm the oil. Add the garlic cloves and sauté until they begin to turn tan, 3–4 minutes. Stir in the nuts and seeds, coating them well with the oil. Add the salt and ground chile, just a pinch at a time, until the taste just tingles the tongue.

Transfer the nuts and seeds to a baking sheet, spreading them evenly. Bake for 15–20 minutes, stirring occasionally. The air will be filled with a rich, nutty aroma. Transfer to a bowl, sprinkle with more salt, if needed, and serve warm or at room temperature.

makes 4 cups (1¼ lb/625 g)

Yucatán

Zicil-P'ak

pumpkin seed dip

The name of this dip or spread, a classic pre-Columbian dish, is a combination of the Maya words for pumpkin seeds and tomato. That is just what this delightful concoction is, with only a few other ingredients thrown in for additional flavor. This version is one I adapted from Restaurante El Príncipe Tutul Xio in Mani, deep in the Puuc hills south of Mérida. Serve it as a dip with crispy totopos *(page 251) or, as the restaurant did, on top of thin slices of grilled pork wrapped in corn tortillas.*

1 cup (5 oz/155 g) raw hulled green pumpkin seeds

1 large, ripe tomato or 4 plum (Roma) tomatoes, roasted (page 250)

1 habanero chile, roasted (page 247)

2 tablespoons finely chopped fresh cilantro (fresh coriander)

2 tablespoons finely chopped fresh chives

1 teaspoon sea salt, or to taste

squeeze of lime juice

Heat a heavy frying pan over medium-low heat until quite hot. Pour in the pumpkin seeds and, as soon as they start to pop, stir constantly until they begin to puff up. Don't let them get brown. Pour onto a plate to cool completely, then grind them quite fine in a spice grinder.

In a blender or food processor, combine the tomato and chile and process briefly. Pour into a small bowl and stir in the ground seeds, cilantro, chives, and salt. Let the mixture stand for 30 minutes.

Just before serving, add the lime juice. The dip should spread easily. If it is too thick, stir in a little water, then serve.

makes about 1 cup (8 fl oz/250 ml)

Chiapas

Sincronizadas

tortilla ham and cheese sandwiches

Chiapas is a state of overwhelming beauty, rich in rivers, lakes, and ocean shorelines, rugged mountains, and lowland jungles. Once part of Guatemala and still peopled by descendants of the Maya civilization that flourished here, it is an unlikely place to be eating these recent, rather commercial additions to the "fast food" of Mexico. While sincronizadas *are now found all over Mexico, with some much better than others, the best I've ever had were at a roadside eatery in the fog-shrouded highlands of Chiapas—just ham and cheese layered between two tortillas and heated on a* comal *until the cheese was softly melted. But it was a tangy cow's milk cheese and an exceptional piece of mountain-cured ham, both specialties of the region. I like to add a little oil to my* comal *when cooking the* sincronizadas, *as they seem to brown better, but it is not necessary.*

1 tablespoon safflower or canola oil (optional)

12 thin corn tortillas, 6 inches (15 cm) in diameter, homemade (page 251) or purchased

6 thin slices Port Salut, white cheddar, or other full-flavored cheese, about 5 oz (155 g) total weight

6 thin slices good-quality ham, about 5 oz (155 g) total weight

6 teaspoons Chipotle Chile Salsa (page 174) or other salsa

guacamole (page 43)

♛ Heat a heavy frying pan or *comal* over medium heat and add the oil, if using. Top 6 of the tortillas with a slice of cheese and a slice of ham, and spread the ham with 1 teaspoon of the salsa. Cover with a second tortilla and place in the hot pan. Toast over medium heat until the cheese begins to melt and the tortilla is freckled with brown. Flip over and toast the other side. Transfer to a plate and keep warm.

♛ Serve each sandwich with a scoop of guacamole on the side.

makes 6 sandwiches

Discadas

farmer's-style burritos

Even a badly dented plow disk is not discarded by farmers in northern Mexico. Instead, it is used over a wood fire for cooking this robust, easy-going dish. Not having a battered disk handy, I suggest substituting the similarly shaped wok. There is no substitute, however, for good-quality chorizo. It's worth the time to make this fresh pork sausage at home (page 248) or seek out the best product you can find in a Hispanic market. Serve the burritos with Well-Fried Beans (page 182).

bottom quarter of a white onion, plus 2 onions, finely chopped

½ lb (250 g) lean bacon, chopped

½ lb (250 g) chorizo, homemade (page 248) or purchased, crumbled

1 red bell pepper (capsicum), seeded and chopped

3 ripe tomatoes, roasted (page 250) and chopped, or 1 can (14½ oz/455 g) diced tomatoes, partially drained

¾ lb (375 g) pork tenderloin or boneless country-style ribs, cut into ¾-inch (2-cm) chunks

1 lb (500 g) beef sirloin tip, cut into ¾-inch (2-cm) chunks

1 serrano chile, finely chopped

sea salt to taste

¼ head lettuce, finely shredded

1 cup (8 oz/250 g) guacamole (page 43) (optional)

salsa of choice

8–10 flour tortillas, 8 inches (20 cm) in diameter, homemade (page 251) or purchased

Heat a wok over medium-high heat and rub the chunk of onion around the pan several times to season it; discard the onion. Add the bacon, and when the fat starts to melt, stir in the chorizo and fry, stirring constantly, until the meats are cooked but not starting to brown or crisp, 8–10 minutes.

Add the chopped onions and bell pepper to the wok, reduce the heat to medium-low, and fry until the onions are golden, about 10 minutes. Spoon the excess fat into a large frying pan. Add the tomatoes to the wok and continue to cook for several minutes until the tomatoes are very soft and some liquid remains.

Meanwhile, heat the bacon and chorizo fat in the frying pan over medium-high heat. Add the pork and beef and cook until any liquid evaporates and the meat begins to caramelize, about 5 minutes. Add the meat to the wok and stir to mix well. Add the chile, season with salt, and heat through.

Set out the lettuce, guacamole, and salsa. Place a *comal,* griddle, or heavy frying pan over medium-high heat. Place a tortilla on the hot surface and heat briefly, turning once. Transfer to a plate and top with some of the meat. Loosely fold the tortilla over the meat, spoon some of the condiments on top, and serve. Alternatively, fold the bottom of the tortilla over the filling, fold in the two sides, left and then right, and finish by rolling up the tortilla until it is completely closed, then eat out of hand.

serves 8

SOPAS Y SOPAS SECAS

Soup appears on the Mexican table for at least one meal of the day.

Preceding pages: In Puerto Vallarta, a beachside feast of grilled fish and shrimp (prawns) is a tempting sight for tourists and residents alike. **Left:** A *rebozo,* or shawl, is essential for hauling home the abundant offerings of the marketplace—or for carrying a young child while shopping. **Above top:** The sixteenth-century Church of Santo Domingo, pride of Oaxaca, boasts an elaborately carved façade and an ornate gilded interior. **Above:** Corn dough, or *masa,* made with dried kernels from ears of red, yellow, or blue corn, is fashioned into tortillas in varying hues.

IF THERE WERE ONLY one reason for me to go to Mexico, it would be for the soups—honest soups made with loving, knowing hands to satisfy my hunger, to delight and comfort me. Luckily, a soup always seems to be on the table for one meal of the day. It is as much a part of life as the laughter of children. It may be just a tiny cup of intensely flavored shrimp (prawn) broth to intrigue the appetite, a ladleful of tomato-enriched *caldo* with a few nuggets of carrots, some grains of rice, and slivers of chicken at the start of dinner, or a bowl so satisfying and nourishing that it serves as the complete meal. I cannot imagine eating in a Mexican home or restaurant without some kind of soup being offered.

But that was not always true. It is thought that the closest the Mayas, Aztecs, and other indigenous people came to soup making may have been thick stews cooked in large clay *ollas.* It was the Spaniards who first brought to Mexico the memories of the traditional robust

Above top: The cool colors and simple stonework of this Yucatecan house are typical of the local architecture. **Above:** *Nixtamal*—a mixture of corn, slaked lime, and water—must soak for hours before being ground into *masa* for tortillas. **Right:** A fisherman greets the morning after a long night trolling the waters north of Puerto Vallarta.

soups that had utilized the cheap and easily obtainable ingredients of the different regions of Spain. Yes, they were able to bring some of these ingredients with them—especially meats—but in re-creating the dishes, their cooks, many of them natives, had to improvise. The local chiles, corn, beans, and tomatoes were put to good use in the homes of the Spanish settlers, and instead of the much beloved *cocido* of boiled beef and chickpeas (garbanzo beans), there was *menudo* of hominy and tripe, or *caldo de res,* a rich beef broth with chunks of beef and vegetables.

Everywhere across Mexico, some soups, like these two, are favorites that are served up in market *fondas* and in small *restaurantes* offering a set-course *comida corrida.* Regional specialties abound. In the lively port of Veracruz, I often start the day with a bowl of invigorating chile-rich crab soup. Only three hours away, in the highlands of the state, I will indulge myself in Xico by eating a brothy black bean soup that is flavored with smoky chiles and an unusual herb, *xonequi,* that is used nowhere else, not even in neighboring Coatepec or Jalapa. With its little blue

MARIELA II

corn *masa* dumplings and satisfying taste, this ebony soup is worth the trip. I am content.

A rich chicken broth is the basis for many of Mexico's soups. Nearly every market has one section given over to chicken, with the biggest and fattest birds hung by their feet over the counter like gigantic sleeping bats, the plucked bodies golden from a diet of brightly colored marigold petals. Prospective buyers carefully select just the right chicken to provide the best soup stock. An old hen is usually preferred, especially if it is complete with eggs. Lots of chicken feet are added to give a welcomed gelatinous quality. The best cooks simmer the chicken in water for a very long time with just a few pieces of onion, parsley, or garlic to give a slight flavor that doesn't overpower the taste of the chicken.

I will always remember the chicken soup I once had in a small restaurant in Tuxtla Gutiérrez, in Chiapas. I had been sick, and all I wanted was something hot, nourishing, and easy to swallow. It was billed as *consomé de pollo* on the menu, and it was just that. But what made it so special was how it was served. The clear broth was brought to the table in a tureen, and after the waitress ladled it up, she added tiny bits of chopped tomato, a chivelike onion, avocado, and a sprinkle of cilantro to the bowl, bringing fresh flavors and crisp textures. I left with my energy restored and good memories of this simple dish.

Similar broths or stocks are used as the base for many other Mexican soups. One classic is tortilla soup—on the menu of almost every eating place in the country—although in Michoacán it will be called *sopa Tarasca,* after the Indians of the region. The broth enlivened with tomatoes and chiles is, again, made special by all the wonderful things that are added. This time, the broth is poured over a handful of crunchy tortilla strips and little fingers of fried ancho chiles, and cubes of cheese are floated on top. One freezing cold night in Pátzcuaro, in a highland valley of Michoacán, I was served this soup as I warmed myself in front of a blazing wood fire with a mound of dozing kittens to keep me company. To make the soup even more special, chunks of avocado and a spoonful of thick *crema* gave it a soothing touch.

Above top: In his backyard, a Yucatecan man tends to rows of plump tomatillos and lantern-shaped habanero chiles. **Above:** *Huitlacoche,* a silvery black fungus that grows on ears of corn, is prized in Mexico for its pungent, smoky-sweet flavor. **Right top:** Poultry, today nearly as prominent on the Mexican table as the more popular pork, stars in dishes as simple as a rich broth studded with avocado and chickpeas (garbanzos) or as complex as Chicken and Squash Blossom Rolls in poblano chile sauce (page 132). **Right:** A vendor and a customer laugh easily with each other at a bustling outdoor street market in Tlacolula, near Oaxaca.

I can still remember the first time I ordered *sopa de arroz* in a Mexico City restaurant. I certainly was not expecting a plate of red rice speckled with peas. I like rice, and not wanting to make a fuss, I just ate it and did not say anything when I was served my main course. The next day, at a rather upscale place, I ordered *sopa de fideos,* and the same thing happened, only this time my plate was covered with thin pasta in a tomato sauce.

By the next time I went out to dinner, I had figured out that the mistake was on my part, as these are considered *sopas secas,* or "dry soups." For a more formal meal it is proper to serve first a wet soup to be followed by the dry, much as pasta is served before a main course in Italy. These days, it is usually one or the other. Rice is the most common of the dry soups, but crepes and various savory vegetable *budines,* or "custards," often take their place, both a reflection of the strong French influence in Mexican cuisine. My favorite filling for crepes is *huitlacoche,* that silvery black fungus that

flourishes on some ears of corn. I remember when those deformed kernels were found on the corn we grew on our Idaho farm. My dad's immediate response was to burn this corn "smut" so it didn't spread throughout our fields. In Mexico, it has long been prized as a gastronomic delight, and its appeal has spread, so that some growers in the United States have begun to specialize in its cultivation.

Whether as filling and down-to-earth as a pot of simmering *pozole,* with its generous measure of hominy and its hearty pork flavor; a refreshing fruit soup; or a plate of chile-fired pasta, there is a soup to satisfy all needs.

Above: Aromatic cumin seeds lend their nutty, piquant flavor to many Mexican dishes. **Right:** A golden sunset is pierced by the spiky silhouette of two agave plants. **Below:** Mexican cuisine benefits from the heat and subtle flavors of a seemingly endless variety of chiles that are added fresh or dried, used whole or chopped, "walked through" a salsa or stuffed with a filling. **Far right:** Mexican architecture is famous for its vibrant character and its love affair with intense colors.

San Luis Potosí

Sopa de Lentejas con Piña, Peras, y Plátanos

lentil soup with pineapple, pears, and plantains

San Luis Potosí, a state best known for the highland gold and silver mines that made it one of seventeenth-century New Spain's richest outposts, also has a small tropical region, La Huasteca, that extends down the slopes of the eastern range of the Sierra Madre. From here, the Spaniards obtained the tropical fruits that, combined with the lentils and pears of their homeland, created this earthy, soul-satisfying soup.

1½ cups (10½ oz/330 g) lentils, preferably brown, well rinsed

8 cups (64 fl oz/2 l) water

1 white onion, stuck with 2 whole cloves

4 cloves garlic, peeled but left whole

1 bay leaf

1 tablespoon olive oil

½ lb (250 g) good-quality chorizo, homemade (page 248) or purchased, crumbled

4 ancho chiles, seeded and toasted (page 247)

boiling water to cover

1 ripe tomato, roasted (page 250), or ¾ cup (4½ oz/140 g) drained canned chopped tomatoes

½-inch (12-mm) piece true cinnamon bark or ½ teaspoon ground cinnamon

1 black-ripe plantain, peeled and cut on the diagonal into slices ¼ inch (6 mm) thick

½ cup (2 oz/60 g) chopped white onion

¼ teaspoon dried oregano, preferably Mexican

pinch of ground allspice

sea salt and freshly ground pepper to taste

1 small pear, peeled, cored, and cut into ½-inch (12-mm) cubes

2 fresh pineapple slices, each ½ inch (12 mm) thick, cut into small triangles

2 limes, quartered

In a large pot, combine the lentils, water, clove-studded onion, garlic, and bay leaf. Bring to a boil over high heat, cover, reduce the heat to medium-low, and simmer gently until the lentils are almost tender, about 30 minutes. Meanwhile, in a frying pan over medium heat, warm the oil. Add the chorizo and brown until it gives off its fat, about 5 minutes. Using a slotted spoon, transfer the chorizo to the lentils. Drain all but 1 tablespoon of fat from the pan, reserving the excess to use later if needed.

In a bowl, combine the ancho chiles with boiling water to cover. Let soak until the chiles are soft, about 15 minutes. Drain and put into a blender or food processor with the tomato, cinnamon, and 1 cup (8 fl oz/250 ml) of the lentil cooking liquid. Blend until smooth.

Reheat the chorizo fat in the frying pan over medium-high heat. Add the plantain slices and fry, turning as needed, until dark brown, 6–8 minutes. Using a slotted spoon, transfer to absorbent paper to drain. Pour some of the reserved chorizo fat into the pan if needed, add the chopped onion, and sauté over medium heat until softened, about 2 minutes. Pour in the chile mixture and add the oregano, allspice, salt, and pepper. Fry, stirring frequently, until the sauce is thickened, about 5 minutes.

Stir the sauce into the lentils and continue to simmer until the lentils are tender, about 15 minutes. The timing will depend on the age and type of lentil used. When tender, stir in the plantain, pear, and pineapple and simmer until the fruit is soft, about 10 minutes longer. Add more water if necessary, although the soup should be thick. Taste and adjust the seasoning.

Ladle into warmed large bowls and accompany with the lime wedges. Serve immediately.

serves 8 as a first course, or 6 as a main course

Local beans, chiles, and corn were put to use in the kitchens of Spanish settlers.

Michoacán

Sopa de Melón

melon soup

I first tasted this unusual soup in the area around the agricultural town of Apatzingán. Its mild, sweet flavor is a perfect contrast to a spicy main course.

corn or peanut oil for frying

3 purchased thin corn tortillas, cut into ½-inch (12-mm) squares

3 very ripe cantaloupes, halved and seeded

2 tablespoons unsalted butter

1 russet potato, peeled and cut into chunks

1 cup (8 fl oz/250 ml) milk

½ cup (4 fl oz/125 ml) water

1 tablespoon medium-dry sherry (optional)

1 teaspoon sea salt, or to taste

¼ teaspoon ground white pepper

1 tablespoon fresh lime juice

In a small frying pan, pour oil to a depth of ½ inch (12 mm) and place over medium-high heat. When very hot, add the tortilla squares and fry, turning at least once, until golden brown, about 3 minutes. Transfer to absorbent paper to drain.

Using the small end of a melon baller, press deep into the flesh of a melon half, twist, and scoop out a whole ball. Repeat until there are about 16 balls. Cut the remaining melon flesh into chunks and purée in a blender until smooth.

In a saucepan over medium heat, melt the butter. Add the potato and cook for 3 minutes, stirring constantly. Add the milk, cover, and simmer over low heat until the potato is soft, about 10 minutes. Let cool slightly, then purée. Return to the pan over medium heat and add the water, stirring constantly. Let the soup come to a slow boil. Add all but ½ cup (4 fl oz/125 ml) of the puréed melon and the sherry (if using), salt, and pepper. Simmer over low heat, stirring often, for 10 minutes. Add the lime juice and remaining melon purée, stir well, and heat through.

Ladle into warmed bowls, garnish with the cantaloupe balls and crispy tortilla squares, and serve.

serves 4–6

Oaxaca

Caldo de Gato

"cat" broth

No, this hearty meat and vegetable soup is not made out of the stray cats that roam the streets of Oaxaca. I have yet to find out why this popular Oaxacan dish was given such a name. The dried and smoked chile pasilla de Oaxaca *is unique to this region of Mexico and is an entirely different chile than the more common* chile pasilla de México. *Canned* chiles chipotles en adobo *may be substituted.*

2 lb (1 kg) beef short ribs, cut into 2-inch (5-cm) cubes, trimmed of excess fat

2 lb (1 kg) sirloin tip roast or other stewing beef, cut into 2-inch (5-cm) cubes

6 cups (48 fl oz/1.5 l) beef broth

1 white onion, thickly sliced

6 cloves garlic, peeled but left whole

2 large fresh mint sprigs

sea salt to taste

10 tomatillos, about ½ lb (250 g), husked, rinsed, and quartered

3 chiles pasillas de Oaxaca, *seeded and toasted (page 247), or 2* chiles chipotles en adobo

1 chayote, about ¾ lb (375 g), peeled and cut into 2-inch (5-cm) pieces, or 2 small zucchini (courgettes), cut into 2-inch (5-cm) pieces

4 small carrots, peeled and quartered crosswise

4 small new red potatoes, unpeeled, quartered

½ cup (3½ oz/105 g) medium- or long-grain white rice

1 small cabbage, about 1 lb (500 g), cut into 8 wedges

¼ lb (125 g) green beans, ends trimmed and cut into 2-inch (5-cm) lengths

1 can (15 oz/470 g) chickpeas (garbanzo beans), drained

3 tablespoons chopped fresh cilantro (fresh coriander)

1 lime, cut into 6 wedges

In a large pot, combine the meats and the broth. Add enough water so that the liquid reaches at least 2 finger joints above the meat. Bring to a boil over medium-high heat and skim off any foam that collects on the surface. Add the onion, garlic, mint, and salt, then reduce the heat, cover, and simmer until the meats are just tender, about 1½ hours. When done, skim the fat from the surface or, if time allows, put it all in the refrigerator for several hours and lift off the fat that congeals on the surface.

Meanwhile, place the tomatillos in a saucepan over medium heat. Bring to a simmer and cook until soft, about 15 minutes. Drain, reserving the cooking liquid. Break the chiles into small pieces and put into a blender. Add the tomatillos and purée to make a smooth sauce, adding some of the reserved cooking liquid if the blades are sticking. Set aside.

Using a slotted spoon, lift the cooked meats from the broth. Strain the broth and return it to the pot. Remove any bones or gristle from the meats and return them to the pot as well. Bring to a simmer over medium heat and add the chayote or zucchini, carrots, potatoes, and rice. Simmer, uncovered, for 10 minutes. Add the cabbage and green beans and continue cooking until the vegetables are tender but not mushy, 8–10 minutes longer. Add the chickpeas and the tomatillo sauce to taste. Adjust the seasoning with salt. Simmer a few minutes more.

Ladle the soup into warmed deep bowls, sprinkle with the cilantro, and serve with lime wedges for squeezing into the soup.

serves 6 generously

Morelos

Crêpas de Hongos

mushroom crepes

Crepes, which are basically another form of tortilla, have long been a favorite dish to order for the dry soup course in upscale restaurants. They also make an elegant light supper when served with a green salad.

CREPES

1¼ cups (6½ oz/200 g) all-purpose (plain) flour

½ teaspoon sea salt

1⅓ cups (11 fl oz/340 ml) milk, or more if needed

3 eggs, lightly beaten

2 tablespoons unsalted butter, melted and cooled

3 tablespoons fresh cilantro (fresh coriander), chopped

additional melted unsalted butter or safflower or canola oil for frying

FILLING

¼ cup (2 fl oz/60 ml) olive oil, or more if needed

4 árbol chiles, seeded

1 cup (5 oz/155 g) finely chopped white onion

4 cloves garlic, minced

1¼ lb (625 g) fresh wild or cultivated mushrooms, brushed clean and diced

½ cup (¾ oz/20 g) finely chopped fresh cilantro (fresh coriander)

sea salt and freshly ground pepper to taste

SAUCE

1 tablespoon unsalted butter

2 cloves garlic, minced

3 tablespoons all-purpose (plain) flour

3 cups (24 fl oz/750 ml) milk

1 cup (8 fl oz/250 ml) crema *(page 248)*

sea salt and freshly ground pepper to taste

½ cup (¾ oz/20 g) finely chopped fresh cilantro (fresh coriander)

GARNISH

1 cup (4 oz/125 g) shredded Manchego or Monterey jack cheese

½ cup (¾ oz/20 g) chopped fresh cilantro (fresh coriander)

To make the crepes, in a bowl, combine the flour and salt. Stir in the 1⅓ cups (11 fl oz/340 ml) milk, eggs, 2 tablespoons butter, and cilantro. Using a handheld mixer, beat until well mixed. Add 1 tablespoon more milk if necessary, as the batter should be very thin. Cover with plastic wrap and let stand at room temperature for 45–60 minutes.

Stir the batter and add a little more liquid if it is too thick. Heat an 8- or 9-inch (20- or 23-cm) crepe pan over medium-high heat. Cover the surface lightly with melted butter or oil and heat for a few seconds. Ladle about 3 tablespoons of the batter in the pan. Remove the pan from the heat and tilt so the batter forms a thin, round crepe. Return to the heat and cook until the bottom is slightly browned, about 1 minute. Using a spatula, loosen the edges of the crepe and turn. Cook until slightly browned on the second side, less than 1 minute, and invert the pan over a large plate. Continue with the remaining batter to make 20–25 crepes.

Preheat an oven to 350°F (180°C). Oil a shallow baking dish measuring 9 by 12 inches (23 by 30 cm).

To make the filling, in a large, heavy frying pan over medium-low heat, warm the ¼ cup (2 fl oz/60 ml) olive oil. Add the chiles and fry for just a few seconds. Transfer to absorbent paper to drain, then crumble. Add the onion and garlic to the oil remaining in the pan over medium heat and sauté until the onion is golden, about 3 minutes. Transfer to a dish. Raise the heat to medium-high, add more oil if needed, and toss in the mushrooms so they form a single layer. Cook the mushrooms, stirring occasionally, until they are soft and brown on all sides, 4–5 minutes. Stir in the reserved chiles, onion, and garlic and add the cilantro, salt, and pepper. Remove from the heat.

To make the sauce, melt the butter in a saucepan over medium-low heat. Add the garlic and sauté for a few seconds. Stir in the flour and cook for a few seconds longer. Add the milk and *crema* and season well with salt and pepper. Bring to a slow boil, reduce the heat to low, and simmer, stirring continuously, for several minutes until the sauce thickens. Mix half of the sauce into the mushroom mixture. Stir the cilantro into the remaining sauce.

Spoon an equal amount of the filling onto each crepe and roll up. Place the filled crepes, seam side down, in a single layer in the prepared baking dish. Top with the sauce and cheese. Bake until the cheese is bubbling and beginning to brown, 8–10 minutes. Garnish with the cilantro and serve.

serves 4–6

Nuevo León

Menudo

hominy and tripe soup

Throughout northern and parts of central Mexico, pieces of tripe are simmered in a rich pork broth to become that popular restorative soup called menudo. *With all of the condiments that are heaped on top, it usually serves as a full meal, traditionally on Sunday, after a night of carousing. In Nuevo León, home cooks like Sra. Villareal de Longoria season the broth with chiles and then add* pozole *(hominy) for more texture. Serve the soup with lots of hot flour tortillas.*

2 lb (1 kg) honeycomb tripe

1 tablespoon cider vinegar

2 pig's feet or 1 calf's foot, split lengthwise

2½ qt (2.5 l) water

1 lb (500 g) packaged freshly prepared pozole *or 2 cans (14 oz/440 g each) white hominy, drained and rinsed*

½ white onion, finely diced

4 bay leaves

3 cloves garlic

1 tablespoon dried oregano, preferably Mexican

1 teaspoon sea salt, or more to taste

3 ancho chiles, seeded and toasted (page 247), then soaked in very hot water for 30 minutes

2 tablespoons safflower or canola oil

CONDIMENTS

6 limes, quartered

¼ cup (¾ oz/20 g) ground pequín chile or 3 serrano chiles, chopped

½ white onion, chopped

3 tablespoons dried oregano, preferably Mexican

Wash the tripe under running cold water and cut into ½-inch (12-mm) squares. Put them into a large pot and add the vinegar and water to cover. Bring to a slow boil over medium-high heat and simmer, uncovered, for 10 minutes. Drain, rinse the tripe, and return to the pot. Add the pig's feet or calf's foot and the 2½ qt (2.5 l) water. If using the freshly prepared *pozole,* add it to the pot. Bring to a boil over medium-high heat, skimming off any foam from the surface. Add the onion, bay leaves, garlic, oregano, and salt. Reduce the heat, cover, and simmer until both the tripe and the *pozole* are tender, 2–4 hours.

While the meat is cooking, drain the chiles, reserving the liquid. Tear the chiles into small pieces and put into a blender along with ½ cup (4 fl oz/125 ml) of the soaking liquid. Blend until smooth, adding more liquid if necessary.

In a frying pan over medium-high heat, warm the oil. Pour in the puréed chiles and cook, stirring constantly, for several minutes. Ladle in 1 cup (8 fl oz/250 ml) broth from the simmering meat, reduce the heat, and simmer for 5 minutes. Add the chile sauce to the tripe. If using canned hominy, add it at this time as well.

Remove the pig's feet or calf's foot and skim off any excess fat from the surface of the *menudo.* When the pig's feet or calf's foot is cool enough to handle, cut off any meaty pieces and return them to the pot, discarding the bone and cartilage. Continue simmering for another 10–15 minutes to heat through and blend the flavors. The *menudo* is even tastier if prepared several days in advance and refrigerated in a tightly sealed container. When ready to finish, remove any congealed fat and reheat.

Ladle the soup into warmed deep bowls. Set out small bowls of the condiments and let everyone choose their own toppings.

serves 8 generously

Tradiciones Gastronómicas Mexicanas

Despite the demands of today's world, the traditional sequence of eating meals still predominates throughout Mexico. To break the long night's fast, many Mexicans enjoy a freshly baked sweet roll and a cup of coffee or chocolate for *desayuno.* I like to make my way to a nearby church, where shawl-wrapped women are selling homemade tamales and *atole,* a nourishing corn *masa* gruel.

This sparse meal may come as early as sunup, followed hours later by *almuerzo,* a much heartier breakfast, brunch, or lunch. On Sunday morning, especially in northern Mexico, *menudo,* a comforting tripe soup consumed after a night of alcoholic indulgence, is a staple. In other regions, a different soup may take its place. Yes, eggs are eaten, but however they are cooked, they will have a sauce of chiles, onions, and tomatoes. Juice, fruit, maybe meat, usually beans, and almost always tortillas will be part of an *almuerzo.*

Sensibly, the main, sustaining meal, or *comida,* is served in midafternoon, usually about two-thirty. If possible, the entire family gathers at home to eat. Sunday, especially, is a time when the extended family assembles for a relaxed midday meal, often at home, but sometimes in a favorite restaurant. It is best to come to the table hungry. Plates of *antojitos* are served in abundance, accompanied with pungent salsas and with beer or tequila to wash them all down. Then a light but tasty soup is presented, often followed by a dry soup of rice or pasta. The main course may be fish, stuffed chiles, a meat dish, or, on special occasions, a mole. If beans have not been part of this plate, they will be served separately in a soupy broth. The dessert, a traditional sweet of flan, rice pudding, or fruit ice, is followed by coffee and maybe a brandy or an aged tequila.

Merienda, a light snack of *antojitos,* soup, tamales, or leftovers, is usually all that is eaten before bed. For special occasions, a more elaborate *cena,* or late supper, is enjoyed with family and friends.

Jalisco

Crema de Flor de Calabaza

golden squash blossom cream soup

One of the glorious market sights of Mexico's summer rainy season is the profusion of vibrant gold squash blossoms. Paula Mendoza Ramos and her daughter, Rosa Maria, use the delicately flavored flowers in elegant crepes and in soups such as this one.

¼ cup (2 oz/60 g) unsalted butter

2 poblano chiles, roasted, peeled, seeded, and deveined (page 247), then diced

½ cup (2½ oz/75 g) finely chopped white onion

3 tablespoons all-purpose (plain) flour

1 lb (500 g) large squash blossoms (about 15, depending on size), stems and pistils removed and coarsely chopped

4 cups (32 fl oz/1 l) milk

3 cups (24 fl oz/750 ml) chicken broth

sea salt and white pepper to taste

In a frying pan over medium-low heat, melt the butter. Add the chiles and sauté lightly until soft, about 3 minutes. Transfer to a plate. Add the onion to the butter remaining in the pan and sauté over medium-low heat until translucent, about 5 minutes. Add the flour and cook, stirring continuously, until lightly golden, about 2 minutes.

Set aside a handful of the chopped squash blossoms. Gently stir the remaining blossoms into the onion mixture over low heat and let them sweat, stirring occasionally, for 5 minutes. Pour in the milk and chicken broth and bring to a gentle simmer. Taste and season with salt and pepper. Cover and keep at a lazy simmer for 10 minutes to blend the flavors. Remove from the heat and let cool slightly.

Working in batches, pour the soup into a blender or food processor and process until smooth. Pass the puréed soup through a sieve back into the pan. Gently reheat over medium-low heat.

Ladle into warmed bowls, top with the sautéed chiles and reserved blossoms, and serve immediately.

serves 6

Sonora

Caldo de Queso con Papas

cheese soup with potatoes

A classic northern Mexican ranch dish, this rich but simple soup is best when made from the local Sonoran cheeses. When you crave comfort food, there is nothing more satisfying.

2 tablespoons unsalted butter or safflower oil

4 small new potatoes, peeled and cut into ¾-inch (2-cm) cubes

1 white onion, finely chopped

1 clove garlic, minced

2 large, ripe tomatoes, peeled and finely chopped

4 cups (32 fl oz/1 l) beef broth

2 Anaheim chiles, roasted, peeled, seeded, and deveined (page 247), then chopped, or 2 canned mild green chiles, drained and chopped

1 cup (8 fl oz/250 ml) half-and-half (half cream) or milk, slightly warmed

sea salt and freshly ground pepper to taste

¾ lb (375 g) white cheddar or Monterey jack cheese, shredded

4 green (spring) onions, including the tender green tops, finely diced

In a dutch oven or other large, heavy pot over medium heat, melt the butter or warm the oil. Stir in the potatoes and onion and sauté until they begin to soften, 6–8 minutes. Do not allow to brown. Add the garlic and sauté for another minute or so.

Raise the heat to medium-high and add the tomatoes. Cook, stirring, until quite thick, about 5 minutes. Pour in the broth and chiles. Simmer, uncovered, until the potatoes are soft but not breaking apart, about 4 minutes. Reduce the heat to very low and add the half-and-half or milk, salt, and pepper. Cook until heated to serving temperature.

Divide the cheese evenly among warmed bowls and ladle in the soup. Garnish with the green onions and serve immediately.

serves 4–6

Michoacán

Sopa Tarasca

tarascan tortilla soup

In the region around Pátzcuaro and Tzintzuntzán, which is the center of the Purépecha or Tarascan Indian culture, two quite different soups go by the name Tarascan. The original, which has a rich bean base, is more of a home-style soup. The other is the delicious version most often served in restaurants. The longtime cook in the small family-owned Hostería San Felipe, where I stop to eat whenever I am in the beautiful lakeside town of Pátzcuaro, is emphatic about the origin of this latter soup. She says it was her robust version that has become so omnipresent that it is considered a traditional regional soup.

6 purchased thin corn tortillas

4 ancho chiles, seeded and deveined

hot water to cover

about 8 tablespoons (4 fl oz/125 ml) safflower or canola oil

½ white onion, chopped

2 cloves garlic, peeled but left whole

1 ripe tomato, roughly chopped, or 1⅓ cups (8 oz/250 g) drained canned chopped tomatoes

6 cups (48 fl oz/1.5 l) rich chicken broth

4 or 5 fresh epazote leaves (optional)

sea salt to taste

¼ teaspoon dried oregano, preferably Mexican

½ lb (250 g) queso fresco *or Monterey jack cheese, cubed*

1 avocado, preferably Haas, pitted, peeled, and cubed

Set 1 tortilla aside. Cut the other tortillas in half and then cut crosswise into strips ½ inch (12 mm) wide. Let them dry for 5–10 minutes. In a bowl, soak 1 chile in the hot water for 10–15 minutes. Cut the other chiles lengthwise into narrow strips about 1 inch (2.5 cm) long.

In a frying pan over medium-high heat, warm 6 tablespoons (3 fl oz/90 ml) of the oil. When hot, add the tortilla strips and fry, tossing, until crisp and golden on both sides, just a few seconds. Using a slotted spoon, transfer to absorbent paper to drain. Fry the chile strips very quickly in the same oil—again for just seconds—then remove and drain on absorbent paper.

If the frying pan is dry, add 1 tablespoon of the oil. Place over medium-low heat, add the onion and garlic, and sauté until a rich golden brown, about 10 minutes. Transfer to a blender or food processor. Drain the soaking chile, discarding the liquid. Tear up the chile and the remaining tortilla and add to the blender or food processor with the tomato. Purée until smooth, adding up to ¼ cup (2 fl oz/60 ml) water if needed to achieve a smooth consistency.

In a dutch oven or other large, heavy pot over medium-high heat, warm 1 tablespoon of the oil. Add the purée and fry, stirring continuously, until the sauce has deepened in color, about 5 minutes. Stir in the broth and the epazote, if using, and simmer for 15 minutes to blend the flavors. Add the salt and oregano at the end of the cooking.

When ready to serve, divide half of the tortilla strips and all of the cheese among warmed bowls, then ladle the hot soup into the bowls. Top with the remaining tortilla strips, the chile strips, and the cubed avocado. Serve immediately.

serves 6

¿Licuadora o Molcajete?

Every Sunday, outside of the city of Oaxaca, there is a Zapotec Indian market in Tlacolula so large that it spills through most of the town. The streets are choked with men leading goats past women seated on blankets with carefully constructed pyramids of chiles in front of them, stalls of cassettes with music blaring, and tables spread with medicinal herbs. It is a chaotic wonderland that links past and present.

The clearest evidence of this are the numerous displays of blender parts, which are prominent among the locks, nails, coils of rope, and batteries being hawked. *Licuadoras,* or blenders, are now among the most important cooking utensils in the Mexican kitchen. All but the very poorest or very traditional families consider this time-saving tool essential.

The *molcajete,* the three-legged mortar of dark volcanic rock that has been used throughout the centuries for grinding, is less evident at the market. Of course, the *molcajetes* that most families already have at home seldom need to be replaced, and except for the making of salsas and guacamole and the grinding of small amounts of whole spices and seeds, the blender is now the main workhorse.

Puebla

Sopa de Chile Poblano

poblano chile soup

The large poblano chile is extremely versatile. It can be stuffed, cut into rajas *(strips), which are used in a variety of ways, or made into this simple, yet elegant traditional soup. Around the town of San Martín Texmelucan, close by the highway between Mexico City and Puebla, is one of the primary growing regions for poblano chiles—a chile named for this state—so it is not surprising that local cooks, like my sometime cooking companion, Mónica Mastretta, who perfected this recipe, use them frequently. The cream sweetens the rich spice of the chiles, and the peas lend a brighter green hue to the finished soup.*

¼ cup (2 oz/60 g) unsalted butter

1 teaspoon safflower or canola oil

4 poblano chiles, roasted, peeled, seeded, and deveined (page 247), then cut into long, narrow strips

1 white onion, chopped

3 cloves garlic, chopped

6 cups (48 fl oz/1.5 l) chicken broth

1 cup (5 oz/155 g) fresh or frozen English peas

sea salt and freshly ground pepper to taste

½ cup (2½ oz/75 g) blanched almonds, finely ground

5 tablespoons (2½ fl oz/75 ml) crema *(page 248)*

In a large saucepan over medium heat, melt the butter with the oil. Stir in the chiles, onion, and garlic and sauté, stirring, until well softened, about 3 minutes. Add the chicken broth, peas, salt, and pepper, and simmer, uncovered, to blend the flavors, about 10 minutes. Remove from the heat and let cool slightly.

Working in batches, pour the chile mixture into a blender, add the ground almonds, and process until smooth. Taste and adjust the seasoning. Reheat the soup if necessary.

Ladle into warmed bowls and garnish with the *crema.* Serve immediately.

serves 4–6

Tlaxcala

Sopa de Bolitas de Carne y Papas

potato and meatball soup

Hearty enough to be a meal, this simple sopa *is thick with tasty balls of meat entwined with shreds of potato. I first sampled this warming soup on a chilly January morning at a tiny market* fonda *in Tlaxcala, the historical capital of Mexico's smallest state of the same name. Since the cook was reluctant to share the recipe, this is my version, with lots of advice from my friend Yolanda Ramos Galicia, an anthropologist and a noted cook from Tlaxcala.*

Tlaxcala, meaning "land of corn," is situated between Mexico City and Puebla and is one of my favorite places to relax in the heartland of this country. It has a fascinating history—without the help of the Tlaxcalans, who were the archenemies of Montezuma, the Spanish would not have defeated the Aztecs. It is also an exquisite colonial city with a very distinctive cuisine. In the surrounding countryside there are abandoned and restored pulque haciendas and glorious churches. Nearby is Cacaxtla, a wonderfully preserved archaeological site with vivid murals.

4 large russet potatoes, about 2 lb (1 kg) total weight

1 lb (500 g) ground (minced) lean pork

1 white onion, one half minced and one half coarsely chopped

1 teaspoon sea salt, or to taste

1 teaspoon freshly ground pepper

½ teaspoon dried oregano, preferably Mexican

2 eggs, lightly beaten

2 tablespoons safflower or canola oil

1 lb (500 g) ripe tomatoes, chopped, or 1 can (14½ oz/455 g) chopped tomatoes, drained

4 cups (32 fl oz/1 l) chicken broth

1 tablespoon all-purpose (plain) flour

1 jalapeño chile, partially slit open

1 fresh flat-leaf (Italian) parsley sprig, chopped

¼ cup (¼ oz/7 g) fresh cilantro (fresh coriander) leaves

Peel the potatoes and grate them on the medium holes of a handheld grater. Wrap the potatoes in a kitchen towel and squeeze out the excess liquid. In a bowl, combine the potatoes and meat, tossing and blending them together with the minced onion, salt, pepper, and oregano. When well mixed, add the eggs and mix again. With your hands, roll the meat-and-potato mixture into 1-inch (2.5-cm) balls.

Heat a large dutch oven or other heavy pot over medium heat and add the oil. When it is sizzling hot, working in batches, gently drop in the meatballs and fry until lightly brown on all sides, about 10 minutes. Using a slotted spoon, transfer the meatballs to a plate and set aside.

While the meatballs are cooking, put the tomatoes and chopped onion into a blender. Process until smooth, adding a little of the chicken broth, if needed, to facilitate the blending.

Sprinkle the flour into the hot oil remaining in the pot and stir for several minutes over medium heat. Slowly pour in the tomato-onion mixture, drop in the chile, and add the parsley. Continue to cook, stirring occasionally, until the mixture thickens and darkens in color, about 3 minutes. Add the remaining broth and the meatballs and let the soup simmer, uncovered, for 10–15 minutes. Remove the chile and discard. Taste and adjust the seasoning.

Ladle into warmed wide bowls and float the cilantro leaves on the surface. Serve immediately.

serves 6

Puebla

Sopa de Hongos

wild mushroom soup

During the summer rainy season, when wild mushrooms appear in the hills surrounding the central plateau of Mexico, I like to select mushrooms for this soup at the market at Cholula, a university town.

¼ cup (2 fl oz/60 ml) safflower or canola oil

1 white onion, finely diced

8 cloves garlic, finely diced

4 serrano chiles, seeded and finely diced

3 ripe plum (Roma) tomatoes, peeled and finely diced

2 tablespoons olive oil, or as needed

2 lb (1 kg) fresh wild mushrooms, brushed clean and sliced

2 teaspoons sea salt, plus salt and freshly ground pepper to taste

9 cups (72 fl oz/1.25 l) chicken broth

4 fresh epazote leaves, finely chopped (optional)

In a dutch oven or other large, heavy pot over medium-high heat, warm the safflower or canola oil. Add the onion and sauté until deep gold, about 6 minutes. Add the garlic and chiles and sauté for 1 minute longer. Stir in the tomatoes and simmer, uncovered, until very soft, about 15 minutes.

Meanwhile, warm the 2 tablespoons olive oil in a large frying pan over medium-high heat. Add the mushrooms and stir with a wooden spoon to coat evenly with the oil, adding more oil if the pan seems dry. Season with the 2 teaspoons salt and cook, stirring occasionally, until the mushrooms release their liquid, about 5 minutes.

Add the mushrooms to the onion mixture, pour in the broth, and bring to a simmer over medium-low heat. Add the epazote, if using, and stir well. Adjust the seasoning with salt and pepper and simmer for at least 15–20 minutes to blend the flavors.

Ladle the soup into warmed individual bowls and serve immediately.

serves 8

Tabasco

Arroz Blanco

seasoned white rice

Seldom in Mexico is rice prepared simply steamed and without seasoning. In this version from Ricardo Muñoz Zurita, the tiny bit of lime juice perks up the flavor of the grains, accents the seasonings, and seems to make the rice whiter. For a richer dish, substitute warm chicken broth for the cooking water. I usually omit the washing of the rice, as the rice I use is coated with water-soluble vitamins.

2 cups (14 oz/440 g) medium- or long-grain white rice

½ white onion, coarsely chopped

2 cloves garlic

3 tablespoons cold water

5 tablespoons (2½ fl oz/75 ml) safflower or canola oil

4 cups (32 fl oz/1 l) hot water

½ teaspoon fresh lime juice

3 fresh flat-leaf (Italian) parsley sprigs

1 teaspoon sea salt, or to taste

♛ Rinse the rice in water, swishing the grains, and then drain. Repeat 2 or 3 times, draining well. It is best if the rice is completely dry, so spread it out on a kitchen towel and leave it out for a few minutes.

♛ Put the onion, garlic, and cold water into a blender and process until smooth.

♛ In a dutch oven or other heavy pot with a lid, heat the oil over medium-high heat until it is smoking. Add the rice and toss until the grains turn a toasty golden color and have a nutty aroma, 7–10 minutes. The rice is ready when it begins to crackle.

♛ Stir the onion mixture into the rice and cook, stirring, for 1 minute. Pour in the hot water and add the lime juice, parsley, and salt. Continue to cook over medium-high heat until the mixture begins to simmer, then reduce the heat to medium-low, cover, and cook for 15 minutes without lifting the lid. Remove from the heat and leave the pot covered for 10 minutes, so the rice continues to steam.

♛ When ready to serve, remove the parsley and toss the rice with a fork, making sure that all the liquid has evaporated, then spoon into a bowl and serve.

makes 6 cups (30 oz/940 g); serves 6–8

Puebla

Sopa de Cilantro

cilantro soup

The distinctive flavor of cilantro is the major ingredient in this light, willow green soup that my friend Mónica Mastretta likes to serve at dinner parties.

2 cups (16 fl oz/500 ml) milk

2 bay leaves

2 tablespoons unsalted butter

1 teaspoon safflower or canola oil

⅓ white onion, coarsely chopped

3 tablespoons all-purpose (plain) flour

2 bunches fresh cilantro (fresh coriander), main stems removed

4 cups (32 fl oz/1 l) chicken broth

¼ teaspoon ground white pepper

sea salt to taste

½ cup (4 fl oz/125 ml) crema *(page 248)*

1 cup (1 oz/30 g) totopos *(page 251)*

¼ lb (125 g) queso fresco, *crumbled*

♛ In a saucepan, combine the milk and bay leaves and bring slowly to a gentle boil. Remove from the heat and set aside to cool slightly.

♛ In a heavy frying pan over medium heat, melt the butter with the oil. Add the onion and sauté until translucent, about 3 minutes. Add the flour and cook, stirring often, for several minutes until quite thick.

♛ Remove the bay leaves from the milk and discard. Gradually add the hot milk to the onion mixture, stirring constantly. Cook over medium heat, continuing to stir, until slightly thickened, about 5 minutes. Remove from the heat and let cool slightly.

♛ Working in batches, pour the onion-milk mixture into a blender, add the cilantro, and process until smooth. Pour the purée into a large saucepan and place over medium heat. Gradually stir in the chicken broth, pepper, and salt and cook, stirring occasionally, for 10 minutes. Stir in the *crema* and simmer only until heated through.

♛ Ladle into warmed bowls and sprinkle on the *totopos* and cheese. Serve immediately.

serves 6

Pozole

Corn—heart, soul, and backbone of the Mexican culinary world—becomes something entirely new when it is transformed into *pozole,* the Mexican word for what is called hominy elsewhere. Fat, meaty kernels of corn are first treated the same as for making tortillas or tamales. But instead of being ground into *masa,* the kernels are kept gently bubbling on the fire for hours until very tender (page 250).

What transforms the *pozole* into a hearty and flavorful soup, one with the same name as its principal ingredient, is something I learned firsthand in Uruapan, Michoacán. One evening, I stopped at an open-air *fonda* crowded with locals to see what made the kitchen's *pozole* so popular. On the counter were bowls of chopped white onions and red radishes, thinly sliced cabbage, and dried oregano so aromatic that I could smell it from my spot far down the line. Not until I was perched on a stool and served a large enamel bowl filled with a fragrant chile-red broth, thick with meat and hominy, did I realize that what makes *pozole* so special is the combination of textures and flavors created when these toppings are stirred into the soup.

Red *pozole* is just one of the several guises taken on by this colorful soup found throughout central Mexico. In Jalisco, it will be plain white, just pork, hominy, and savory broth, a dish that appears rather dull until the condiments are added: a *picante* árbol chile salsa, onions, radishes, and shredded lettuce. In Acapulco and other parts of Guerrero, Thursday is green *pozole* day, and small stands serve only this earthy version, its flavor and color enhanced by ground pumpkin seeds, an assortment of greens, jalapeño chiles, and tangy tomatillos. The locals usually top off the soup with crisp-fried pork rinds and chunks of avocado, along with chopped onion, cabbage, and pungent dried oregano. A squirt of lime juice is the final benediction.

Sinaloa

Pozole Sinaloense

pork and hominy soup

Pozole *refers to both the dish itself and the large corn kernels processed to make hominy. Variations of this rustic soup are found in most regions of Mexico. This red version from the state of Sinaloa is a family recipe from a young man who convinced me that his mother's* pozole *was every bit as exceptional as others I had sampled in my travels.*

SOUP

½ small pig's head, about 3 lb (1.5 kg), and 2 pig's feet, cleaned and halved, or 4 pig's feet, cleaned and halved

3 lb (1.5 kg) pork soup bones

1 lb (500 g) country-style pork ribs

2 lb (1 kg) boneless pork loin, cut into large chunks

1 small head garlic, outside papery skin removed, then halved crosswise

1 white onion, peeled but left whole

½ lb (250 g) ancho chiles (12–14), seeded

about 4 cups (32 fl oz/1 l) very hot water

3 lb (1.5 kg) packaged freshly prepared pozole *or 4 cans (14 oz/440 g each) white hominy, drained and rinsed*

1 tablespoon dried oregano, preferably Mexican

sea salt to taste

boiling water, if needed

CONDIMENTS

½ head lettuce or cabbage, shredded

20 small radishes, thinly sliced or diced

2 white onions, finely chopped

2 avocados, preferably Haas, pitted, peeled, and cubed (optional)

8 limes, halved

To make the soup, rinse the pig's head, if using, and the pig's feet in several changes of water. Place in a large pot and add water to cover. Bring the water to a boil over high heat, reduce the heat to medium, and simmer, uncovered, for 1 hour. Remove the pig's head and feet and set aside to cool. Reserve the liquid in the pot. With a knife, cut the meat from the head, discarding the bone, skin, and fat. The ear is a delicacy and should be cut up and returned to the broth with the other pieces of meat. Cut the meat from the pig's feet and add to the broth.

Add the soup bones, pork ribs, pork loin, garlic, and onion to the broth and simmer over medium heat. Cover, reduce the heat to medium-low, and cook until the meat is tender, about 2 hours.

Meanwhile, in a bowl, completely cover the chiles with the hot water and let soak for 20 minutes.

When the meat is tender, remove the big pieces from the pot along with the onion and garlic. Squeeze out the garlic from the skin and place in a blender with the onion and the chiles and 1 cup (8 fl oz/250 ml) of their soaking liquid. Blend until smooth, then pour through a medium-mesh sieve and return to the simmering broth.

When the meat is cool enough to handle, shred with the grain into large pieces. Discard any fat, bones, and gristle. Add the *pozole* or hominy, oregano, and salt and continue to simmer, uncovered, for about 30 minutes longer to blend the flavors. Add boiling water if necessary to keep the meats immersed. Using a large spoon, skim off the fat from the surface.

To serve, ladle the *pozole* into warmed bowls. Serve the condiments in small bowls on the side, to be added to taste.

serves 12 generously

Tabasco

Arroz Rojo con Achiote

red rice with achiote

As I explore Mexico, Ricardo Muñoz Zurita, one of the country's leading young chefs, often travels with me, and together we have discovered many unusual dishes, including this one from Tabasco, the state where he was born. This garlicky orange-red rice looks like the familiar Mexican red rice, but achiote *paste gives it a subtle spark of flavor.*

2 medium-large ripe tomatoes, chopped, or 1 can (14½ oz/455 g) chopped tomatoes, drained

½ cup (2½ oz/75 g) chopped white onion

2 cloves garlic, chopped

1 tablespoon achiote *paste (page 246)*

⅓ cup (3 fl oz/80 ml) safflower or canola oil

2 cups medium- or long-grain white rice

3 cups (24 fl oz/750 ml) chicken broth

1 green bell pepper (capsicum), roasted, seeded, and deveined (page 246), then cut into short, narrow strips

5 fresh flat-leaf (Italian) parsley sprigs, chopped, plus a few sprigs for garnish

1 teaspoon sea salt, or to taste

In a blender, purée the tomatoes, onion, and garlic. Add the *achiote* paste and blend until well mixed. Pass the mixture through a sieve.

In a heavy saucepan over medium heat, warm the oil. Add the rice and cook, stirring, until it starts to turn light gold, about 5 minutes. Stir in the tomato purée and fry, scraping the pan bottom occasionally, until the purée is absorbed, about 3 minutes. Stir in the broth and add the bell pepper, parsley sprigs, and salt. Reduce the heat to medium-low, cover, and cook the rice for 25 minutes. When the rice is almost cooked through, remove the pan from the heat and leave covered for 10 minutes.

Toss the rice with a fork, then spoon into a warmed bowl, garnish with parsley sprigs, and serve.

serves 8–10

Sopa Seca de Fideos con Tres Chiles

three chiles pasta

That triumvirate of Mexican chiles, the ancho, pasilla, and guajillo, is used by Marco Beteta to create an intensely flavored pasta dish that is served as a dry soup course. Fideos, *very thin noodles coiled into an oval, is the most common form of pasta in Mexico.*

2 ancho chiles
4 pasilla chiles
4 guajillo chiles
3 cloves garlic, unpeeled
1 tomato
¼ white onion
½ teaspoon cumin seeds, toasted
sea salt and freshly ground pepper to taste
2 tablespoons safflower or canola oil
14 oz (440 g) dried fideos
2 cups (16 fl oz/500 ml) chicken broth
¼ cup (2 fl oz/60 ml) crema *(page 248)*
¼ cup (1½ oz/45 g) crumbled queso fresco

Seed and toast the chiles (page 247), soak in hot water for 10 minutes, then drain. Roast the garlic (page 248), tomato (page 250), and onion (page 249). Tear the chiles into pieces and put into a blender along with the garlic, tomato, onion, and cumin seeds. Blend until smooth, adding a tablespoon or so of water, if necessary. Pass through a sieve. Season with salt and pepper.

In a large frying pan over medium-high heat, warm the oil. Add the *fideos,* breaking each coil into 3 parts. Stir and toss constantly until covered with oil and just beginning to turn golden brown. Add the chile sauce and cook, stirring often, for 5 minutes, reducing the heat when the sauce begins to bubble. Add the broth and stir until the sauce is absorbed into the pasta and the pasta is tender, about 5 minutes.

Scoop the *fideos* onto a warm serving dish and top with the *crema* and cheese. Serve immediately.

serves 6

Veracruz

Chilpachole de Jaiba

crab in a spicy broth

Veracruz is a riotously joyous land, with a people who delight daily in the pleasures of their senses regardless of what life may bring them tomorrow. Today is for living—and living means eating. On Sundays and holidays, families from the port of Veracruz flock south over the Rio Jamapa to spend the day at one of the rickety seafood restaurants perched among the roots of the mangrove trees that surround Laguna Mandinga. Every table is crowded with boisterous patrons eating boiled shrimp (prawns) by the kilo, as well as mojarra, *a freshwater fish caught just hours earlier from the lagoon. The local fishermen receive stiff competition from the equally experienced green kingfishers that hover over the water just waiting to plunge after the smallest of the young fish swimming below. Another favorite dish is a netful of tiny blue crabs simmered in a pungent, deeply red tomato broth.*

The Atlantic Ocean blue crabs are usually available, freshly caught, with their claws bound to their bodies. The larger Dungeness crabs from the Pacific are more often preboiled and sold in the shell, which is important, as the shells are needed for the broth. If you are buying live crabs, I suggest putting the crabs in a pot with a couple of inches (5 cm) of cold water, then very gradually heating it until it is lukewarm. The crabs seem to die peacefully, but since they aren't yet cooked, they can immediately be used as if they were alive and plunged into 3 quarts (3 l) boiling water and cooked until the shells turn bright red, 5–6 minutes, then the crabs are swiftly removed.

8 blue crabs or 2 Dungeness crabs, cooked

8 cups (64 fl oz/2 l) water

sea salt to taste

4 cloves garlic, unpeeled, roasted (page 248)

1 large white onion, quartered and roasted (page 249)

1 can (14½ oz/455 g) diced tomatoes, drained

3 jalapeño chiles, roasted (page 247), or 2 chiles chipotles en adobo

3 tablespoons olive oil

1 large fresh epazote sprig or 4 fresh epazote leaves

2 limes, quartered

Place each crab on its back, remove the tail section, and set aside. Turn, grasp the large top shell, lift off, and reserve. Remove and discard the white gills and any other organs. Gently crack the claws, but leave the meat in the shell. Pick out the meat from the rest of the crab, place in a bowl, cover, and refrigerate along with the claws. Save all of the shells, rinse them, smash them lightly, and put them into a large saucepan. Add the water and season lightly with salt. Bring to a boil, reduce the heat, cover, and simmer for 20 minutes. Remove from the heat and strain the broth through a fine-mesh sieve lined with a double layer of cheesecloth (muslin). (The broth can be refrigerated overnight before continuing.)

Peel the garlic and put in a blender or food processor with the onion, tomatoes, and chiles. Purée until smooth, adding a little of the broth if necessary.

In a dutch oven or other deep, heavy pot over medium-high heat, warm the olive oil. When the oil is shimmering hot but not smoking, quickly pour in the tomato purée all at once. Be careful, as it will splatter. Reduce the heat just a bit and stir frequently until the sauce is thick, about 5 minutes.

Add 6 cups (48 fl oz/1.5 l) of the crab broth, then taste and adjust the seasoning. Simmer for 20 minutes. (The broth can be prepared in advance to this point, cooled, covered, and refrigerated for up to 6 hours before continuing.)

Add the epazote to the simmering broth and continue cooking for 10 minutes. Add the crabmeat and claws and cook until just heated through.

Ladle into warmed bowls, making sure that the crab claws are evenly divided. Serve immediately with the lime quarters for squeezing into the broth at the table.

serves 4–6

Soup is nearly as much a part of daily life as the laughter of children.

Navidad en Michoacán

It was a cold, clear December night in Pátzcuaro, Michoacán, where my husband and I were out walking. Hearing laughter, we looked down a narrow passageway lined on both sides with *rebozo*-clad men and women cheering on a swarm of children swatting a fruit- and candy-filled purple piñata. An old woman soon noticed our interest and pulled us in to meet the host, Chava, and his family. We were immediately offered small earthenware cups of steaming hot chocolate, and room was made for us to warm our hands over a squat charcoal-burning stove.

Soon, holding candles, we became part of a *posada,* a procession following a teenage boy and girl reenacting the roles of Joseph and Mary searching for lodging in Bethlehem before the birth of the baby Jesus. At each door, they knocked, singing a request for lodging, always to be refused. Finally at Chava's home, the couple was admitted, and all of us were invited to partake of bowls of *pozole.* We returned many times over the years for another cup of welcoming hot chocolate and bowl of *pozole,* which I will forever associate with our first Christmas in Michoacán.

México, D.F.

Pozole Verde con Hongos

mushroom and hominy soup

Every region has its own version of pozole, *but the one thing they usually have in common is their use of pork for flavoring. It took Mexico City's María Dolores Torres Yzábal, a classical but inventive cook, to come up with a rather quick-and-easy alternative using mushrooms in place of the meat. As many Mexican cooks no longer have time to make their own chicken broth, chicken bouillon granules and water are often substituted. For a totally vegetarian* pozole, *use vegetable broth instead of chicken bouillon granules.*

3 tablespoons canola or peanut oil, or more if needed

1 lb (500 g) fresh white mushrooms, brushed clean and sliced

1 purchased thin corn tortilla, left out overnight to dry

2 thin slices baguette, left out overnight to dry

7 cups (56 fl oz/1.75 l) water

5 teaspoons chicken bouillon granules

1 lb (500 g) tomatillos, husked, rinsed, and chopped

1 cup (1 oz/30 g) fresh cilantro (fresh coriander) sprigs, loosely packed

3 tablespoons finely chopped white onion

2 cloves garlic, finely chopped

1 serrano chile, finely chopped

3 tablespoons sesame seeds, toasted

3 tablespoons pumpkin seeds, toasted (page 250)

1-inch (2.5-cm) piece true cinnamon bark

2 whole cloves

1 fresh epazote sprig (optional)

2 cups (12 oz/375 g) packaged freshly prepared pozole *or drained canned hominy, rinsed*

sea salt to taste

CONDIMENTS

1 cup (5 oz/155 g) finely chopped radishes

1 cup (5 oz/155 g) finely chopped white onions

1 cup (3 oz/90 g) shredded cabbage

½ cup (¼ oz/7 g) dried oregano, preferably Mexican

2 serrano chiles, finely chopped (optional)

In a cast-iron frying pan over high heat, warm the 3 tablespoons oil. Add the mushrooms and toss and stir until you can smell their earthy aroma, 1–2 minutes. Remove immediately with a slotted spoon. Reduce the heat to medium and fry the tortilla, turning once, until browned, just a few seconds on each side. Using the slotted spoon, transfer the tortilla to absorbent paper to drain. Pat off any excess oil. If needed, add a little more oil to the pan and reheat, then lay the bread slices in the pan and brown on both sides in the same way. Transfer the bread slices to absorbent paper. When the tortilla and bread are cool, break into pieces.

Pour the water into a large pot and bring to a boil over high heat. Add the bouillon granules and, when they have dissolved, add the mushrooms, reduce the heat to medium-low, and simmer, uncovered, until soft, about 5 minutes. Drain the mushrooms, reserving the broth.

Working in batches, put the tortilla and bread pieces, tomatillos, cilantro, onion, garlic, serrano chile, and ½ cup (4 fl oz/125 ml) of the broth into a blender or food processor and blend until smooth.

Reheat the oil in the frying pan over medium-high heat until just starting to smoke, adding more if necessary. Pour in the purée all at once and fry, stirring occasionally, for a couple of minutes. Reduce the heat to medium and simmer, uncovered, until the mixture thickens, about 10 minutes.

Meanwhile, put the sesame and pumpkin seeds into a spice grinder and grind very finely. Put the seeds and 2 cups (16 fl oz/500 ml) of the reserved broth into a blender and blend until smooth. Stir into the tomatillo sauce.

Return the remaining broth to the pot and bring to a simmer. Place the cinnamon bark, cloves, and epazote (if using) on a piece of cheesecloth (muslin). Bring the corners together, tie securely with kitchen string, and drop the pouch into the broth. Add the tomatillo-seed sauce and stir in the mushrooms and *pozole* or hominy. Simmer the soup, uncovered, for 10–15 minutes. Season with salt. Remove and discard the pouch before serving.

Ladle the soup into warmed bowls. Set out small bowls of the condiments and let everyone choose their own toppings.

---

serves 6

Veracruz

Ostiones Alvarado

oyster stew, alvarado style

Fifty miles south of the port city of Veracruz lies the wind-lashed fishing port of Alvarado. Never mind that there is little of scenic interest in the town itself. This is a place to eat seafood. This rustic soup, with its perfume of fresh oysters, is one of my favorite dishes. Use very small oysters, or you may, as I sometimes do, substitute small clams or scallops for the oysters.

1-inch (2.5-cm) piece true cinnamon bark or ½ teaspoon ground cinnamon

10 peppercorns or ¼ teaspoon freshly ground pepper

2 whole cloves or pinch of ground cloves

½ teaspoon dried oregano, preferably Mexican

1 cup (8 fl oz/250 ml) water

2 pt (1 l) extra-small shucked oysters in their liquid (20–24)

6 small russet potatoes, peeled and cut into ½-inch (12-mm) cubes

2 teaspoons sea salt, plus salt to taste

4 jalapeño chiles

2 tablespoons safflower or canola oil

½ white onion, finely chopped

2 cloves garlic, finely minced

2 ripe tomatoes, peeled and coarsely chopped, or 1 can (1 lb/500 g) chopped tomatoes, drained

freshly ground pepper to taste

2 tablespoons chopped fresh flat-leaf (Italian) parsley leaves

lemon wedges

If using cinnamon bark, peppercorns, and whole cloves, put them in a spice grinder and grind to a powder. Place the freshly ground or already-ground spices in a bowl and add the oregano and water. Add the oysters and their liquid, cover, and refrigerate.

In a saucepan, combine the potatoes with water to cover. Add 2 teaspoons salt, bring to a boil over high heat, reduce heat to medium-high, and cook until just tender, 6–8 minutes. Using a slotted spoon, remove all but about 4 tablespoons of the potatoes and set aside. Raise the heat to high and reduce the remaining potato water to 2 cups (16 fl oz/500 ml), mashing the potatoes remaining in the liquid until they are well incorporated.

Seed and devein 3 of the chiles (page 247) and cut them lengthwise into strips ¼ inch (6 mm) wide. Leave the remaining chile whole.

In a large, heavy pot over medium heat, warm the oil. Add the onion and the chile strips and sauté until the onion is golden and the chiles are soft, about 4 minutes. Add the garlic and cook for 3 minutes longer. Raise the heat to medium-high and add the tomatoes, stirring frequently with a wooden spoon until most of the liquid has evaporated, about 4 minutes. Reduce the heat and stir in the potato water along with the whole jalapeño. (The stew can be prepared ahead up to this point, then cooled, covered, and refrigerated for up to 12 hours.)

Position a sieve over the pot and pour in the oysters and their liquid, allowing the liquid to flow into the soup. Bring to a slow boil over medium-low heat, and simmer, uncovered, for 5 minutes. Add the reserved potatoes and the oysters and heat just until the oysters plump, about 2 minutes. Taste the soup for seasoning and adjust with salt and pepper.

Remove from the heat, discard the whole chile, and ladle immediately into warmed bowls. Garnish with the parsley and serve with the lemon wedges on the side.

serves 4 as a main course, or 6 as a first course

México, D.F.

Caldo Tlalpeño

chicken and chickpea soup

The rambunctious flavor of the smoky chipotle chile in this classic soup from Mónica Mastretta is tamed by the addition of earthy chickpeas.

6 cups (48 fl oz/1.5 l) chicken broth

1 whole chicken breast, skinned

1 fresh mint sprig

1 tablespoon safflower or canola oil

½ large white onion, chopped

1 large carrot, peeled and diced

2 cloves garlic, chopped

1 chile chipotle en adobo, *finely chopped*

1 fresh epazote sprig

½ teaspoon sea salt

½ teaspoon freshly ground pepper

1 can (15 oz/470 g) chickpeas (garbanzo beans), drained and rinsed

1 avocado, preferably Haas, pitted, peeled, and diced

1 lime, cut into 6 wedges

In a saucepan over medium heat, bring the broth, chicken, and mint to a simmer and cook, partially covered, until the chicken is opaque throughout, about 15 minutes. Using tongs, lift out the chicken and mint. Discard the mint. Let the chicken cool until it can be handled, then bone the chicken and shred the meat. Set aside. Reserve the broth.

In a large saucepan over medium heat, warm the oil. Add the onion and carrot and sauté until the onion is translucent, about 5 minutes. Add the garlic and sauté for 1 minute longer. Pour in the broth and add the chile, epazote, salt, and pepper. Bring to a simmer, cover, and cook for 20 minutes. Stir in the chickpeas and simmer, uncovered, for 10 minutes longer. Add the shredded chicken and heat through.

Ladle the soup into warmed bowls, top with the avocado, and pass the lime wedges at the table.

serves 6

Michoacán

Sopa Fría de Aguacate

chilled avocado soup

When I eat at the home of Enrique Bautista, I know that at least one of the dishes will be made from the avocados that grow in abundance on the hillsides surrounding the house. On hot days, this quickly prepared cold soup, pale green and with the rich but delicate flavor of the avocados, is a perfect way to start a meal.

4 cups (32 fl oz/1 l) chicken broth

1 small white onion, quartered

3 peppercorns

4 avocados, preferably Haas

¼ cup (2 fl oz/60 ml) fresh lime juice

1 clove garlic, minced

3 tablespoons chopped white onion

1 cup (8 fl oz/250 ml) crema *(page 248) or buttermilk*

1 cup (1½ oz/45 g) chopped fresh cilantro (fresh coriander)

½ cup (1 oz/30 g) coarsely chopped fresh spinach

2 serrano chiles, chopped

sea salt to taste

Fresh Tomato and Chile Salsa (page 173)

Pour the broth into a saucepan and place over medium-high heat. Add the onion quarters and peppercorns, bring to a boil, and boil until the broth is reduced to 3 cups (24 fl oz/750 ml), about 5 minutes. Strain, discard the solids, and let the broth cool.

Cut the avocados in half, remove the pits, and scoop out the pulp into a blender or food processor. Add half of the reduced chicken broth and the lime juice and process until smooth. Pour into a bowl and stir in the remaining broth.

Put the garlic, chopped onion, *crema* or buttermilk, cilantro, spinach, and chiles into the unrinsed blender and process until smooth. Stir into the avocado mixture until thoroughly blended. Taste for seasoning and add salt as needed. Cover and refrigerate in the coldest part of the refrigerator. Chill the soup bowls at the same time.

Taste the soup and add more salt if necessary. Pour into the bowls, garnish with the salsa, and serve.

serves 6

México, D.F.

Caldo Guadiana

black bean and corn soup

Corn, beans, and chiles are the triad of ingredients essential to the Mexican diet. Marco Beteta has imaginatively combined them into this soup.

2 tablespoons safflower or canola oil

1 white onion, coarsely chopped

1 clove garlic, coarsely chopped

8 cups (56 oz/1.75 kg) undrained Pot Beans (page 201) made with black beans

3 cups (24 fl oz/750 ml) chicken broth

1 fresh epazote sprig (optional)

1 cup (6 oz/185 g) fresh or frozen corn kernels

2 scant teaspoons chicken bouillon granules

sea salt and freshly ground pepper to taste

CONDIMENTS

1 cup (1 oz/30 g) crumbled chicharrones *(page 246)*

1 cup (5 oz/155 g) crumbled queso fresco

½ cup (2 oz/60 g) grated queso añejo *or Parmesan cheese*

2 pasilla chiles, sliced and toasted (page 247)

5 serrano chiles, finely chopped

3 chiles chipotles en adobo, *finely chopped*

1 avocado, pitted, peeled, and diced

½ white onion, finely chopped

2 tablespoons minced fresh cilantro (fresh coriander)

In a large, heavy pot over medium heat, warm the oil. Add the onion and sauté until softened, about 5 minutes. Add the garlic and sauté for 1 minute. Transfer to a food processor or blender and add the beans. Purée until smooth, adding the chicken broth as needed. Pass the puréed beans through a medium-mesh sieve to remove any remaining bits of skin.

Heat the oil remaining in the pan over medium heat. Pour the beans into the hot oil and simmer, uncovered, for 2 minutes. Add the epazote, if using, and the corn kernels and season with the bouillon granules, salt, and pepper. Stirring occasionally, simmer until the corn is tender, about 4 minutes. Add a bit more broth, if necessary. Ladle into heated bowls and set out small bowls of the condiments.

serves 6

Puebla

Arroz de Fandango

fiesta rice

This colorful rice is usually cooked and served in a clay cazuela *as a substantial side dish alongside grilled chicken or meat, such as Marinated Steak with Herbs (page 155). It also makes a tasty main dish.*

3 tablespoons safflower or canola oil

½ white onion, cut vertically and then into thin slices

4 poblano chiles, roasted, peeled, seeded, and deveined (page 247), then cut lengthwise into narrow strips

4 cups (20 oz/625 g) Seasoned White Rice (page 91), at room temperature

½ cup (3 oz/90 g) frozen or lightly cooked fresh corn kernels

2 cups (16 fl oz/500 ml) crema *(page 248)*

sea salt and freshly ground pepper to taste

½ teaspoon dried oregano, preferably Mexican

1 cup (8 fl oz/250 ml) milk

½ lb (250 g) Manchego or Monterey jack cheese, shredded

Preheat an oven to 325°F (165°C). Butter or oil a shallow 1½-qt (1.5-l) baking dish, such as an attractive ovenproof ceramic dish.

In a frying pan over medium heat, warm the oil. Add the onion and sauté until just translucent, about 3 minutes. Stir in the chile strips and sauté, stirring occasionally, for about 10 minutes.

Spoon half of the rice into the bottom of the prepared baking dish, spreading it in an even layer. Spread half of the onion-chile mixture and half of the corn over the rice, then dribble half of the *crema* on top. Sprinkle with salt and pepper and the oregano. Repeat the layering with the remaining rice, onion-chile mixture, and *crema*. Pour the milk evenly over the top and sprinkle with the cheese.

Bake the rice until the cheese is bubbling hot, about 20 minutes. Serve hot directly from the dish.

serves 6

Jalisco

Sopa Verde de Tortilla

green tortilla soup

Paula Mendoza Ramos is the cook for the Roma de la Peña family, which for generations has owned the beautiful hacienda and distillery that produce Herradura tequila. Sra. Mendoza and her daughter, Rosa Maria, oversee the preparation of all of the important banquets, but I particularly like this simple, homey dish that, like chilaquiles, *makes use of the leftover corn tortillas from an earlier meal.*

In Mexico, this dish is considered a dry soup, traditionally served before the main course, as pasta is in Italy. It is equally fitting as a light supper dish accompanied with a salad.

15 purchased thin corn tortillas

corn or peanut oil for frying

2 tablespoons unsalted butter

½ cup (1½ oz/45 g) coarsely chopped green (spring) onion tops or chives

5 poblano chiles, roasted, peeled, seeded, and deveined (page 247)

½ bunch fresh epazote

1½ cups (12 fl oz/375 ml) water

1 tablespoon safflower or canola oil

sea salt to taste

½ cup (4 fl oz/125 ml) crema *(page 248)*

½ cup (2 oz/60 g) grated queso asadero, *Manchego, or white cheddar cheese*

Preferably a day ahead, cut the tortillas into strips about ¾ inch (2 cm) wide by 2 inches (5 cm) long and set them out on a countertop to dry. The process can be speeded up by laying them on a baking sheet and placing in a warm oven until crisp.

In a wide saucepan or frying pan, pour corn or peanut oil to a depth of at least 1 inch (2.5 cm) and heat until very hot but not smoking. Add a handful of tortilla strips and fry, tossing with a slotted spatula, until crisp and lightly golden on both sides, just a few seconds. Watch carefully so that they do not get too dark. Using the slotted spatula, transfer the strips to absorbent paper to drain. (The tortilla strips can be fried up to 1 day in advance and kept in a tightly closed paper sack at room temperature.)

Preheat an oven to 350°F (180°C). Butter a shallow 9-inch (23-cm) round baking dish with 1 tablespoon of the butter.

In a blender, combine the green onion tops or chives, chiles, epazote, and water and blend until smooth. Pass through a sieve, pressing with the back of a spoon.

In a frying pan over medium-high heat, warm the canola or safflower oil until it is smoking. Add the chile sauce and fry it, reducing the heat to medium when it begins to bubble, until the sauce is thick, about 10 minutes. Stir frequently, scraping the pan bottom with a wooden spoon. Season with salt. Remove from the heat, stir in the *crema,* and then return the sauce to medium heat. Just before it starts to boil, drop in the tortilla strips and lightly stir, just for a few seconds, to soften them.

Pour the mixture into the prepared baking dish. Cut the remaining 1 tablespoon butter into small bits and use to dot the top. Sprinkle evenly with the cheese. Bake until the cheese has melted and the mixture is bubbling, about 15 minutes.

Remove from the oven and serve immediately directly from the dish.

serves 6

PLATOS FUERTES

Main dishes—moles, tamales, grilled fish, stuffed chiles, carnitas—reflect regional differences.

Preceding pages: At the southernmost tip of Baja California Sur, spiny cacti stretch toward the sky between the twin tourist destinations of San José del Cabo and Cabo San Lucas. **Above top:** Residents of Guadalajara are known for their love of conversation, a pastime that they regularly pursue in the city's many outdoor cafés. **Above:** Spices for various regional *moles*—cumin, aniseed, cloves, black pepper—are displayed in brilliantly colored heaps. **Right:** Fresh chiles—*chiles de agua,* jalapeños, serranos, habaneros—impart a hint of fruity heat or a sizzling shot of fire, depending on which type is used.

IT TURNED OUT TO BE a riotous birthday celebration for my friend Ana Elena. A group of us had spent most of the day sipping and comparing tequilas from several distilleries high in the hills east of Guadalajara and wanted to finish up with an appropriately festive dinner. Our choice was a *birriería,* a casual restaurant that had as its *plato fuerte,* or main dish, the regional specialty of chile-drenched slow-cooked lamb or goat. One of our group suggested a spot off the highway rumored to serve up the most flavorful *birria* in town, so off we went.

We arrived too late for midday *comida* and too early for *cena,* so we spent some time talking to the kitchen help who were peeling mountains of plump garlic heads to purée with freshly toasted guajillo chiles for the next day's *birria.* The heady aroma made us even hungrier, and as we snacked on crispy *chicharrones* and chunky guacamole, other customers began to arrive. Soon everyone was spooning up savory broth and wrapping chunks of meat in hot tortillas daubed with more guacamole and

lots of pungent white onions. A large group of mariachi musicians encircled us and songs were sung, toasts were drunk, and other patrons joined us in an off-key rendition of "Las Mañanitas," Mexico's birthday song. The meal was simple, but the vibrant flavors and rustic textures made it one to remember. And the communal socializing with extended family of new and old friends is what makes eating out in Mexico so special.

At home, although *comida* (the main meal of the day) is served in midafternoon, the family gathers for a leisurely eating ritual. Children arrive from school, and the men from work. On Sundays, other relatives and friends show up to share in the food and conversation.

I knew I was in for a treat when my friend Ricardo asked me to join him at the home of his aunt in southern Tabasco. The thick sun-jelled air surrounded us as we drove through rolling, green hills with only an occasional tree to serve as cattle shade. An iguana crossed the road on our way into town. Upon arrival, I was given the place of honor on the couch, facing a large fan. Introductions completed, we gathered around the big table. I counted sixteen people at one point, but some of the children would vanish periodically, so I lost track.

After soup was served, a tureen holding one of the best dishes I have ever eaten was placed on the table. It was *tortuga en sangre,* made from the highly prized turtles collected from the

Above left: Centuries of Spanish Catholicism left an indelible impression upon Mexico's indigenous religions, and today shrines to the dark-skinned Virgin of Guadalupe, who appeared in a trio of visions to a local peasant in 1531, can be found all over the country. **Left:** The complex preparation of *cochinita pibil*—seasoned pork wrapped in banana leaves and buried for hours above a smoldering wood fire in a stone-lined pit—ensures an almost unimaginably tender dish. **Above:** Meaty ribs, thin strips of beef, tender tripe, and pearly white fat, the last for rendering into flavorful lard, are all available at the local *carnicería.*

RR 8612

slow-moving rivers that snake their way through Tabasco's flatlands. I was relieved to learn that this is not an endangered species, but still, in order to have the large turtles desired for dishes like this, most families have holding tanks by their houses, where they feed and raise the more easily obtained smaller turtles. The tender meat was flavored with *achiote,* spices, and herbs and presented with sweet chiles and plantains. The grandmother and I were each served several of the eggs as a special treat. Everyone was watching for my reaction as I ate my first one, making me a bit nervous. That initial swallow completed, I smiled, thanked my hostess, and shared the rest with Ricardo.

On an Acapulco beach, I have dined on just-caught fish simply cooked on sticks over a fire of dried coconut shells. I ate *carnitas,* tasty morsels of crisp pork, in a little town in Michoacán, where a garage was turned into a dining room for the locals. In Tamaulipas, a main course may be an enormous slice of unadorned beef accompanied with enchiladas.

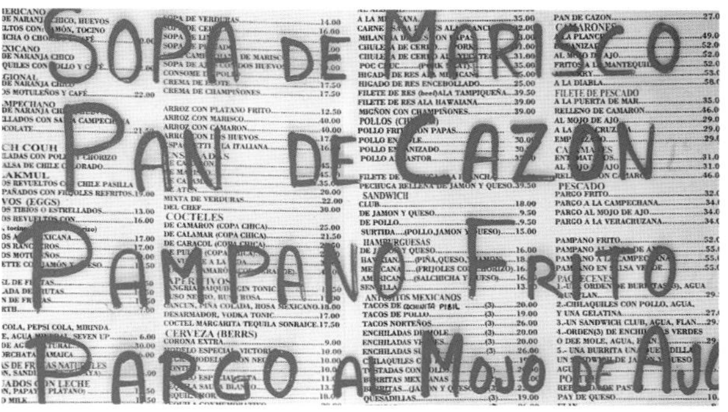

Left: A goat vendor sells his finest specimens for slow-cooked, tender *birria,* a specialty of Jalisco. **Above top:** A waiter at Morelia's Villa Montaña Hotel prepares for dinner. **Above middle:** Market stalls in Yucatecan cities offer local seafood dishes. **Above:** Crispy *chicharrones* (fried pork skin) are eaten as a snack or used as a flavorful topping.

Above top: Over the heat of an open-air kitchen in a Oaxacan marketplace, a quartet of local women prepares a typical quick meal of seared meat and chiles with tortillas. **Above:** Basket making is just one of Mexico's many craft traditions, which also include woodcarving, cloth weaving, metalwork, and pottery.

But most main-course dinners are not plain grilled or fried meat or fish. They are served in or with a sauce, and when you order, it is often by the name of the sauce—a *pipián verde* or a *mole negro.* The cooked meat, poultry, or fish sometimes seems almost incidental and interchangeable. These dishes are presented alone or, at the most, with a mound of rice.

Vegetables stuffed with any of a wide gamut of ingredients can themselves become the focus of the meal. Chiles (fresh and dried), chayotes, and squashes are those most often used as casings, and in every region the results are quite different. Walking down the streets of Puebla and Mexico City in early autumn, you will pass by seated women, shelling and breaking out the meat from young walnuts picked just before they have fallen from the trees. They are ground to make the sauce that covers the classic *chiles en nogada,* which is served on September 16 to honor Mexico's Independence Day. Green poblano chiles are filled with a sweet-crunchy *picadillo* of meat, fruit, and nuts, covered with the white walnut

Oaxaca

Codorniz en Salsa de Pétalos de Rosas

quail in rose petal sauce

Among the many poignant scenes depicted in Laura Esquivel's book and subsequent movie, Like Water for Chocolate, *none is more moving than what occurs when the daughter and family cook, Tía, is given a bouquet of pink roses by the man she loves—a man married to her sister. In order to dispose of the lovely flowers, now splashed with blood from her thorn-pricked hands, and at the same time retain their meaning, she kills six quail that she had raised and skillfully creates a sauce of the rose petals. The resulting dish is so voluptuously sensuous that, acting as an aphrodisiac on the eaters, it brings about actions that change the normal pattern of their lives. Alas, this similar dish, created by my Oaxacan friend Emilia Arroyo, may not produce the same effect on you and your guests, but you should be prepared nonetheless.*

2 teaspoons unsalted butter

2 cloves garlic, finely minced

1 teaspoon aniseeds, crushed

2 small tunas *(page 176), peeled and cut into chunks, or 1 tablespoon canned beet juice*

12 pesticide-free red or pink rose petals, plus petals from a red or pink rose for garnish

12 chestnuts or 36 blanched almonds

5 cups (40 fl oz/1.25 l) water, or as needed

2 tablespoons honey

1½ teaspoons ground white pepper

sea salt to taste

1 or 2 drops rose water

8 quail

freshly ground black pepper to taste

In a saucepan over medium-low heat, melt the butter. Add the garlic and aniseeds and sauté until the garlic is lightly browned, about 4 minutes. Remove from the heat and set aside.

Place the *tunas* or beet juice and the 12 rose petals in a blender and purée until smooth. Pour into a small bowl and set aside.

If using the chestnuts, score them in quarters with a sturdy, sharp knife, making an X at the top. Place in a deep frying pan over medium-high heat and toast, shaking the pan occasionally (the chestnut hulls will break open), for 5 minutes. Add 4 cups (32 fl oz/1 l) of the water, raise the heat to high, bring to a boil, reduce the heat to medium-low, and simmer until the centers of the chestnuts are easily pierced with a fork, about 20 minutes. Drain the chestnuts well and, when they can be handled, peel away the skins. Put the nuts, several at a time, into the blender, processing after each addition, until pulverized.

If using almonds, toast them over low heat in a dry frying pan until golden, about 5 minutes. Let cool, pulverize in a spice grinder, and add in batches to the blender, processing after each addition.

Pour the rose petal mixture and the remaining 1 cup (8 fl oz/250 ml) water into the blender with the ground nuts and process until smooth.

Put the garlic butter and the nut–rose petal mixture in a deep saucepan and place over low heat. Cook, stirring frequently, for 10 minutes to blend the flavors. Add the honey, white pepper, and salt. Taste and adjust the seasoning. Pass the sauce through a medium-mesh sieve, pressing on the sauce with the back of a spoon. Stir in the rose water to taste.

Preheat an oven to 450°F (230°C).

Season the quail inside and out with salt and black pepper. Fold the wing tips under the birds and tie the legs together with kitchen string. Place on a rack in a roasting pan.

Roast the quail for 10 minutes. Reduce the temperature to 375°F (190°C), baste with a little of the sauce, and roast for about 10 more minutes. To test if the quail are done, pierce a thigh joint with a fork. The juice should be slightly pink. Remove the quail from the oven and put on a large platter. Loosely cover with aluminum foil and set aside; allow to rest for about 5 minutes.

Gently reheat the rose petal sauce and pour it over the quail. Garnish with rose petals and serve.

serves 4

Oaxaca blends the vibrant culture of indigenous peoples with the elegance of colonial Spain.

México, D.F.

Albóndigas en Salsa Verde

meatballs in spicy tomatillo sauce

Well-known cook Margarita Carrillo de Salinas prepares these plump balls of ground meat in the classic fashion, with a hidden surprise of chopped egg.

1 lb (500 g) tomatillos, husked and rinsed

2 small white onions, 1 quartered and 1 finely chopped

2 cloves garlic, unpeeled

2 chiles chipotles en adobo

1 cup (8 fl oz/250 ml) beef or chicken broth, plus up to 1 cup (8 fl oz/250 ml), if needed

sea salt to taste, plus 1 teaspoon

2 lb (1 kg) ground (minced) lean beef

1 cup (4 oz/125 g) fine dried bread crumbs soaked in ¼ cup (2 fl oz/60 ml) milk

2 eggs, lightly beaten

6 tablespoons (½ oz/15 g) finely chopped fresh cilantro (fresh coriander)

½ teaspoon freshly ground pepper

3 eggs, hard-boiled and cut into cubes

Roast the tomatillos (page 250), onion quarters (page 249), and garlic (page 248). Peel the garlic and place in a blender with the tomatillos and roasted onion. Add the chiles and the 1 cup (8 fl oz/250 ml) broth and process until smooth. Pour into a saucepan and bring to a boil. Reduce the heat and simmer, uncovered, for 10 minutes. Season with salt.

Mix the meat, bread crumbs, beaten eggs, chopped onion, 4 tablespoons (⅓ oz/10 g) of the cilantro, salt to taste, and pepper in a bowl. For each meatball, flatten 1 rounded tablespoon of the mixture. Add several cubes of egg and wrap the meat around them. Shape into a ball. Drop the balls into the simmering sauce, cover, and cook, stirring occasionally, 20–30 minutes. Add more broth as needed.

Spoon onto a warmed platter, sprinkle with the remaining 2 tablespoons cilantro, and serve.

serves 6–8

Michoacán

Trucha en Salsa de Hierbas

trout in herb sauce

Once abundant with trout, black bass, and catfish, the streams and lakes of Mexico's high tablelands are now quite polluted. Particularly in a state like Michoacán, with a name that even translates to "the place of fish," it is no wonder that the scarcity has forced the locals to turn to fish farming to satisfy the demand. Señora Livier de Suarez, one of Morelia's outstanding cooks, passed on this tasty recipe to me. Garlicky French bread makes a good accompaniment, as do Tiny Garlic Potatoes (page 195).

SAUCE

1 cup (1½ oz/45 g) chopped fresh cilantro (fresh coriander)

1 cup (1½ oz/45 g) chopped fresh flat-leaf (Italian) parsley

1 cup (8 fl oz/250 ml) dry white wine

3 cloves garlic, chopped

1 teaspoon Worcestershire sauce

1 teaspoon chopped fresh oregano or ½ teaspoon dried, preferably Mexican

¼ teaspoon Tabasco sauce or other hot-pepper sauce

3 tablespoons extra-virgin olive oil

sea salt to taste

½ teaspoon freshly ground pepper

TROUT

4 rainbow trout, cleaned with heads intact, 6–8 oz (185–250 g) each

sea salt to taste, plus 1 teaspoon

1 teaspoon freshly ground pepper

1 cup (5 oz/155 g) all-purpose (plain) flour

½ cup (2½ oz/75 g) masa harina *for tortillas (page 249)*

1 cup (8 fl oz/250 ml) milk

6 tablespoons (3 oz/90 g) unsalted butter

1 teaspoon safflower or canola oil

2 limes or lemons, quartered

To make the sauce, put the cilantro, parsley, wine, garlic, Worcestershire sauce, oregano, and Tabasco sauce in a blender and process briefly. Slowly pour in the oil, blending until just absorbed. Season with salt and the pepper. Pour the sauce into a saucepan and bring to a simmer. Keep warm over low heat.

Rinse the fish and pat dry. Season the cavities with salt to taste and ½ teaspoon of the pepper. In a shallow dish, mix together the flour, *masa harina,* 1 teaspoon salt, and remaining ½ teaspoon pepper. Pour the milk into a shallow bowl.

In a large frying pan over medium heat, melt the butter with the oil. Dip each trout into the milk and then into the seasoned flour. When the butter is just bubbly but not yet browned, gently slide in the fish. Fry, turning once, until lightly golden and the flesh is just becoming opaque, 4–5 minutes per side.

Transfer the fried trout to warmed individual plates. Pour the warmed sauce over the top, arrange the lime or lemon wedges on the side, and serve.

serves 4

México, D.F.

Tamalitos Rancheros

tiny rustic tamales

Noted Mexican cook Margarita Carrillo de Salinas prepares the masa *and filling in advance and then gets friends or family together to assemble these tamales. The reward is tasty tamales for supper served with Mexican Hot Chocolate (page 239).*

MEAT

½ white onion

2 whole cloves

1½ lb (750 g) boneless pork butt or shoulder, in large chunks

4 cloves garlic

about 1½ teaspoons sea salt

SAUCE

6 ancho chiles, seeded and deveined (page 247)

½ lb (250 g) tomatillos, husked and rinsed

1 white onion, coarsely chopped

4 cloves garlic

¾ teaspoon ground cumin

⅛ teaspoon ground allspice

6 tablespoons (3 fl oz/90 ml) safflower or canola oil

2 bay leaves

sea salt to taste

TAMALES

50 corn husks

⅔ cup (5 oz/155 g) lard or vegetable shortening

4 cups (2½ lb/1.25 kg) masa harina *for tamales*

1½ teaspoons baking powder

1½ teaspoons sea salt, or to taste

To prepare the meat, stud the onion with the cloves and put it into a large pot. Add the pork, garlic, salt, and water to cover and bring to a boil, skimming off any foam from the surface. Reduce the heat to low, cover, and simmer for 1½–2 hours. Let the meat cool in the broth, then remove, reserving the broth. Shred the meat very finely. Skim off as much of the fat from the broth as possible.

To make the sauce, in a bowl, soak the chiles in very hot water to cover for 15–20 minutes. Drain, reserving the water. In a saucepan over medium-high heat, combine the tomatillos with water to cover, bring to a boil, and cook until soft, about 8 minutes. Drain well. In a blender or food processor, combine the chiles, the tomatillos, half of the chopped onion, the garlic, the cumin, the allspice, and ½ cup (4 fl oz/125 ml) of the chile water. Blend until smooth.

In a deep, heavy frying pan over medium-high heat, warm the oil. Add the remaining onion; sauté for about 5 minutes. Add the chile purée and bay leaves and let sizzle for a few seconds. Reduce the heat to low and simmer uncovered, stirring occasionally, until the sauce begins to thicken, about 15 minutes. Stir in the meat, season with salt, and cook until the sauce becomes thick and a little dry, about 20 minutes. If it becomes too dry, add a little broth.

To make the tamales, rinse the corn husks and soak in very hot water until pliable, about 15 minutes. In a bowl, using an electric mixer, beat the lard or shortening until fluffy, about 5 minutes. Add the *masa harina,* baking powder, and salt and mix well. Reheat the broth and stir 3 cups (24 fl oz/750 ml) into the *masa harina* mixture, 1 cup (8 fl oz/250 ml) at a time, adding more broth if it is too dry. Beat for at least another 10–15 minutes. The dough should be very light. Taste and add more salt if necessary. The *masa* (dough) is ready when a spoonful of it dropped into cold water floats to the surface.

Drain the husks and pat dry. Put 4 or 5 of the torn ones in the bottom of a steamer basket. Line up the husks, *masa,* and meat on a work surface. Hold a husk in the palm of your hand, with the pointed end on your wrist. Spread 1 tablespoon of the dough in the center of the upper half, leaving a margin on all sides. Put 1 rounded teaspoon of the meat filling in the center of the dough. Fold the sides of the husk over the filling and bring up the pointed end until even with the cut or cupped end. If desired, tie the open end with narrow strips of soaked husks.

Place each tamale vertically in the steamer basket, folded side down. Start in the center, propping the tamales around an inverted small funnel. Fill a large pot with water to a depth of at least 2 inches (5 cm), but not enough to touch the basket once it is in the pot. Bring the water to a low boil. Add the basket, cover the tamales with corn husks and a kitchen towel, then cover the steamer with a tight lid.

Steam, without uncovering, for 1 hour. Remove a tamale, unwrap it, let it sit for several minutes, then break into it to see if the dough is firm. Serve the tamales hot, piled on a platter, letting each person unwrap his or her own tamales.

---

makes about 40 tamales; serves 8–10

Los Ingredientes en la Cocina Maya

Many dishes from Campeche, Yucatán, and Quintana Roo, the states that make up the Yucatán peninsula, are unique. In fact, diners from other parts of the country consider the food an almost foreign cuisine. What makes it so different—some unusual ingredients—will be apparent to anyone who meanders through a local market.

Large stalls display bewildering mounds of seasoning pastes called *recados.* The most common is the brick red *recado rojo,* which includes ground *achiote,* the hard, red seeds from annatto trees, which is rubbed over pork, chicken, or even fish before pit-roasting and grilling. Each *recado* is made with different spices, and each is used to flavor specific dishes. Although citrus fruits are not indigenous to Mexico, precarious-looking pyramids of squat, aromatic *naranjas agrias* are constructed by Maya vendors. The juice of these bitter, or Seville, oranges is used to dilute the *recados* and is often substituted for vinegar when pickling chiles and onions. The odd-shaped *lima agria* will be here, too. Its most distinguishing characteristic is the protruding nipple on the blossom end of the green fruit, and its most popular use is in the distinctively flavored soup named for it, *sopa de lima.*

The cooking of this region does not rely on numerous varieties of chile, but the ones used are unfamiliar to most outsiders. Among them are the rather mild, pale yellow or blond *chile x-cat-ik;* a very hot one called, simply, *chile seco,* the dried form of the local *chile verde;* and *chile dulce,* a sweet fresh chile. Finally, there is the habanero, a flavor-rich chile so incendiary that local cooks often just "walk it through the sauce." In recent years, these small green, yellow, and orange lanternlike chiles are found almost any season of the year in stores outside Mexico, but here they are used only in Yucatecan cooking.

Yucatán

Pollo en Lima Agria

chicken in lime-flavored broth

This dish is typical of the hybrid stews of Yucatán in which grilled meats are served in a seasoned broth enriched with mint, sweet and mild chiles, tomatoes, and slices of lima agria, *or bitter lime. Regular limes can be substituted but lack the distinctive flavor. Silvio Campos first marinates the chicken in a seasoning paste, or* recado, *made with* achiote, *a red seed that changes the color of anything with which it is cooked. The final embellishment is a tangle of tangy red onion rings.*

8 chicken thighs and half breasts, about 3 lb (1.5 kg) total

2 qt (2 l) plus 1 cup (8 fl oz/250 ml) water

3 fresh oregano sprigs or 1 teaspoon dried, preferably Mexican

sea salt to taste, plus ½ teaspoon

½ cup (4 oz/125 g) achiote *paste (page 246)*

¾ cup (6 fl oz/185 ml) fresh bitter orange juice (page 249)

2 tablespoons safflower or canola oil

½ white onion, finely chopped

2 red or green bell peppers (capsicums), seeded and finely chopped

1 güero chile or any pale yellow chile, finely diced

4 ripe tomatoes, coarsely chopped

6 limes, sliced

½ cup (¾ oz/20 g) chopped fresh cilantro (fresh coriander)

⅓ cup (½ oz/15 g) chopped fresh mint

¼ teaspoon freshly ground pepper

Pickled Red Onions (page 190)

♛ Place the chicken in a large pot, add the water, and bring to a boil over high heat, skimming off any foam that forms on the surface. Add the oregano and salt to taste, reduce the heat to medium-low, and simmer, uncovered, for 20 minutes. Using a slotted spoon, transfer the chicken to a plate and let cool. Let the broth cool, then cover and refrigerate.

♛ In a bowl, mix the *achiote* paste with the ½ teaspoon salt. Thin with the orange juice. Place the chicken in a shallow dish and pour the juice mixture over it. Turn the chicken to coat evenly. Cover and refrigerate for at least 6 hours or as long as 12 hours.

♛ About 30 minutes before serving time, prepare a medium-hot fire in a charcoal grill. Alternatively, preheat an oven to 400°F (200°C).

♛ Meanwhile, remove the chicken from the marinade and, using paper towels, blot off the excess moisture. Lift off and discard the congealed fat from the broth and reheat in a large saucepan to a simmer.

♛ While the broth is heating, in a frying pan over medium-high heat, warm the oil. Add the onion, bell peppers, and chile and sauté until soft, about 10 minutes. Add the tomatoes and simmer until they break down, about 10 more minutes. Remove from the heat and let cool slightly, then pour the mixture into a blender or food processor and blend until smooth. Pass the purée through a medium-mesh sieve placed over the simmering broth, pressing on the purée with the back of a spoon. Add the lime slices, cilantro, mint, and pepper. Taste and adjust the seasoning. Simmer 10 minutes to blend the flavors.

♛ When the coals are ready, place the chicken pieces on the grill rack and grill, turning once, until toasty brown, 5–10 minutes on each side. If cooking in the oven, place on a rack in a large roasting pan and bake, turning once, for about the same amount of time.

♛ To serve, place a piece of chicken in each bowl, add some of the broth, and top with pickled onions.

serves 8

México, D.F.

Chiles Rellenos de Quelites

poblano chiles stuffed with greens and cheese

Roberto Santibañez from Mexico City, now the executive chef at Fonda San Miguel in Austin, Texas, shared this vegetarian recipe with me. He takes the poblano chile and fills it with the unusual combination of cheese and quelites. *Quelites are a wild green sometimes known as lamb's-quarters, pigweed, or goosefoot. The spinachlike leaves have a delightful flavor and are said to be even more nutritious than spinach and Swiss chard, to which they are related. It is extremely important to wash the greens well. Green Salad with Jicama and Mango (page 187) complements the chiles.*

CHILES

2½ lb (1.25 kg) quelites *(see note) or spinach leaves, stems removed*

sea salt to taste

¼ cup (2 fl oz/60 ml) olive oil

⅓ cup (2 oz/60 g) raisins

⅓ cup (2 oz/60 g) pine nuts

½ cup (4 fl oz/125 ml) water

6 oz (185 g) queso fresco, *in 6 narrow pieces*

6 poblano chiles, roasted (page 247) and left whole

½ cup (4 fl oz/125 ml) crema *(page 248)*

SAUCE

1½ lb (750 g) plum (Roma) tomatoes

1 slice small white onion

2 cloves garlic, unpeeled

about ½ cup (4 fl oz/125 ml) water, if needed

1½ teaspoons olive oil

sea salt to taste

To prepare the chiles, place the *quelites* or spinach in a saucepan with only the rinsing water clinging to the leaves and sprinkle with salt. Place over medium heat and cook, stirring often, until wilted, about 5 minutes. Drain well, squeeze out any excess moisture, and chop coarsely.

Preheat an oven to 350°F (180°C). In a large frying pan over medium-high heat, warm the oil. Add the raisins, pine nuts, and greens and cook, stirring constantly, until totally dry, about 3 minutes. Pour in the water and add salt, if needed; remember that the cheese may be quite salty. Continue to stir until the liquid has evaporated, about 5 minutes. Remove from the heat; let cool. Carefully peel the chiles. Leaving the stem end intact, make a lengthwise slit in each chile and remove the seeds and veins, taking care not to break the walls.

Divide the greens and cheese among the chiles, stuffing them carefully so as not to tear them and allowing them to close completely with overlapping edges. Place in a shallow baking dish and cover with aluminum foil. Bake the chiles until they are heated through and the cheese is softened, 20–30 minutes.

To make the sauce, roast the tomatoes (page 250), onion (page 249), and garlic (page 248). Peel the garlic and put in a blender or food processor with the tomatoes and onion. Process until smooth, adding up to ½ cup (4 fl oz/125 ml) water if needed.

In a frying pan over medium-high heat, warm the oil until it is smoking. Pour the tomato mixture into the pan all at once—be careful, as it will splatter—and fry, stirring, for 1–2 minutes. Reduce the heat to medium-low and continue cooking until the sauce is quite thick, 15–20 minutes. Season with the salt and keep warm.

Remove the chiles from the oven and transfer to a serving platter or individual plates. Pour the sauce around them, swirl on the *crema,* and serve warm.

serves 6

Jalisco

Camarones con Naranja y Tequila

shrimp with orange and tequila

This coastal dish from María Dolores Torres Yzábal has an orange-and-chile sauce for a tangy accent. Serve with Seasoned White Rice (page 91).

1 orange

6 tablespoons (3 oz/90 g) unsalted butter

2 tablespoons finely chopped white onion

2 cloves garlic

16 large shrimp (prawns), peeled with final tail segment intact and deveined

1 chile chipotle en adobo *or 2 serrano chiles, finely chopped*

¼ cup (2 fl oz/60 ml) tequila reposado

3 tablespoons minced fresh cilantro (fresh coriander)

sea salt to taste

With a zester or vegetable peeler, cut the zest from the orange in very narrow strips, being careful to avoid any of the white pith. Bring a saucepan of water to boil. Place the strips in a small sieve or slotted spoon, plunge them into the boiling water, remove immediately, and rinse under running cold water. Repeat three times to remove the bitter taste. Pat the orange strips dry with paper towels.

In a frying pan over medium heat, melt the butter. Add the onion and sauté until translucent, 3–4 minutes. Add the garlic and shrimp and cook, stirring frequently, until the shrimp turn pink and begin to curl, 4–5 minutes. Do not overcook the shrimp; they should be tender, not rubbery.

Add the chipotle chile or serrano chiles and the orange strips. Stir briefly to mix. Pour the tequila over the shrimp, carefully ignite with a long match, and let the flames burn out. Add the minced cilantro, season with salt, and serve on a warmed platter or individual plates.

serves 4

Zacatecas

Gallina Rellena Estilo Zacatecas

stuffed chicken, zacatecas style

This is a cherished recipe of my friend María Elena Lorens, whose grandmother, Mamá Jesusita, cooked it every Sunday for the whole family. With its fragrant, crisp brown skin, succulent meat, and unusual filling, this stuffed chicken is a perfect dish to showcase at a small holiday dinner party. For a colorful contrast, set out Spinach Salad (page 188) and Baked Sweet Potatoes (page 198).

1 roasting chicken, 5–6 lb (2.5–3 kg)
2 cups (16 fl oz/500 ml) dry sherry
1 cup (8 fl oz/250 ml) white wine vinegar
1 large white onion, sliced into rings
2 bay leaves
1 teaspoon peppercorns
¼ teaspoon ground cumin

STUFFING

2 tablespoons safflower or canola oil
1 lb (500 g) ground (minced) lean pork
1 cup (4 oz/125 g) chopped white onion
2 ripe tomatoes, peeled, seeded, and chopped
1 cup (4 oz/125 g) peeled chopped apple
½ cup (3 oz/90 g) raisins
½ cup (2½ oz/75 g) slivered blanched almonds, toasted
½ cup (2½ oz/75 g) pimiento-stuffed green olives, chopped
2 slices French or Italian bread, lightly toasted and cut into small cubes
1 egg, lightly beaten
1–2 tablespoons chicken broth, if needed
¼ teaspoon ground cumin
¼ teaspoon ground cinnamon
sea salt and freshly ground pepper to taste

3 tablespoons lard or unsalted butter
sea salt and freshly ground pepper to taste
6–8 inner romaine (cos) lettuce leaves
8 radishes, sliced

Rinse the chicken and pat dry. In a bowl, stir together the sherry, vinegar, onion, bay leaves, peppercorns, and cumin to make a marinade. Combine the chicken and marinade in a large bowl, cover, and refrigerate, turning occasionally to marinate the chicken evenly, for 4–6 hours.

To make the stuffing, in a frying pan over medium heat, warm the oil. Add the pork and sauté until cooked through, about 5 minutes. Using a slotted spoon, transfer the pork to a plate. Pour off all but 2 tablespoons of the oil and pork fat. Add the onion and sauté until translucent, 3–5 minutes. Stir in the tomatoes, apple, raisins, almonds, and olives and sauté until the tomatoes and apples soften, about 2 minutes. Transfer to a large bowl. Stir in the cooked pork, bread cubes, and beaten egg. Add the broth if the dressing is too dry. Sprinkle with the cumin and cinnamon, mix well, and season with salt and pepper.

Preheat an oven to 350°F (180°C).

Remove the chicken from the marinade and pat dry, reserving the marinade in a small saucepan. Bring the marinade to a boil, then set aside. Rub the bird with the lard or butter; sprinkle inside and out with salt and pepper. Loosely fill the body and neck cavities with the warm stuffing. Lap the skin over the openings and secure by sewing with a trussing needle and kitchen string or with skewers or toothpicks. Fold the wing tips under the bird. If desired, truss the legs together with a piece of string. Spoon any remaining stuffing into a lightly buttered baking dish, cover, and slip it into the oven to heat during the last 10–15 minutes the chicken is cooking.

Place the chicken on one side on a rack in a roasting pan and roast for 10 minutes, basting often with the reserved marinade. Turn the chicken on its other side and roast for another 10 minutes. Turn breast side up and continue cooking, basting frequently with the marinade, until the juices run clear when a knife is inserted into the thigh joint. Total cooking time is about 1½ hours. Transfer the chicken to a serving platter and let rest for 5 minues before carving.

Clip the strings or remove the skewers or toothpicks. Spoon the stuffing into a warmed bowl, adding the stuffing that was baked separately. Carve the chicken and arrange on a platter garnished with lettuce leaves and radish slices. Strain the pan juices, skim off the fat from the surface, reheat, and pour into a warmed bowl. Pass the pan juices at the table.

serves 6–8

Oaxaca

Pollo a la Cazuela

chicken in a clay pot

One of my favorite recipes from Socorrito Zorrilla is her version of the traditional chicken in a pot: pieces of chicken flavored with chiles and avocado leaves and wrapped in banana leaves before cooking.

4 guajillo chiles, seeded and toasted (page 247)

4 plum (Roma) tomatoes, roasted (page 250), or 1 can (14½ oz/455 g) diced tomatoes, drained

1 tablespoon finely chopped white onion

4 cloves garlic, coarsely chopped

1 tablespoon fresh oregano leaves or 1 teaspoon dried, preferably Mexican

sea salt to taste, plus 1 teaspoon

freshly ground pepper to taste, plus ½ teaspoon

3–4 lb (1.5–2 kg) chicken pieces (12–16 pieces)

4 fresh or thawed frozen banana leaves

16 avocado leaves (optional)

In a small bowl, soak the chiles in boiling water to cover until soft, 10–20 minutes. Drain and tear them into pieces. In a blender, combine the chiles, tomatoes, onion, garlic, and oregano. Blend until very smooth. Strain through a medium-mesh sieve. Season with salt and pepper.

Preheat an oven to 350°F (180°C). Rinse the chicken, pat dry, and season with the 1 teaspoon salt and ½ teaspoon pepper.

Cut the banana leaves into 8-inch (20-cm) squares and soften them by passing over a burner. Set each leaf on a 10-inch (25-cm) square of aluminum foil. Center 2 avocado leaves (if using) on each banana leaf. Douse the chicken with the chile sauce. Place 3 or 4 chicken pieces on the leaves. Cover with 2 more avocado leaves (if using). Fold the foil tightly around the chicken. Place the packets on a baking sheet. Bake until the chicken is cooked throughout, about 30 minutes.

Remove the foil and the top avocado leaves. Slide the chicken and bottom leaves onto individual plates or combine in a shallow clay pot. Serve at once.

serves 4–6

México, D.F.

Chiles Tolucos

ancho chiles stuffed with cheese, chorizo, and beans

Stuffed dried chiles, such as large red wine–colored anchos, are typical of the high valleys in central Mexico. This dish, a favorite of Mexico City cook Margarita Carrillo de Salinas, features the famous chorizo from nearby Toluca. She adds cheese and either black beans or the light tan frijoles de Mayo, *for which you can substitute pinto beans. Start the meal with spicy Chicken and Chickpea Soup (page 101) and close with Corn Cake (page 219).*

6 ancho chiles

1 cup (8 fl oz/250 ml) cider vinegar

1 cup (8 fl oz/250 ml) fresh orange juice

½ lb (250 g) piloncillo *cone (page 249), chopped, or 1 cup (7 oz/220 g) firmly packed dark brown sugar*

5 cloves garlic

1 bay leaf

1 teaspoon dried oregano, preferably Mexican

1 teaspoon dried thyme

2 tablespoons safflower or canola oil

¼ lb (125 g) good-quality chorizo, homemade (page 248) or purchased, crumbled

1 cup (7 oz/220 g) Well-Fried Beans (page 182) (see note)

sea salt to taste

½ lb (250 g) Monterey jack or other good melting cheese, cut into strips 2 inches (5 cm) long by ½ inch (12 mm) wide by ½ inch (12 mm) thick, plus ⅓ lb (5 oz/155 g), shredded

1 cup (8 fl oz/250 ml) crema *(page 248)*

1 firm but ripe avocado, preferably Haas, pitted, peeled, and sliced

10 radishes, thinly sliced

Leaving the stem and top intact, make a lengthwise slit in each chile and remove the seeds and veins, taking care not to break the walls.

In a saucepan over medium heat, combine the vinegar and orange juice and bring to a simmer. Add the *piloncillo* or brown sugar, garlic, bay leaf, oregano, and thyme and cook, stirring, until the sugar has dissolved. Remove from the heat. Add the chiles and soak until they feel fleshy, 15–20 minutes.

In a frying pan over medium heat, warm the oil. Add the chorizo and fry until thoroughly cooked, 6–8 minutes. Pour off the excess fat and stir in the beans. Season with salt. Let cool.

Preheat an oven to 350°F (180°C).

Using tongs or a slotted spoon, transfer the chiles to absorbent paper to drain. Strain the soaking liquid and set aside to use as a sauce.

Carefully stuff the chiles with the chorizo-bean mixture and strips of cheese; the chiles should be plump. (At this point the chiles can be refrigerated for up to 1 day.) Arrange the filled chiles, seam side down, in a baking dish, and spoon the *crema* over the top. Sprinkle the top with the shredded cheese.

Bake the chiles until the cheese on top is melted and the chiles are heated through, about 15 minutes. Meanwhile, reheat the sauce.

Put 1 or 2 chiles on each individual plate, spoon the sauce around the sides, and garnish with the avocado and radish slices. Serve immediately.

serves 4–6

Moles

The most remarkable of Mexico's culinary achievements is the mole—the quintessential fiesta dish since before recorded history. The term may come from *molli,* the Nahuatl word for "sauce" or "mixture." It is a broth thickened with ground toasted nuts, seeds, or even tortillas or bread; flavored by chiles, herbs, and spices; and served with a few pieces of meat or vegetables.

The arrival of the Spanish changed the native mole. Visiting dignitaries were entertained in the convents of seventeenth-century Mexico, and no preparation was as lauded as the silky black *mole poblano* from the Convent of Santa Rosa in Puebla. It contained over a hundred different ingredients from both continents, as well as exotic spices from Asia.

Whenever there is a special event to celebrate, the women of the family will begin the preparation of their treasured version of mole, a dish that spans a full spectrum of colors and flavors. In Oaxaca, it might be *mole amarillo,* its yellow sauce usually surrounding various vegetables and meat, or *mole verde,* with an aromatic fresh herb sauce served with pork and tiny white beans. In Michoacán, a fruity *manchamanteles* with its lighter red sauce is common, while in Guerrero, a brick-red mole rules. I

Oaxaca

Mole Amarillo de Res

yellow mole of beef and vegetables

Abigail Mendoza, who lives in the valley of Oaxaca, serves this mole with hot corn tortillas (page 251) to scrape up every bit of sauce.

2 lb (1 kg) boneless stewing beef, trimmed and cut into 1-inch (2.5-cm) cubes

1 beef soup bone

1 tablespoon sea salt, or to taste

4 guajillo chiles, seeded and toasted (page 247)

2 ancho chiles, seeded and toasted (page 247)

4 cloves garlic, coarsely chopped

⅛ teaspoon ground cumin

½ cup (2½ oz/75 g) masa harina *for tortillas (page 249)*

1 lb (500 g) new potatoes, cut into large chunks

1 chayote, peeled, seeded, and cut into chunks

1 lb (500 g) green beans, ends trimmed and cut into 1½-inch (4-cm) lengths

2 fresh epazote sprigs or 1 teaspoon dried oregano, preferably Mexican

3 limes, cut into wedges

Put the beef and bone into a large, heavy pot. Add water to cover and the salt. Bring to a slow boil over medium heat, skimming off any foam from the surface. Cover, reduce heat to medium-low, and simmer for about 45 minutes. Discard the soup bone.

Tear the chiles into large pieces and place in a bowl. Add very hot water to cover and soak for 10–15 minutes. Drain and place in a blender with the garlic and cumin. Add ½ cup (4 fl oz/125 ml) of the broth from the beef. Pulse to form a very smooth purée. Scrape into a bowl. Put 1 cup (8 fl oz/250 ml) broth into the blender, add the *masa harina,* and blend until smooth. Stir into the chile mixture.

Add the potatoes and chayote to the meat and cook, covered, for 10 minutes. Add the green beans and cook for about 10 minutes. Stir in the chile-*masa* mixture and add the epazote or oregano. Reduce the heat to low and cook uncovered, stirring occasionally, for about 10 minutes. Taste and adjust the seasoning. Ladle into bowls. Serve with the limes.

serves 6–8

Puebla

Pechugas Rellenas con Flor de Calabaza

chicken and squash blossom rolls

Mexico's native squash provides cooks like Mónica Mastretta with an almost year-round supply of the vivid golden yellow flowers. In this dish she throws caution to the wind and adds the delicate flowers to a robust combination of corn and roasted poblano chiles and enrobes it all in a thin slice of chicken. While you have squash blossoms on hand, don't hesitate to serve Cheese-Stuffed Squash Blossoms (page 39) as a starter. For dessert, try something equally special, such as Mangoes Flambéed with Tequila (page 216).

8 boneless, skinless chicken breast halves

sea salt and freshly ground pepper to taste

1½ cups (9 oz/280 g) fresh or frozen corn kernels

¼ cup (2 fl oz/60 ml) safflower or canola oil

1 white onion, finely chopped

6 poblano chiles, roasted, peeled, seeded, and deveined (page 247), then cut into 1-inch (2.5-cm) strips

3 cups (3 oz/90 g) chopped squash blossoms, pistils and stems removed

½ cup (½ oz/15 g) epazote or fresh cilantro (fresh coriander) leaves, finely chopped

¼ cup (2 oz/60 g) unsalted butter

1 cup (8 fl oz/250 ml) chicken broth

1 tablespoon chicken bouillon granules

½ lb (250 g) cream cheese, at room temperature

½ cup (4 fl oz/125 ml) heavy (double) cream

3 tablespoons chopped fresh cilantro (fresh coriander), optional

Preheat an oven to 350°F (180°C). Butter a small baking dish.

One at a time, place the chicken breasts between 2 sheets of waxed paper and pound evenly with a meat mallet until about ¼ inch (6 mm) thick. Season with salt and pepper and set aside.

Bring a small saucepan three-fourths full of water to a boil, add the fresh corn kernels, and cook until just tender, 3–4 minutes. Drain well and set aside. If using frozen corn kernels, thaw briefly.

In a frying pan over medium heat, warm the oil. Add the onion and chile strips and sauté until quite soft, about 5 minutes. Remove half of the chiles to use for the sauce and set aside. Add the squash blossoms to the pan and sauté until wilted and well seasoned, about 10 minutes. Add the corn kernels and epazote or cilantro. Season with salt and pepper. Mix well and remove from the heat.

Center 3 tablespoons of the filling on each of the chicken breasts. Gently roll and secure with a toothpick. In a frying pan over medium heat, melt the butter. Add the chicken rolls and sauté, turning as needed, until the rolls are golden brown on all sides, about 8 minutes. Carefully transfer the rolls, toothpick sides down, to the prepared baking dish. Add the chicken broth and bake until the rolls are cooked through, about 20 minutes.

Meanwhile, put the remaining chile strips, bouillon granules, cream cheese, and cream in a blender or food processor. Process until smooth. Season with salt and pepper. Pour into a small saucepan and warm over very low heat until ready to serve.

Remove the toothpick from each chicken roll, place the rolls on a serving plate, and cover with the sauce. Garnish with the 3 tablespoons cilantro, if using, and serve.

serves 6–8

Jalisco

Carne en Su Jugo Estilo Tapatío

meat in a spicy broth, guadalajara style

Bold and brash, this simple but unusual beef dish justly typifies the foods of Tapatíos—a word that identifies a person or anything else as being from Guadalajara, the capital of Jalisco.

½ lb (250 g) lean, thin bacon slices, finely chopped

1 lb (500 g) beef sirloin tip or top round, thinly sliced diagonally, then coarsely chopped

4 cups (32 fl oz/1 l) rich beef broth

2 chiles chipotles en adobo

2 bay leaves

2 teaspoons sea salt, or to taste

1 teaspoon freshly ground pepper, or to taste

2 cups (14 oz/440 g) drained Pot Beans (page 201) made with pinto beans, or drained canned pinto beans

½ cup (¾ oz/20 g) chopped fresh cilantro (fresh coriander)

12 large green (spring) onions, grilled (page 249)

5 serrano chiles, chopped

3 limes, quartered

In a frying pan over medium-low heat, slowly fry the chopped bacon until crisp. Transfer to absorbent paper to drain. Raise the heat to medium-high, add the beef to the bacon drippings, and fry for about 2 minutes. Transfer the beef to a large, heavy pot.

Put about 1 cup (8 fl oz/250 ml) of the beef broth in a blender, add the *chiles chipotles,* and blend until smooth. Add to the pot along with the rest of the broth and the bay leaves, salt, and pepper. Bring to a boil, reduce the heat to low, cover, and simmer until the meat is very tender, about 20 minutes.

Heat the beans in a saucepan over medium-low heat. Divide among bowls. Ladle the meat with its broth into the bowls and sprinkle with bacon and cilantro. Put 2 or 3 onions on the side of each bowl. Pass the serrano chiles and limes at the table.

serves 4–6

Querétaro

Mole Fandango de Guajolote

fiesta black turkey mole

Both the turkey and the mole can be cooked in advance and combined right before serving. In fact, the flavors mellow if the mole is allowed to rest at least overnight.

1 whole turkey breast, 6–8 lb (3–4 kg), halved
6 cloves garlic
1 white onion, thickly sliced
sea salt to taste

MOLE

12 ancho chiles
15 dried pasilla chiles
15 cascabel chiles
7 tablespoons (1½ oz/45 g) sesame seeds
8 tablespoons (4 oz/125 g) flavorful lard (page 249) or (4 fl oz/125 ml) safflower oil
6 tomatillos, husked, rinsed, and quartered
1 white onion, finely chopped
2 cloves garlic, minced
¼ teaspoon aniseeds
¼ teaspoon ground cumin
1 bay leaf
1 day-old corn tortilla
1 slice day-old French bread or French roll
25 almonds
30 peanuts
2 tablespoons raisins
about ½-inch (12-mm) piece true cinnamon bark
3 whole cloves
1 disk Mexican chocolate, about 1½ oz (45 g)
1 teaspoon sugar
1 teaspoon sea salt, or to taste, if needed

In a large pot, combine the turkey, garlic, onion, salt, and water to cover. Bring to a slow boil over medium-high heat, skimming off any foam from the surface. Reduce the heat and simmer until the turkey is partially cooked, about 30 minutes. Remove from the broth. Strain the broth. Cover the turkey and broth and refrigerate until needed. Before using the broth, spoon off the congealed fat from the surface.

To make the mole, seed the chiles, reserving the seeds, then devein. Put 1½ tablespoons of the seeds of each chile type in a heavy frying pan over medium heat. Toast until golden, then pour into a dish. Toast the sesame seeds lightly. Set 2 tablespoons of the sesame seeds aside. Add the rest to the chile seeds.

In a large frying pan, warm 2 tablespoons of the lard or oil over medium heat. Add the tomatillos and onion and cook until deeply browned, 10–15 minutes. Stir in the garlic and fry until soft, 3–4 minutes. Stir in the aniseeds, cumin, and bay leaf. Transfer to a blender. Process until a smooth paste forms.

Wipe out the pan and add another 2 tablespoons of the lard or oil. Place over medium-high heat and heat until shimmering. Line a baking pan with absorbent paper. Quickly fry the tortilla, turning once, and drain on the paper. Fry the bread, turning once, until golden, just a few minutes; drain on the paper. In the following order, one at a time, fry the almonds, peanuts, raisins, cinnamon, and cloves for just a few seconds, immediately draining on the paper. Add along with about 1 cup (8 fl oz/250 ml) of the broth to the blender holding the tomatillo paste. Process to form a thick paste.

Add the remaining lard or oil to the same pan and place over medium heat. Fry the chiles, a few at a time and tossing constantly, until blistered, just a few seconds. Discard any burned chiles. Place the chiles in a bowl, add hot water to cover, and soak for about 30 minutes. Drain and tear into small pieces. Add with ½–1 cup (4–8 fl oz/125–250 ml) of the broth to the blender. Process until a smooth purée forms.

Pour off most of the fat from the pan, leaving about 1 tablespoon. Place over medium-high heat, add the seed, tomatillo, and tortilla mixture, reduce the heat, and simmer, stirring often, about 3 minutes. Add the puréed chiles and stir well for several minutes. Break the chocolate into chunks and add it with the sugar, stirring until it melts. Slowly stir in 4 cups (32 fl oz/1 l) of the broth and simmer for about 2 minutes. Season with salt.

Place the turkey in the mole. Simmer, turning occasionally and basting often, for about 45 minutes. An instant-read thermometer inserted into the thickest part should register 150–155°F (66–68°C). Remove from the heat and let stand in the mole for 10–15 minutes. Lift out the turkey, scraping off the sauce, and cut into thick slices. Arrange on a serving platter or individual plates and spoon the mole over the top. Sprinkle with the 2 tablespoons sesame seeds and serve immediately.

serves 10–12, with extra for enchiladas or tamales

Guerrero

Pato con Tamarindo

grilled duck with tamarind

Using tamarind with Muscovy duck is a contemporary idea, but one that seems a natural. It is necessary to start this dish a day in advance.

1 lb (500 g) tamarind pods (page 250)
2 tablespoons unsalted butter
8 cloves garlic, mashed
1 cup (8 fl oz/250 ml) chicken broth
2 tablespoons honey
1 tablespoon Worcestershire sauce
1½ teaspoons cayenne pepper, or more to taste
sea salt to taste
4 boneless Muscovy duck breasts with skin intact, 12–14 oz (375–440 g) each

Place the tamarind pods in a bowl, add boiling water to cover, and let soften for 1 hour. Drain, squeeze out the seeds, mash the pulp, and pass through a sieve. In a frying pan over medium heat, melt the butter. Add the garlic and sauté for 3 minutes. Stir in the tamarind and broth and simmer for 5 minutes. Add the honey, Worcestershire sauce, cayenne, and salt and simmer several more minutes, stirring often. Let cool. Set aside half for serving, cover, and refrigerate. Score the skin sides of the breasts down to the meat in a diamond pattern. Roll in the marinade, seal in a tightly covered container, and refrigerate at least 8 hours.

Prepare a medium-low fire in a charcoal grill. Lift the duck from the marinade. Pour the marinade into a small saucepan and bring to a boil, adding water if needed to thin it slightly. Place the breasts, skin side down, on the grill rack and grill, basting with the heated marinade, until brown and crisp on the first side, 10–12 minutes. Turn and cook on the second side for about 3 minutes for medium-rare. Transfer to a cutting board, cover loosely with aluminum foil, and let rest.

Reheat the reserved tamarind mixture. Slice each breast on the diagonal. Fan the slices out on individual plates, top with the warm sauce, and serve.

serves 6–8

México, D.F.

Pipián de Ajonjolí

sesame seed pipián with chicken

Savory pipianes *are similar to moles in appearance, and for some types of moles the names are interchangeable. So what, if anything, distinguishes a* pipián *from a mole? Just as the* mole poblano *is quite different from a* mole amarillo, verde, *or* manchamanteles, *it helps me to think of a* pipián *as just another type of mole. Fewer spices are typically used in a* pipián, *and although it still includes chiles and tomatoes or tomatillos in the sauce, it is more apt to be thickened just with seeds, providing a seductive, creamy texture. Pair this elegant dish with Seasoned White Rice (page 91). You might end with Coconut Flan (page 217).*

CHICKEN

8 cups (64 fl oz/2 l) water

4 chicken thighs

¼ white onion

2 cloves garlic

1 teaspoon sea salt

4 chicken breast halves

PIPIAN

4 small ripe tomatoes, about 1 lb (500 g)

2 thick slices white onion

4 cloves garlic, unpeeled

2 dried chipotle chiles or canned chiles chipotles en adobo

1½ cups (4½ oz/140 g) plus 2 tablespoons sesame seeds

2-inch (5-cm) piece true cinnamon bark

6 tablespoons (3 fl oz/90 ml) safflower or canola oil

½ teaspoon sea salt

To prepare the chicken, in a large pot, bring the water to a boil. Add the chicken thighs, onion, garlic, and salt, skimming off any foam from the surface. Reduce the heat to medium, cover partially, and simmer for 10 minutes. Add the chicken breasts, return the water to a simmer, and cook for 15 minutes. Let the chicken cool in the broth. Lift out the chicken, reserving the broth. Remove the skin and tear the meat into large pieces, discarding the bones. Strain the broth, then spoon off the fat.

To make the *pipián,* roast the tomatoes (page 250), onion (page 249), and garlic (page 248). Toast the dried chiles (page 247), if using. In a small bowl, soak the dried chiles in very hot water for 10 minutes, then drain. Place the tomatoes, onion, and garlic in a blender or food processor with 2 cups (16 fl oz/500 ml) of the broth. Process briefly, add the chiles, and process until smooth.

Warm a large frying pan over medium heat. Add the 1½ cups (4½ oz/140 g) sesame seeds and toast, stirring constantly, until golden brown, about 2 minutes. Spread on a plate to cool completely. Finely grind the seeds in a spice grinder. Pour into a small bowl. Finely grind the cinnamon and add to the seeds.

In a large, flameproof earthenware casserole or a dutch oven over medium-high heat, warm the oil. When just starting to smoke, pour in the tomato mixture, reduce the heat to medium-low, and simmer, stirring occasionally, until the mixture thickens and changes color, about 10 minutes. Add the ground sesame seeds and cinnamon, salt, and 2 cups (16 fl oz/500 ml) of the broth, whisking until smooth. Add the chicken and simmer over low heat, stirring to prevent the sauce from sticking, until the oil rises to the surface, 10–15 minutes. Add up to ¾ cup (6 fl oz/180 ml) more broth if needed to thin the sauce.

Place the chicken on a warmed platter or on individual plates, spoon on the sauce, and garnish with the 2 tablespoons sesame seeds. Serve immediately.

serves 8

México, D.F.

Manchamanteles

red mole with chicken, pork, and fruit

This light red mole with the delightfuly descriptive name of manchamanteles, *or "tablecloth stainer," is a stewlike dish found throughout central Mexico. Combining fruit and meat is a common practice in Mexico, with the fruit adding a slightly sweet and welcome tart flavor. Fresh corn tortillas (page 251) are a necessity, and Seasoned White Rice (page 91) is also nice for absorbing the sauce.*

¼ cup (2 fl oz/60 ml) safflower or peanut oil, or as needed, plus 1 tablespoon

1 white onion, coarsely chopped

6 cloves garlic, coarsely chopped

6 ancho chiles, seeded, deveined, and torn into large pieces

4–4½ cups (32–36 fl oz/1–1.1 l) chicken broth

½ cup (4 fl oz/125 ml) water, or as needed

20 almonds

¼ cup (1 oz/30 g) pecans

1 lb (500 g) boneless pork shoulder, cut into 1½-inch (4-cm) pieces, trimmed of excess fat

sea salt to taste

1 lb (500 g) chicken thighs, halved

½ lb (250 g) good-quality chorizo, homemade (page 248) or purchased, crumbled (optional)

½-inch (12-mm) piece true cinnamon bark or ½ teaspoon ground cinnamon

6 peppercorns or 2 large pinches of freshly ground pepper

4 whole cloves or 2 pinches of ground cloves

½ teaspoon dried oregano, preferably Mexican

1 tablespoon unsalted butter

2 slices pineapple, cored and cut into large cubes

1 small ripe plantain or green banana, about ¼ lb (125 g), peeled, quartered lengthwise, and cut into large cubes

1 small jicama, about ½ lb (250 g), peeled and cut into large cubes

In a large frying pan or *cazuela* over medium heat, warm the ¼ cup (2 fl oz/60 ml) oil. Add the onion and fry until lightly browned and soft, about 5 minutes. Add the garlic and cook until softened, a few more minutes. Using a slotted spoon, transfer the onion and garlic to a blender. In the same pan, quickly fry the chiles, flattening them with a spatula until they just start to blister and change color, only a few seconds. Using the slotted spoon, transfer to a work surface and let cool, then tear into small pieces and add to the blender. Add 1 cup (8 fl oz/250 ml) of the chicken broth and process until smooth, adding ½ cup (4 fl oz/125 ml) broth or the water only if necessary to create a good consistency. In the oil remaining in the pan, quickly sauté the nuts until fragrant, and transfer to the blender.

Raise the heat to medium-high and add more oil if necessary. Working in batches, add the pork in a single layer, salt lightly, and brown well on all sides, turning as needed. Using the slotted spoon, transfer to absorbent paper to drain. Add more oil to the pan if it is dry and heat over medium-high heat. Fry the chicken in the same manner, until lightly browned on all sides. Drain on absorbent paper. Add the chorizo (if using), brown it, and drain on the paper.

Grind the cinnamon bark, peppercorns, and cloves in a spice grinder and add to the blender holding the nuts, or add the preground spices. Process thoroughly, adding more water if needed to create a very smooth sauce. If it is too granular, strain through a medium-mesh sieve.

Reheat the oil remaining in the frying pan over medium-high heat until it starts to smoke, scraping up any meat particles from the pan bottom. Pour in the chile sauce, stirring constantly, being careful that it doesn't splatter. Add the oregano, then stir in the remaining 3–3½ cups (24–28 fl oz/750–875 ml) broth and bring to a simmer. Reduce the heat to low, add the pork, season with salt, cover, and cook until tender, about 45 minutes.

Meanwhile, melt the butter with the 1 tablespoon oil in a separate frying pan over medium heat. Add the pineapple and fry, turning as needed, until browned on all sides, about 5 minutes. Using a slotted spoon, transfer to a plate. Repeat with the plantain or banana and jicama in separate batches.

When the pork is tender, add the chicken, chorizo, pineapple, and plaintain or banana, cover, and simmer over low heat, stirring occasionally, until the chicken is cooked throughout, about 10 minutes longer. Add the jicama, taste for salt, and add a bit of water if the sauce is too thick.

Transfer the chicken and chunks of meat and fruit to a warmed serving bowl. Spoon the sauce on top and around them. Serve immediately.

serves 8

México, D.F.

Pescado Marco

red snapper with smoked chile sauce and cheese

Only a step or two away from the hotel where I stay in Mexico City is a bar-restaurant little known to tourists. In the early afternoon, polished cars block the street, the chauffeurs oblivious to those trying to drive past. Inside Guadiana, people are conducting business while drinking tequila or wine and enjoying the superb food of owner Marco Beteta. Later in the day, the sound level increases as more people crowd in to throw dice on the now-cleared tables. It was years ago, tired, disheveled, and hungry from a long plane ride, that I first pushed through the revolving doors of the packed restaurant. Instead of being ignored or turned away, as I obviously did not match the usual clientele, I was given a place at the marble bar and made to feel welcome. I have returned over and over and always enjoy the food as much as the atmosphere. This dish is a popular item on his menu.

¼ cup (2 fl oz/60 ml) safflower or canola oil
½ white onion, sliced
4 cloves garlic
2½ tablespoons all-purpose (plain) flour
4 cups (32 fl oz/1 l) water
6 tomatoes, sliced
1 bay leaf
1 teaspoon chicken bouillon granules
½ teaspoon ground allspice
2 chiles chipotles en adobo
⅓ lb (5 oz/155 g) bacon, chopped
juice of ½ lime
6 drops Worcestershire sauce
3 drops Maggi seasoning sauce (page 249)
sea salt and freshly ground pepper to taste
6 red snapper fillets or other firm white-fleshed fish fillets, about 6 oz (185 g) each
6 thin slices white cheddar or Monterey jack cheese

In a saucepan over medium heat, warm the oil. Add the onion and sauté until translucent, about 5 minutes. Add the garlic and sauté for 1 minute longer. Stir in the flour and cook, stirring, until golden, about 3 minutes. Gradually pour in the water while stirring constantly. Add the tomatoes, bay leaf, bouillon granules, and allspice. Bring to a simmer and cook until thickened, about 10 minutes. Remove from the heat and let cool slightly.

Working in batches, pour the sauce into a blender, add the chiles, and process until smooth. Pass the purée through a medium-mesh sieve, pressing down with the back of a spoon, and set aside.

In a frying pan large enough to hold the fish in a single layer, fry the bacon over medium heat until almost crispy, about 3 minutes. Using a slotted spoon, transfer to absorbent paper to drain. Pour off the bacon fat, wipe out the pan, and return to medium-high heat. Pour in the chile sauce, lime juice, and Worcestershire and Maggi sauces. Season with salt and pepper. Bring to a boil, reduce the heat to low, and simmer for 5 minutes to blend the flavors.

Rinse the fish fillets and pat dry. Sprinkle them with salt and pepper and carefully lay them in the sauce. Cook until the flesh is opaque throughout, 4–5 minutes. Turn the fillets halfway through cooking if the sauce does not quite cover the fish, or spoon the simmering sauce over the top.

When the fish is ready, place a cheese slice on top of each fillet, cover the pan, and cook just until the cheese melts. Transfer to a warmed platter or individual plates, sprinkle the chopped bacon over the top, and serve immediately.

serves 6

Pescados

After a morning exploring Dzibilchaltún, ten square miles (26 sq km) of ancient Maya buildings, I headed for Puerto Chuburna, on the very end of the Yucatán peninsula. There, friends prepared *tikin-xic* for me. Large fillets of fish, rubbed with *achiote* paste, were grilling over a smoldering fire built right on the sand, and on the table were tortillas, explosive salsas, and tiny *chivitas,* river snails that took a toothpick to pry out and eat. It was a meal that will stand out among the many I have eaten over years of travel in Mexico.

With thousands of miles of shoreline, Mexico is blessed with an abundance of seafood. More than half of the states are washed by the waters of the Pacific Ocean, the Gulf of Mexico, the Caribbean, or the Sea of Cortés, and each has its own culinary specialties. It is on the Gulf of Mexico, however, where the most varieties and the most elaborate preparations are found. Never will I forget my visit to the market at Villahermosa and my first sighting of *pejelagartos:* rows of smoked fish with a crocodile-like skin, run through, mouth to tail, with wooden sticks. Appearance aside, they make a tasty taco filling. In Campeche, *pan de cazón,* a double-decker tortilla sandwich with layers of sand shark meat, black beans, and a feisty habanero chile sauce, is a traditional dish. In all of the coastal communities, restaurants offer whatever was caught that day prepared almost any way imaginable.

One shouldn't leave, though, without sampling the spectacular *huachinango a la Veracruzana,* red snapper with an olive, caper, and tomato sauce, or that other classic dish, *robalo en hoja santa,* sea bass wrapped in the leaves of an herb with a sense-tickling aroma.

Yucatán

Costillas al Carbón

grilled pork ribs

I have wonderful memories of eating these addictive ribs at the home of Silvio and Angelica Campos in the small village of Tixkokob in the Yucatán.

4 lb (2 kg) meaty pork back ribs

sea salt to taste

2 tablespoons achiote *paste (page 246)*

½ cup (4 fl oz/125 ml) fresh bitter orange juice (page 249)

4 cloves garlic, minced

2 large ripe tomatoes

¼ white onion

1 habanero chile

¼ cup (⅓ oz/10 g) coarsely chopped fresh cilantro (fresh coriander)

♛ Cut the ribs into sections of 4 or 5 ribs each and place in a large pot. Add water to cover and the salt. Bring to a boil, skimming off any foam from the surface. Reduce the heat to low, cover, and simmer until nearly cooked, about 35 minutes. Transfer the ribs to a glass bowl. In a bowl, dissolve the *achiote* paste in the orange juice. Stir in the garlic and a good amount of salt. Pour over the ribs, mix well, cover, and refrigerate for at least 6 hours or up to 24 hours.

♛ Prepare an indirect-heat fire in a charcoal grill. Meanwhile, roast the tomatoes (page 250), onion (page 249), and chile (page 247). Remove the ribs from the marinade, place on the grill rack, and grill, turning often, until crispy brown, about 15 minutes.

♛ Combine the tomatoes, onion, and chile in a blender or food processor and blend until smooth. Pour the purée into a saucepan and heat to serving temperature.

♛ Remove the ribs from the grill and cut into 1-rib portions. Add the ribs to the sauce and simmer, uncovered, over low heat, for 10 minutes. Taste and adjust the seasoning with salt.

♛ Arrange the ribs on a platter, spoon the sauce over them, and sprinkle with the cilantro. Serve at once.

serves 4–6

México, D.F.

Torta Azteca

savory layered tortilla cake

Two of my most prized cookbooks are slender, hand-bound, mimeographed copies of the recipes of Gaby Buerba, a most talented cook. Gaby would use the much-esteemed huitlacoche, *a delicious fungus that grows on corn, for this rustic layered tortilla dish, but any type of edible mushroom will add the needed earthy taste. Well-Fried Beans (page 182) are the traditional accompaniment.*

1 large chicken breast half

1 thick slice white onion

2 cloves garlic

½ teaspoon sea salt, plus salt to taste

1 lb (500 g) tomatoes, roasted (page 250) and quartered, or 1 can (14½ oz/455 g) diced tomatoes, with juice

3 serrano chiles, coarsely chopped

¼ cup (1 oz/30 g) coarsely chopped white onion

1 teaspoon safflower or canola oil

freshly ground pepper to taste

8 purchased thin corn tortillas, each cut into 6 wedges, or 48–50 unsalted commercial tortilla chips

1 tablespoon unsalted butter

¼ lb (125 g) fresh mushrooms, brushed clean and sliced

2 poblano chiles, roasted (page 247) and sliced (optional, but highly recommended)

⅔ cup (5 fl oz/160 ml) crema *(page 248)*

½ cup (2 oz/60 g) shredded queso Chihuahua *or Monterey jack cheese*

6 radishes, thinly sliced

Place the chicken in a saucepan with the onion slice, 1 of the garlic cloves, and the ½ teaspoon salt. Add water to cover and bring to a boil. Reduce the heat to medium, cover, and simmer for 15–20 minutes. Lift out the chicken and shred the meat, discarding the skin and bones. Reserve the broth, skimming off any fat from the surface.

In a blender or food processor, purée the tomatoes with the chiles, chopped onion, and remaining garlic clove. In a small saucepan over medium heat, heat the oil until smoking. Add the tomato mixture and fry, stirring occasionally, until the color darkens, 3–4 minutes. Add ½ cup (4 fl oz/125 ml) of the reserved broth and season with salt and pepper. Bring the sauce to a boil, reduce the heat to medium-low, and simmer, uncovered, until thickened, 8–10 minutes. Remove from the heat and keep warm.

Preheat an oven to 350°F (180°C). Lightly oil an 8-inch (20-cm) square baking dish.

If using tortillas, place the wedges in a single layer on a baking sheet and cover with a wire rack to keep them from curling. Bake for about 10 minutes, then set aside. Leave the oven on.

In a small frying pan over medium-high heat, melt the butter. Add the mushrooms and sauté until any liquid evaporates, 5–8 minutes.

Put one-third of the tortilla wedges or chips in the bottom of the baking dish. Top with half of the poblano chiles (if using), chicken, mushrooms, and *crema*. Spoon on one-third of the sauce and cheese. Top with half of the remaining tortilla wedges or chips and add the remaining chiles, chicken, mushrooms, and *crema*. Top with half of the remaining sauce and cheese. Finish with the remaining tortilla wedges or chips and the remaining sauce and cheese.

Bake until the sauce starts to bubble and all the layers are heated through, 15–20 minutes. Remove from the oven, scatter the radish slices on top, and serve immediately directly from the dish.

serves 4

Arroz con Azafrán y Almejas

saffron rice with clams

This recipe from Tabasco-born Ricardo Muñoz Zurita is similar to one from nearby Campeche, where oysters are often substituted for the clams. Sautéed bell peppers (capsicums) are usually added for color and a slightly different flavor. I have enjoyed it both ways in the restaurants of Campeche.

large pinch of saffron threads

3 tablespoons hot water

2 cups (14 oz/440 g) medium- or long-grain white rice

2 ripe tomatoes, about ⅔ lb (10 oz/315 g), cut into chunks, or 1 can (14½ oz/455 g) chopped tomatoes, drained

¼ cup (1 oz/30 g) chopped white onion

2 teaspoons chopped garlic (about 6 small cloves)

⅓ cup (3 fl oz/80 ml) safflower or canola oil

3 cups (24 fl oz/750 ml) warm water

2 lb (1 kg) small clams, well scrubbed

4 fresh flat-leaf (Italian) parsley sprigs, chopped

2 teaspoons sea salt

In a small bowl, soak the saffron threads in the hot water for about 10 minutes. In a medium bowl, soak the rice in warm water to cover for 10 minutes. Drain the rice and rinse under cold running water until the water runs clear. Drain thoroughly. Put the tomatoes in a blender. Add the onion, garlic, and saffron with its soaking water. Process until smooth.

In a *cazuela* or heavy saucepan over medium heat, warm the oil. Stir in the rice and sauté until golden, about 5 minutes. Pour the tomato mixture through a sieve placed over the saucepan. Simmer, stirring occasionally, to combine the flavors, 6–8 minutes. Put the 3 cups (24 fl oz/750 ml) warm water into the unrinsed blender, swirl it around, and add to the rice. Bring to a boil and add the clams (discard any that do not close to the touch), parsley, and salt. Stir once, cover, and simmer over low heat until the rice is fluffy and the clams have opened, 20–25 minutes.

Spoon the rice and clams into a wide, shallow serving bowl or into individual plates with rims, discarding any clams that failed to open. Serve at once.

serves 6–8

Michoacán

Enchiladas a la Plaza

enchiladas with red chile–coated chicken and vegetables

At one time, numerous vendors frequented a little side plaza in downtown Morelia, where they prepared these classic red chile enchiladas with their accompanying sauce-drenched chicken and vegetables. Although once in awhile I still find a lone vendor in the plaza, there are now many small restaurants where the enchiladas are featured. I have eaten similar enchiladas from the plazas and streets of towns elsewhere in central Mexico, but never as abundant a dish as in Morelia.

SAUCE

3 guajillo chiles

6 ancho chiles

5 cloves garlic, unpeeled

2 cups (16 fl oz/500 ml) chicken broth, or as needed

1½ teaspoons sugar

1 teaspoon sea salt

¼ teaspoon freshly ground pepper

¼ teaspoon ground cumin

3 tablespoons safflower or canola oil

ACCOMPANIMENTS

6 chicken breast halves or thighs

¼ white onion

2 cloves garlic

3 teaspoons sea salt

2 large red potatoes, peeled and cut into large chunks

2 carrots, peeled and cut into large chunks

3 tablespoons cider vinegar

CONDIMENTS

½ small head cabbage, finely shredded

2 tablespoons cider vinegar

1 teaspoon sea salt

2 thin slices white onion

½ cup (2½ oz/75 g) crumbled queso fresco

12 purchased thin corn tortillas

5 tablespoons (2½ fl oz/75 ml) safflower or canola oil, plus more as needed

To make the sauce, seed the guajillo and ancho chiles, then toast (page 247). Roast the garlic (page 248). In a saucepan, combine the chiles with water to cover. Bring to a simmer over medium heat and simmer for 15 minutes. Let cool. Drain the chiles, tear them into large pieces, and place in a blender. Peel the garlic and add to the blender along with the 2 cups (16 fl oz/500 ml) broth and the sugar, salt, pepper, and cumin. Process until smooth.

In a large frying pan over medium heat, warm the oil until it is smoking. Add the sauce and fry, stirring often, until the color deepens, 3–5 minutes. Add more broth if the sauce thickens too much.

Meanwhile, to prepare the accompaniments, place the chicken in a saucepan with the onion, garlic, and 2 teaspoons of the salt and add water to cover. Bring to a boil, reduce the heat to medium, cover, and simmer until the chicken is tender and cooked throughout, 20–25 minutes. Lift out the chicken, saving the broth for another use.

In a saucepan over medium-high heat, combine the potatoes and carrots with water to cover. Add the vinegar and remaining 1 teaspoon salt and bring to a boil. Cook until tender, about 10 minutes, then drain.

To prepare the condiments, in a bowl, combine the cabbage with the vinegar and salt. Toss, then set aside with the onion slices and the cheese. About 15 minutes before serving, place the cabbage in the center of a platter or divide among individual plates. Have the sauce, chicken, and tortillas ready.

In a large frying pan over medium-high heat, warm the 5 tablespoons (2½ oz/75 ml) oil until it is smoking. Drag each piece of chicken through the sauce, turn, and repeat. Drop the chicken into the hot oil and cook for just a few minutes, then turn and cook the other side until heated through. Using a slotted spoon, transfer to a plate and keep warm.

Add the potatoes and carrots to the same oil over medium heat and cook, turning frequently, until hot, about 3 minutes. Transfer to a plate and keep warm. Add more oil to the pan, wait until it is hot, then drag each tortilla through the remaining sauce, coating both sides, and fry briefly, turning once. Be careful not to tear the tortilla when turning it. While the tortilla is still in the pan, fold it in half and then in half again lengthwise. With a slotted spatula, lift from the pan and keep warm on a plate.

Put the enchiladas on the cabbage and arrange the chicken and vegetables on each side. Garnish with the onion and cheese. Serve at once.

serves 6

Coahuila

Pierna de Carnero Asada

roast leg of lamb

Northern Mexico is cattle country—no doubt about it. In some areas, though, the Spanish Basque ranchers introduced sheep even before the large herds of cattle were established, and even today the young lambs are cooked al pastor, *on a metal rod over hot coals. For special occasions, especially Easter, a spring leg of lamb with an earthy chile-laced gravy is a dish that satisfies a festive group of friends and family.*

2 tablespoons olive oil

5 cloves garlic, finely minced

2 teaspoons freshly ground pepper

1 teaspoon sea salt

1 teaspoon dried thyme

1 cup (8 fl oz/250 ml) tequila reposado

1 bone-in leg of lamb, 4–5 lb (2–2.5 kg), trimmed of excess fat

GRAVY

2 ancho chiles, seeded and toasted (page 247)

1 teaspoon cider vinegar

about 2 cups (16 fl oz/500 ml) boiling water

3 cups (24 fl oz/750 ml) chicken broth

2 tablespoons olive oil or drippings from roasting lamb

3 cloves garlic, unpeeled, roasted (page 248)

2 tablespoons all-purpose (plain) flour

½ teaspoon sea salt, or to taste

In a heavy frying pan over medium heat, warm the oil. Add the garlic and sauté until light gold, 3–4 minutes. Remove from the heat. Sprinkle in the pepper, salt, and thyme. Add the tequila and stir well.

Place the lamb in a large, shallow baking dish and pour the garlic-tequila mixture over the top, massaging it well into the meat on all sides. Let the meat rest for 30–40 minutes, turning it often.

Meanwhile, position a rack in the lower third of an oven and preheat to 425°F (220°C).

Lift the lamb from the marinade, reserving the marinade in a saucepan. Set the lamb on a rack in a roasting pan, meaty side up. Place in the oven and reduce the heat to 325°F (165°C). Bring the marinade to a boil; set aside. Roast, basting occasionally with marinade, until an instant-read thermometer inserted into the thickest part of the lamb away from the bone registers 125°–130°F (52°–54°C) for medium-rare, about 1½ hours, or until the desired doneness. Transfer to a platter, cover loosely with aluminum foil, and let stand for 10 minutes.

Meanwhile, begin making the gravy: In a bowl, combine the chiles and vinegar. Add the water, making sure the chiles are submerged, and soak until soft, about 30 minutes. Transfer the chiles to a blender or food processor with ¼ cup (2 fl oz/60 ml) of the soaking water and process until smooth, adding more soaking water if needed. Pour the broth into a saucepan, bring to a simmer, and keep warm.

In a heavy frying pan over medium-low heat, warm the oil or lamb drippings. Peel the garlic, mince finely, add to the pan, and sauté for just a few seconds. Stir in the flour and cook, stirring, until it turns light gold, about 1 minute. Whisk in the chile paste, stirring constantly until well blended. Slowly pour in the broth, stirring constantly, then add the salt. Continue to cook, stirring, until smooth and thickened, about 5 minutes.

Slice the lamb on the diagonal across the grain and arrange on the platter. Pour the gravy into a warmed bowl and pass at the table.

serves 8

Guerrero

Conejo en Chileajo

rabbit in chile sauce

This local specialty comes from Diana Kennedy, an authority on Mexico's regional cuisines, who discovered it in a roadside shack near Taxco.

¾ cup (2½ oz/75 g) thinly sliced white onion

⅓ cup (3 fl oz/80 ml) fresh lime juice

sea salt to taste

1 rabbit, 2½–3 lb (1.25–1.5 kg), cut into serving pieces

6 green (spring) onions, coarsely chopped

2 cloves garlic, unpeeled, plus 2 peeled cloves

20 large guajillo chiles, seeded and deveined

6 ancho chiles, seeded and deveined

½ white onion, coarsely chopped

½ teaspoon cumin seeds, crushed

½ cup (4 fl oz/125 ml) safflower oil

1½ cups (12 fl oz/375 ml) chicken broth

Mix together the sliced onion, lime juice, and salt in a glass bowl. Let macerate for about 2 hours.

Rinse the rabbit pieces well. Place in a saucepan with the green onions, unpeeled garlic, and salt. Add water to cover, and simmer, covered, for 1½ hours. Lift out the rabbit; discard the cooking liquid.

Place the guajillo and ancho chiles in separate bowls. Add very hot water to cover and let soak until very soft, about 15 minutes. Drain the anchos and transfer to a blender. Add the chopped onion, peeled garlic, cumin, and ¾ cup (6 fl oz/180 ml) water. Blend to form a slightly textured purée. Pour into a bowl. Pour 1¼ cups (10 fl oz/ 310 ml) water into the blender and gradually add the guajillo chiles, blending after each addition until almost smooth. Press through a sieve into the ancho purée. In a heavy, deep frying pan over medium heat, warm the oil until smoking. Add the chile sauce and fry, stirring, for 5 minutes. Add the rabbit and broth and cook until the sauce is thick, about 15 minutes. Season with salt.

Divide the rabbit evenly among individual plates and top with the sauce. Crown with a tangle of onion.

serves 4

México, D.F.

Calamares en Salsa de Tres Chiles

squid in sauce of three chiles

At Restaurante Isadora in Mexico City, Carmen Ortuña creates intriguing dishes that combine traditional Mexican ingredients in an innovative manner. This is one of her newest offerings.

1 each ancho chile, mulato chile, and guajillo chile
1½ teaspoons olive oil
1½ teaspoons minced garlic, plus 1 clove, minced
juice of 1 lime
1 teaspoon Maggi seasoning sauce (page 249)
1 teaspoon Worcestershire sauce
½ cup (4 fl oz/125 ml) dry white wine
1 cup (8 fl oz/250 ml) fish broth or bottled clam juice
1 lb (500 g) squid, cleaned (page 250)
sea salt and freshly ground pepper to taste
2 tablespoons unsalted butter
Seasoned White Rice (page 91)
¼ cup (½ oz/15 g) finely chopped fresh flat-leaf (Italian) parsley

Cut each chile in half from top to bottom. Remove the seeds and veins. Slice the chiles crosswise into narrow strips ¾ inch (2 cm) long.

In a saucepan over medium-low heat, warm the oil. Add the 1½ teaspoons garlic and sauté for about 1 minute. Add the chiles, lime juice, Maggi and Worcestershire sauces, and wine and cook for 2 minutes. Add the fish broth or clam juice. Bring to a boil, reduce the heat to low, and simmer for 10 minutes.

Cut the squid bodies into rings ¼ inch (6 mm) wide. Leave the tentacles whole. Pat dry and sprinkle with salt and pepper. Melt the butter in a frying pan over medium heat. Add the minced garlic clove and sauté until translucent, about 30 seconds. Add the squid and sauté until opaque, just a couple of minutes. Stir in the chile sauce and heat through.

Scoop some rice onto warmed individual plates and spoon the squid and sauce over it. Garnish with the parsley and serve at once.

serves 4

Comida Negra

An oft-stated principle of my introduction to cooking was that the appearance of a dish is almost as important as its taste. If food is garnished with a bit of color, it will appeal to the eater. Remember that maraschino cherry on your dinner plate? The black *(negro),* unadorned dishes of Mexico refute that premise. The supreme dishes of most regions are, let's face it, singularly monochromatic.

One of the most prized of Yucatecan dishes is *relleno negro,* stuffed turkey seasoned with *chirmole,* a paste of burnt black chile. In states bordering the Gulf of Mexico, *calamares en su tinta* is a favorite. Tiny squid are cooked in a subtly flavored but disconcertingly black sauce made from liquid that has been extracted from the squid's ink sacs. Even the accompanying rice turns gray.

In Mexico City's sophisticated restaurants, *huitlacoche,* a black fungus that grows on ears of corn, is a great delicacy in soups and as a crepe filling. The exotic mushroomy flavor of the fungus, often compared with that of truffles, even transforms a simple taco or quesadilla. To convey an idea of its appearance, its Aztec-derived name roughly translates as "sleeping excrement."

Remember, too, that the queen of all fiesta dishes is *mole poblano* with its chile-rich black sauce, and, in Oaxaca, the *mole negro.*

Jalisco

Birria

slow-cooked lamb

Birria, *one of the rustic dishes I most closely identify with Jalisco, is a richly spiced type of the traditional* barbacoa. *No longer steamed in buried underground pots, the chile-marinated meat, usually mutton or kid, is still long-cooked until it turns into a tender stew with plenty of flavorful broth. Laura Caraza, a friend from Mexico City, makes a sophisticated version with fresh ginger and sherry.*

8 ancho chiles

6 guajillo chiles

5 cloves garlic, unpeeled

1 cup (8 fl oz/250 ml) mild white vinegar

2-inch (5-cm) piece true cinnamon bark, ground, or 1 teaspoon ground cinnamon

½-inch (12-mm) piece fresh ginger, peeled and grated

2 teaspoons dried oregano, preferably Mexican

½ teaspoon ground cumin

½ teaspoon freshly ground pepper

1 teaspoon sea salt, or to taste

4–5 lb (2–2.5 kg) bone-in lamb shoulder, trimmed of excess fat

1 lb (500 g) tomatoes, boiled or roasted (page 250), or 1 can (14½ oz/455 g) chopped tomatoes

½ cup dry sherry (optional)

GARNISH

shredded cabbage

finely chopped white onion

lime wedges

Seed the chiles, then toast (page 247). Roast the garlic (page 248). Put the chiles in a saucepan, add water to cover, and bring to a boil. Remove from the heat, press the chiles down in the water, and let soak until very soft, about 20 minutes. Drain and set aside.

Peel the garlic and place in a blender along with the chiles and vinegar. Process until very smooth. Add the cinnamon, the ginger, 1 teaspoon of the oregano, the cumin, the pepper, and the 1 teaspoon salt and blend again. You can add a spoonful of water to be sure the mixture blends smoothly, but this is a paste, so do not add more water than necessary. Taste and add more salt, if needed. If the paste is not perfectly smooth, pass it through a medium-mesh sieve.

Place the meat in a bowl and coat evenly with the paste. Cover and refrigerate for at least 5 hours or, preferably, overnight.

Preheat an oven to 350°F (180°C).

Place a rack in the bottom of a dutch oven or roasting pan large enough to hold the meat. You may have to devise your own rack. The important thing is to allow the steam to rise and the pungent sauce to drip into the water. The pan must have a tight-fitting lid as well. Pour in enough water to reach just to the top of the rack (3–4 cups/24–32 fl oz/750 ml–1 l) and then pile the meat on top of the rack, scraping any chile paste clinging to the bowl over the top. Seal the top of the pan tightly with aluminum foil and cover with the lid. Bake for 3 hours.

Remove from the oven and raise the oven temperature to 375°F (190°C).

Lift the meat from the pan, tear into large pieces, and spread them on a baking sheet, removing any large pieces of fat and gristle and the bones. Reserve the broth in the pan. Brown the meat in the oven for 15 minutes, turning at least once.

Pour the broth into a saucepan, skimming off as much of the fat as possible. In a blender, combine the tomatoes, the remaining 1 teaspoon oregano, and 1 cup (8 fl oz/250 ml) of the broth and purée until smooth. Pour the purée into the saucepan holding the broth. Add the sherry, if using, and bring to a gentle simmer over low heat. Season with salt, if necessary. Simmer gently, uncovered, for 15 minutes to blend the flavors.

To serve, spoon the meat into individual bowls and ladle in the broth. Pass the cabbage, onion, and lime wedges in separate small bowls at the table.

serves 10

Birrierías line the roads leading in and out of Jalisco's bustling capital of Guadalajara.

Veracruz

Pollo en Ciruela

chicken sauced with prunes and oranges

On a rainy day in Xico, high on the slopes of the Sierra Madre, I took refuge in the Restaurant El Mesón Xixqueño. My main course was this voluptuous chicken dish, smothered in a thick prune and orange sauce. The cook had no idea of its origin, except that it had been in her family "forever." Accompany with Seasoned White Rice (page 91).

1 cup (8 fl oz/250 ml) fresh orange juice

½ cup (4 fl oz/125 ml) medium-sweet white wine or sherry, or as needed

½ orange, unpeeled, thinly sliced

2 chiles chipotles en adobo, *finely chopped*

1 tablespoon olive oil, plus extra as needed

sea salt to taste

3 lb (1.5 kg) chicken breasts and thighs

¼ lb (125 g) bacon, chopped

¼ cup (¾ oz/20 g) narrow orange zest strips, about ¾ inch (2 cm) long

SAUCE

½ lb (250 g) dried prunes, pitted (about 30)

¾ cup (7½ oz/235 g) Seville orange marmalade

½ cup (4 fl oz/125 ml) water, or as needed

¼ cup (2 fl oz/60 g) fresh orange juice

3-inch (7.5-cm) piece true cinnamon bark

zest of 1 orange, cut into narrow strips about ¾ inch (2 cm) long

In a glass bowl, mix together the orange juice, wine or sherry, orange slices, chiles, 1 tablespoon oil, and salt. This dish requires more salt than usual to bring out the distinct flavors, so taste as you add it. Cut each chicken breast into 4 pieces and each thigh in half. Add the chicken to the orange juice mixture, cover, and refrigerate for several hours or, preferably, overnight. Stir from time to time.

To make the sauce, in a saucepan, stir together the prunes, marmalade, water, orange juice, cinnamon, and orange zest. Bring to a boil over medium-high heat. Reduce the heat to low and simmer, stirring often, until the sauce is thickened, 10–15 minutes. Let cool, cover, and set aside for at least 2 hours to blend the flavors. Discard the cinnamon bark.

Remove the chicken from the marinade and dry on absorbent paper. Reserve the marinade.

In a large, heavy frying pan over medium-low heat, slowly fry the bacon until golden, 3–5 minutes. Using a slotted spoon, transfer the bacon to absorbent paper to drain. Raise the heat to high and add oil to the bacon drippings to a depth of ¼ inch (6 mm). When the oil is crackling hot, working in batches, add the chicken, reduce the heat to medium, and cook, turning as needed, until golden and crisp on the outside but still moist inside, 15–20 minutes. Transfer the chicken to absorbent paper to drain.

Drain the excess oil from the pan and return the pan to low heat. Add the reserved marinade and gradually raise the heat to medium. Cook until reduced by half, scraping up any browned bits from the pan bottom. Add the prune sauce, bacon, and chicken, stir well, and cook, uncovered, over low heat until the chicken is tender, 20 minutes. Turn the chicken occasionally, adding more water or wine as needed to keep it from scorching.

Transfer the chicken to a warmed serving platter. Remove the cooked orange zest from the sauce and spoon the sauce over the chicken. Garnish with the ¼ cup (¾ oz/20 g) fresh zest and serve immediately.

serves 6

Puebla

Carne Asada con Hierbas

marinated steak with herbs

This recipe began with one given to me by Diana Kennedy, who received it from an acquaintance, Antonio Sanchez. She also knew a person who used serrano or jalapeño chiles en escabeche *for a marinade, juice and all. I've combined the two recipes.*

1 slice of large section beef tenderloin, 2½–3 lb (1.25–1.5 kg) and 2 inches (5 cm) thick

1 can (14 oz/440 g) pickled serrano or jalapeño chiles, with liquid

½ cup (4 fl oz/125 ml) safflower or canola oil

4 cloves garlic

¼ white onion, coarsely chopped

4 large fresh marjoram sprigs or ½ teaspoon dried

4 fresh thyme sprigs or ½ teaspoon dried

2 bay leaves

sea salt and freshly ground pepper to taste

Place the beef in a shallow glass baking dish. In a blender or food processor, combine the chiles, oil, garlic, onion, marjoram, thyme, bay leaves, salt, and pepper. Process to form a purée with some texture. Pour the purée over the steak, cover, and refrigerate for at least 4 hours or as long as 12 hours, turning the steak once or twice.

Prepare a hot fire in a charcoal grill with a cover.

Lift the meat from the marinade, brushing off any excess. Place on the grill rack and sear for about 10 minutes on the first side. Turn the meat and sear the second side until well browned, about 7 minutes. Push the coals to one side of the grill bed, place the steak on the grill rack not directly over the coals, cover the grill, and grill for about 6 minutes longer for medium-rare. Do not leave the meat too long, as it will continue to cook when it is removed from the grill. Transfer to a cutting board, cover loosely with aluminum foil, and let rest for 5 minutes.

Slice the meat diagonally across the grain into strips ½ inch (12 mm) thick. Serve at once on a warmed platter.

serves 4

México, D.F.

Chiles Anchos Rellenos de Picadillo de Pollo

ancho chiles stuffed with chicken picadillo

It is traditionally the poblano chile that is stuffed to create the classic chile relleno. *If the same chile is prepared in its dried form—the rich, chocolate-sweet ancho chile—a very different dish is the result. When Roberto Santibanez was the chef/owner of two Mexico City restaurants, he still liked to entertain at home. This was an ideal dish, as the chiles and filling are prepared in steps, assembled, and then put in the oven to cook at the last minute. Serve with Seasoned White Rice (page 91), black beans, or both.*

PICADILLO

½ cup (4 fl oz/120 ml) mild olive oil

1 cup (5 oz/155 g) finely chopped white onion

2 tablespoons minced garlic

2 lb (1 kg) ripe plum (Roma) tomatoes, finely chopped

¼ teaspoon dried thyme

2 bay leaves

½ cup (3 oz/90 g) raisins

2 lb (1 kg) boneless, skinless chicken thighs, ground (minced) or finely chopped

sea salt to taste

½ cup (2½ oz/75 g) manzanilla *or other meaty green olives, pitted and coarsely chopped*

½ cup (3 oz/90 g) slivered blanched almonds

¼ cup (2 oz/60 g) capers, well rinsed

¼ cup (⅓ oz/10 g) firmly packed finely chopped fresh cilantro (fresh coriander)

¼ cup (⅓ oz/10 g) firmly packed finely chopped fresh flat-leaf (Italian) parsley

leaves from 6 fresh mint sprigs, finely chopped

CHILES

8 large ancho chiles

4 cups (32 fl oz/1 l) water

¼ lb (125 g) piloncillo *(page 249), grated, or ½ cup (3½ oz/105 g) firmly packed dark brown sugar*

½-inch (12-mm) piece true cinnamon bark

⅔ cup (5 fl oz/160 ml) cider vinegar

½ teaspoon sea salt

SAUCE

2 cups (16 fl oz/500 ml) crema *(page 248)*

½ cup (2½ oz/75 g) finely chopped white onion

½ teaspoon sea salt

¼ cup (⅓ oz/10 g) firmly packed finely chopped fresh cilantro (fresh coriander)

To make the *picadillo,* in a saucepan over medium heat, warm ¼ cup (2 fl oz/60 ml) of the olive oil. Add the onion and cook until translucent, about 2 minutes. Add the garlic and cook for 1 minute longer. Add the tomatoes, thyme, and bay leaves, stir well, and simmer until the mixture begins to dry out, about 15 minutes. Add the raisins and continue to cook for 10 minutes longer to meld the flavors and absorb any excess liquid.

In a large sauté pan over medium-high heat, warm the remaining ¼ cup (2 fl oz/60 ml) oil and heat until smoking. Add the chicken and cook, stirring constantly, until lightly browned, about 4 minutes. Salt lightly, then pour the tomato sauce into the pan and cook for 5 minutes to season the chicken. Stir in the olives, almonds, capers, cilantro, parsley, and mint. Remove from the heat; let cool.

Preheat an oven to 350°F (180°C).

To prepare the chiles, leaving the stem end intact, make a lengthwise slit in each chile and remove the seeds and veins, taking care not to break the walls.

In a small saucepan, combine the water, *piloncillo* or brown sugar, cinnamon, vinegar, and salt and bring to a boil over medium-high heat, stirring to dissolve the sugar. Reduce the heat to medium and let simmer for 5 minutes. Add the chiles, cover, and remove the pan from the heat. Let the chiles soak until soft, 15–20 minutes. Carefully transfer the chiles to absorbent paper to drain, reserving the liquid.

Carefully stuff the chiles with the *picadillo* and place them, just touching, in a baking dish. Cover and bake until heated through, about 15 minutes.

While the chiles are baking, make the sauce: In a small saucepan over low heat, combine the *crema,* onion, and salt, bring to a bare simmer, and cook for 5 minutes. Strain, add the cilantro, and keep warm until ready to serve.

Remove the chiles from the oven and arrange on individual plates. Pour the sauce over them and serve.

serves 4–6

Puebla

Tinga Poblana

pork stew with chipotle chiles

Tinga is a classic regional dish. This tasty concoction of highly seasoned pork is also shredded and used as a topping for tostadas and as a filling for tacos and tortas.

2 lb (1 kg) *boneless pork shoulder, excess fat removed, cut into 1-inch (2.5-cm) cubes*

2 *white onions,* 1 *thinly sliced and* 1 *finely chopped*

3 *whole cloves garlic, plus* 3 *cloves, chopped*

1 *teaspoon sea salt, plus salt to taste*

2 *tablespoons safflower or canola oil*

¼ lb (125 g) *good-quality chorizo, homemade (page 248) or purchased, crumbled*

1 *can (14½ oz/455 g) chopped tomatoes*

1 *teaspoon dried oregano, preferably Mexican*

1 *teaspoon dried thyme*

3 *bay leaves*

4 chiles chipotles en adobo, *chopped*

1 *teaspoon sugar (optional)*

2 *firm avocados, preferably Haas, pitted, peeled, and sliced*

In a saucepan, combine the pork, half of the onion slices, and the whole garlic cloves. Add water to cover and the 1 teaspoon salt. Bring to a boil; skim off any foam from the surface. Simmer, uncovered, over medium-low heat until tender, about 1½ hours. Transfer the pork to a bowl.

In a frying pan over medium heat, warm the oil. Add the chorizo and fry, stirring often, until just cooked through, about 5 minutes. Add the chopped onion and garlic and sauté for about 5 minutes. Remove any excess oil. Add the pork, tomatoes, oregano, thyme, bay leaves, and chiles. Cook, stirring occasionally, for about 15 minutes, adding up to 1 cup (8 fl oz/250 ml) of the broth to keep the mixture moist. Season with salt and a little sugar, if needed, to mellow the dish. Ladle the stew into bowls and garnish with the avocado and the remaining onion slices.

serves 8–10, with leftovers

México, D.F.

Enchiladas Verdes

chicken enchiladas with tomatillo sauce

These traditional green-sauced enchiladas from Mexico City are a favorite of chef Ricardo Muñoz Zurita. The recipe comes from nearby Xochimilco, where, long before the Spanish conquest, the Aztecs were raising vegetables, chiles, and herbs on floating gardens encircling Tenochtitlán, their island capital. For a starter, serve Ricardo's tomato-red ceviche (page 40) with shrimp as a color and taste contrast.

CHICKEN

2 lb (1 kg) chicken breasts

¼ white onion

1 head garlic, halved crosswise

1 tablespoon sea salt

SAUCE

3 lb (1.5 kg) tomatillos, husked and rinsed

9 serrano chiles

3 cloves garlic, chopped

¼ cup (2 fl oz/60 ml) safflower or canola oil

1 tablespoon sea salt, or to taste

ENCHILADAS

⅓ cup (3 fl oz/80 ml) safflower or canola oil

18 purchased thin corn tortillas

1 cup (8 fl oz/250 ml) crema *(page 248)*

1 white onion, thinly sliced

1 cup (5 oz/155 g) crumbled queso fresco

To prepare the chicken, place in a saucepan with the onion, garlic, and salt and add water to cover. Bring to a boil over high heat, reduce the heat to medium, cover, and simmer until the chicken is cooked through, 20–25 minutes. Let cool and lift out the chicken, saving the broth for another use. (The chicken can be wrapped and refrigerated for up to 1 day before continuing.) Discard the skin and bones and shred the meat with your fingers. There should be 4 cups (1½ lb/750 g) chicken.

To make the sauce, in a saucepan, combine the tomatillos and chiles with water to cover. Bring to a boil over medium-high heat and cook until tender, 10–15 minutes. If some of the tomatillos remain firm, the pan should still be removed from the heat. Drain and, working in batches, place the tomatillos and chiles in a blender along with the garlic. Process until a smooth sauce forms.

In a frying pan over medium-high heat, warm the oil until it is smoking. Quickly add the tomatillo sauce and fry, stirring constantly, until the sauce begins to bubble. Reduce the heat to low and cook until the sauce starts to thicken, 5 minutes longer. Add the 1 tablespoon salt; taste and add more salt if needed. Keep warm. When the sauce is combined with the tortillas and chicken, the taste of salt will be quite diminished; it should be highly seasoned at this point. You should have 3 cups (24 fl oz/750 ml) of sauce. If needed, add some of the chicken broth.

Preheat an oven to 350°F (180°C).

To make the enchiladas, in a frying pan, heat the oil over medium-high heat until sizzling hot. Using tongs, quickly pass each tortilla through the oil to soften and drain on absorbent paper.

Using your fingers, dip each tortilla briefly in the warm sauce, place on a plate, put a large spoonful of shredded chicken near one edge, roll up the tortilla, and place, seam side down, in a baking dish. Cover with the remaining sauce. Place in the oven and bake until thoroughly heated, about 10 minutes.

Remove the enchiladas from the oven and top with the *crema,* onion slices, and crumbled cheese. Alternatively, arrange the enchiladas on individual warmed plates and garnish before serving. Serve immediately—enchiladas become soggy quickly.

serves 6

GUARNICIONES

Vegetables, fruits, and beans—the foundation of Mexican cuisine—show up in myriad guarniciones.

Preceding pages: The white blossoms of the yucca, a type of agave that grows wild in parts of Veracruz, are traditionally sold during Holy Week and are a delicious treat when mixed into scrambled eggs, topped with tomato sauce, or stirred into a red mole. **Above top:** Two *nopal* vendors give their fleshy, oval inventory a high-level display as they walk along the streets of Mitla, in Oaxaca. **Above:** Respect for the freshness and flavor of ingredients—such as perfectly ripe red tomatoes—is as apparent in the country's humblest eateries as it is in its finest restaurants.

WHENEVER I AM in a market in Mexico today, I visualize the shock that an unsophisticated foot soldier from a faraway province in Spain must have experienced when he first entered the great marketplace in Teotihuacán, the center of the Aztec empire now buried under present-day Mexico City. He would have encountered some of these new ingredients on the trek over the range of volcanic mountains that separated the coast from his commander's highland goal, but not the inconceivably abundant array of unfamiliar foodstuffs. Just try to imagine never having seen chiles or dried beans before, or a ripe crimson tomato, the implausible-looking pineapple, or a green avocado with skin like leather—and, then, in front of you, lay literally acres of these colorful fruits, vegetables, and legumes. This market brought nearly twenty-five thousand people to trade and shop each day for produce that, along with corn, made up the heart of their daily diet.

These ingredients are still the foundation of Mexican cuisine, many of which show up as *guarniciones,* or side dishes. To most food lovers, though, it is the incendiary chile that evokes the tastes of Mexico. People munch on pickled chiles, add roasted strips to tacos, and devour all kinds of stuffed whole fresh and dried chiles. But when the often mind-blowing flavor of one or a combination of chiles is balanced with tomatoes or tomatillos and a tad of onion and garlic, chiles assume their most familiar form—as the very essence of salsa. It might be a simple one with chunks of all raw ingredients, or one of toasted dried chiles combined with charred onions and garlic, then blended and cooked over high heat to add depth of flavor, but there will always be a salsa. It would be a barren table that does not have at least one to enliven the dishes served. And don't forget, without chiles, the classic moles would lose their exotic, sensual spiciness. As an anonymous conqueror described in *Narrative of Some Things of New Spain and of the Great City of Tempestitán, Mexico,* "They have one [plant]—like a pepper—as a condiment which they call chile, and they never eat anything without it." That is still true today.

What is not true is that all chiles are the same. And they are not related to the piquant black pepper Columbus set out to find in India, landing in the Bahamas instead. Chiles are a part of the nightshade family, as are potatoes, tomatoes, and eggplants (aubergines), but they are in the separate genus, *Capsicum,* which has around thirty different species, all native to the New World. The most common species is *C. annuum,* with varieties ranging from the sweet bell pepper (capsicum) to the spicy serrano chile.

Don't think that you can use chiles interchangeably. The degree of heat varies, but just as important are the subtle yet important differences in flavor. It is not hard to get to know the fresh and dried chile workhorses, all of which are quite easy to find outside Mexico. The only problem is that they are often mislabeled, so you must know their distinguishing characteristics. I discovered the reason for one of the most serious but common mistakes when I was in Michoacán. Vendors call the fresh, green poblano chile by the name pasilla chile, which means "raisin." Throughout the rest of Mexico, a pasilla chile is the dried

Below: Freshly grilled ears of corn topped with *crema,* crumbled cheese, chile powder, and lime juice are common street vendors' fare. **Below bottom:** Locally raised lettuce is most frequently used as a refreshing addition to tacos and is also found in increasingly popular green salads.

chilaca chile, which is a dark raisin color. This confusion has spread, as many of the growers of chiles in the western United States are from Michoacán and give the suppliers the name most familiar to them. It does get confusing, and since every region of Mexico has its own favorite varieties and may call them by any number of names, it becomes a challenge to identify the more localized ones.

Chiles may add spirit to the foods of the Mexican people, but it is that humble protein-rich legume, the bean, that has always provided the fundamental nourishment. It is not just a foodstuff to sustain the poor, however. Beans play the same role that rice does in Asia, being a part of almost every meal, every day, for every person. In the southern states, the black bean is omnipresent. Cooks in the central region, in contrast, use red, white, tan, yellow, and multi-colored beans, while in the north, the pinto bean reigns. I often tell the story of my first lesson in the importance of beans in the culinary life of Mexico. My husband and I were guests for *comida* in the home of old friends in Morelia, in Michoacán. It was a formal, elegant meal, with course after course of elaborate dishes. There was a lull in the procession of serving platters, the table was partially cleared,

Left: Thousands of tamales are wrapped, steamed, sold, and enjoyed every day in the main market in Pátzcuaro, in Michoacán. **Below:** *Quesillo de Oaxaca,* a mild, white cow's milk cheese that, like mozzarella, becomes softly stringy when melted, is a specialty of its namesake. **Below bottom:** Golden orange squash blossoms, beautiful to look at and delectable to eat, are used as fillings for dishes as humble as quesadillas and as elegant as crepes.

Below: The *molcajete,* a three-legged mortar fashioned from volcanic rock, is the classic tool for making guacamole and fresh salsas. **Below bottom:** At the market in Tlacolula, customers can find beans for hearty soups, almonds for delicate cakes, and chiles for spicy moles. **Right:** The handmade violins and guitars from Paracho, Michoacán, are justly famous for their high-quality craftsmanship.

and small earthenware bowls were set before each diner. They were brimming with brothy beans and dotted with cubes of soft white cheese. The aroma was wonderful, the taste superb, and I scraped my bowl clean, participating in the tradition of guests being offered a bowl of beans at the end of a meal so that they will not go away hungry from the table.

Like most women who cook, when I am in Mexico, visiting the market is almost a daily experience. Only for me, it is a constant learning experience, not a necessity. I see the pear-shaped chayote, both smooth varieties and those with sharp prickles, and carefully arranged pyramids of tiny avocados or ones the size of grapefruits. Squash flowers, and squashes of all varieties, including one that could double as a watermelon; bundles of different greens; and lush ripe tomatoes and their ancestors, the marble-sized *miltomates,* are on display. I always seek out the bins of look-alike root vegetables. I can identify jicamas, sweet potatoes, yams, and potatoes, but especially in the markets in states bordering the Caribbean, there are so many unknown long tubers that I have to ask their names and uses. Women with

sharp knives sit in the crowded passages, scraping the spines from emerald *nopales* (cactus paddles), and young boys weave their way through the shoppers, offering clumps of small purple heads of garlic.

The challenge for me is to determine how each one of these market finds is used in the regional kitchen. One seldom sees vegetables as a side dish on the dinner plate or served as a salad. I have noticed, however, as the "eating light" concept has gained in acceptance, an increasing array of salads being offered, particularly in the upscale restaurants of resorts and metropolitan areas. Mostly, vegetables are part of some other course. Lettuce and cabbage are essential for tacos and tostadas. Mix chiles and tomatoes together and you have a salsa, then add an avocado and it becomes guacamole. Combine them with nuts and seeds and the dish turns into a mole or a *pipián*. Squashes show up in soups and stews, *nopales* are mixed with eggs for breakfast, jicama and beets appear as a condiment, and potatoes are a common filling for tacos and quesadillas.

Mexican food doesn't easily fit into categories, and while people may eat almost anything for any meal, or even for a snack, beans and vegetables are definitely not members of the supporting cast at the Mexican table. They have been groomed to play a leading role.

Left: In many Yucatecan villages, Spanish colonial churches such as this one can be found not far from crumbling Maya ruins. **Below:** Bundles of fresh spring onions are ready to be taken home and thrown on the grill, for serving alongside soft tacos filled with richly spiced grilled beef. **Below bottom:** Every meal—from a light breakfast at home to a dinner taken at a restaurant—is an occasion to relax and enjoy the company of family and friends.

Puebla

Timbales de Elote y Calabacita

corn and zucchini timbales

One morning, my friend Mónica Mastretta and I spent time at the huge tianguis, *or wholesale market, outside of Puebla. We walked in, sniffed, then sniffed again, and completely relaxed into a dream world of rich and exotic air so perfumed with the scent of melons, guavas, and chiles that it was hours later before we emerged. On the way home, we talked about food, and she dictated this recipe to me. Every time I make these savory custards, I think of that special day. Mónica likes to decorate each timbale with strips of green zucchini peel, but this step can be omitted if it seems too complicated.*

1 tablespoon unsalted butter

2½ cups (15 oz/470 g) fresh or briefly thawed frozen corn kernels

½ cup (4 fl oz/125 ml) water

5 eggs

1 tablespoon sugar

1 tablespoon all-purpose (plain) flour

1 tablespoon heavy (double) cream

1 teaspoon sea salt, plus extra for sprinkling

3 small zucchini (courgettes), trimmed

½ teaspoon dried thyme

SAUCE

4 tablespoons (2 oz/60 g) unsalted butter

½ white onion, finely chopped

4 poblano chiles, roasted, seeded, and deveined (page 247)

3 cups (24 fl oz/750 ml) milk, scalded

¼ cup (1½ oz/45 g) all-purpose (plain) flour

sea salt and freshly ground pepper to taste

♛ Preheat an oven to 350°F (180°C). Rub six 1-cup (8–fl oz/250-ml) timbale molds with the butter.

♛ In a blender or food processor, combine the corn kernels and water. Add the eggs, sugar, flour, cream, and 1 teaspoon salt and blend just until well mixed.

♛ If garnishing the timbales with zucchini peel, using a zester or sharp knife, remove long, narrow strips of peel from 1 zucchini. Cut each strip into strips 3 inches (7.5 cm) long. You will need 12 strips in all. Bring a small saucepan of water to a boil, add the strips, and cook for 2 minutes. Drain, rinse under running cold water, and lay out on a plate.

♛ Using the large holes on a handheld grater, grate the zucchini, including the one just peeled. There should be 1 cup (5 oz/155 g). Sprinkle the zucchini with salt, toss well, and let stand for 10 minutes or so. Squeeze the zucchini in a kitchen towel to remove the excess liquid, then stir it into the corn mixture along with the thyme. Divide the corn mixture evenly among the prepared molds.

♛ Place the molds in a baking pan, being careful that they do not touch. Pour hot water into the pan to reach halfway up the sides of the molds. Carefully place the baking pan in the oven and bake the timbales until a knife inserted in the middle of a mold comes out slightly oily but clean, about 45 minutes.

♛ To make the sauce, in a saucepan over medium heat, melt 1 tablespoon of the butter. Add the onion and sauté until translucent, 4–5 minutes. Transfer to a blender with the chiles and ½ cup (4 fl oz/125 ml) of the hot milk. Purée until very smooth.

♛ In a frying pan over medium-low heat, melt the remaining 3 tablespoons butter. Sprinkle in the flour and stir for 2 minutes. Add 1 cup (8 fl oz/250 ml) of the hot milk and whisk until smooth. Stir in the remaining 1½ cups (12 fl oz/375 ml) milk and the puréed chiles. Cook, stirring often, until the sauce is reduced and thickened, about 4 minutes. Add a generous pinch each of salt and pepper. Keep warm.

♛ Remove the timbales from the baking pan and let stand for several minutes. Then, to unmold, run a knife around the edge of each mold, place a plate on top, and turn the timbale out on the plate. If using the zucchini strips, arrange 2 strips on top of each timbale. Spoon the sauce around or over the timbales and serve immediately.

serves 6

The tile-domed Puebla cathedral, Mexico's most beautiful, contains fourteen relic-filled gilded chapels.

Veracruz

Ensalada de Chayotes

festive chayote salad

It was a hot, muggy afternoon in the countryside outside of Xalapa, the capital of Veracruz, and Ricardo Muñoz Zurita had prepared an elaborate fish dish with olives, tomatoes, and capers for dinner. We were trying to think of a simple salad to accompany it. Lightly dressed chayote, with its clear cucumber flavor and a hint of zucchini (courgette), was perfect. This more colorful version with golden corn and bright red tomatoes is now one of my favorite side dishes for grilled fish or chicken.

3 chayotes, halved and seeded

2 teaspoons salt

3 ears corn, husks and silk removed, or 2 cups (12 oz/375 g) frozen corn kernels

1 lb (500 g) cherry tomatoes, quartered

½ red (Spanish) onion, thinly sliced and separated into rings

boiling water as needed

DRESSING

¼ cup (2 fl oz/60 ml) canola oil

¼ cup (2 fl oz/60 ml) olive oil

¼ cup (2 fl oz/60 ml) pineapple or other mild vinegar (page 250)

1 tablespoon fresh lime juice

1 teaspoon dried oregano, preferably Mexican

2 teaspoons sugar

1 teaspoon red pepper flakes

3 drops Tabasco or other hot-pepper sauce

½ teaspoon sea salt

freshly ground black pepper to taste

Place the chayotes in a large saucepan with water to cover generously. Add the salt, bring to a boil over high heat, reduce the heat to medium, and cook until tender but still firm, about 30 minutes. A fork should pierce all the way through a chayote half. If using the ears of corn, add to the pan during the last 5 minutes of cooking. Drain the chayotes and corn. When cool enough to handle, peel the chayotes and cut into ½-inch (12-mm) dice. Cut the kernels off the corn cobs. If using frozen corn kernels, cook in a small amount of boiling water for 2 minutes, then drain well. Place the chayotes, corn, and tomatoes in a bowl and set aside.

Place the onion slices in a heatproof bowl and add boiling water to cover. Let soak just long enough for the slices to lose some of their crispness but not become limp, 2–3 minutes. Drain the onions well, cover, and refrigerate until cold.

To make the dressing, in a bowl, whisk together the canola and olive oils. Whisk in the vinegar and lime juice and then add the oregano, sugar, red pepper flakes, hot-pepper sauce, salt, and black pepper. Taste and adjust the seasoning. Pour ½ cup (4 fl oz/125 ml) of the dressing over the chayotes, tomatoes, and corn and toss gently. (The mixture can be covered and refrigerated for up to 1 day before continuing.)

Just before serving, toss the chayote mixture lightly once again. Taste and adjust the seasoning or add more dressing. Scatter the onion rings on top and serve.

serves 6–8

Jalisco

Salsa Mexicana

fresh tomato and chile salsa

Salsa mexicana, *also known as* salsa fresca, *is the reigning condiment of Mexico. It is found on the tables of both fancy restaurants and neighborhood* taquerías. *For some reason, in many parts of the country, it is also known as* pico de gallo, *or "rooster's beak," a designation also given to a regional specialty of Jalisco composed of pieces of jicama, with cucumber, melon, or pineapple, all sprinkled with ground dried chiles. The commonality seems to be either the sharply cut pieces of ingredients or the sharp tastes.*

The clean flavor and texture of freshly prepared vegetables are essential to this relishlike salsa of hand-chopped tomatoes, crisp white onions, and fiery green chiles, all mixed together with pungent cilantro. Salt is a magnet for flavors, so be generous with its use here.

1 lb (500 g) ripe tomatoes, cut into ¼-inch (6-mm) pieces

⅓ cup (2 oz/60 g) finely chopped white onion

¼ cup (⅓ oz/10 g) chopped fresh cilantro (fresh coriander)

2 serrano chiles, finely chopped

2 teaspoons fresh lime juice

sea salt to taste

In a bowl, toss together the tomatoes, onion, cilantro, chiles, and lime juice. Sprinkle with salt and toss again. If the salsa is too dry, add a splash of water.

Cover and let stand for 10–15 minutes to allow the flavors to mingle, then serve immediately.

makes 2 cups (16 fl oz/500 ml)

Puebla

Salsa de Chile Chipotle y Jitomate

chipotle chile salsa

The smoke-dried jalapeño, known as the chipotle chile, adds a distinctive wood-fire flavor to this simple tomato table salsa from Puebla. Although similar versions are found in other parts of Mexico, this one is different because of the use of tart and tangy tomatillos. Throughout Mexico, salsas are always made by hand by grinding with a lava rock tejolote *(pestle) in a three-legged lava rock* molcajete *(mortar).*

3 dried chipotle chiles or canned chiles chipotles en adobo

2 cloves garlic, unpeeled, roasted (page 248)

2 ripe tomatoes, about ¾ lb (375 g), roasted (page 250)

sea salt to taste

If using dried chiles, simmer them in salted water to cover until softened, 10–15 minutes. Drain, reserving the liquid, and place the chiles in a blender or food processor along with about ¼ cup (2 fl oz/60 ml) of the liquid. If using canned chiles, scrape off some of the *adobo* sauce and put the chiles in a blender or food processor.

Peel the charred skin from the garlic and add the garlic to the blender along with the tomatoes. Process very briefly. The mixture should be thick and slightly chunky.

Pour into a bowl, season with salt, cover, and let the flavors meld for 20–30 minutes before serving.

makes about 1 cup (8 fl oz/250 ml)

It would be a barren table that does not have at least one chile-laden salsa.

Tamaulipas

Frijoles con Tequila

tipsy beans

Not content just to drink tequila, Mexican cooks also pour it into a pot of beans. Serve with Farmer's-Style Burritos (page 63).

2 rounded cups (1 lb/500 g) dried pinto beans

2 white onions, 1 quartered and 1 finely chopped

2 heads garlic, outside papery skin removed, then halved crosswise

sea salt to taste

2 ancho chiles, seeded, deveined, and toasted (page 247)

1 cup (8 fl oz/250 ml) tequila blanco

½–¾ cup (4–6 oz/125–185 g) flavorful lard (page 249) or (4–6 fl oz/125–185 ml) corn or safflower oil

2 cups (10 oz/315 g) crumbled queso fresco

totopos *(page 251)*

Chipotle Chile Salsa (recipe at left) or other salsa

Pick over the beans and discard any debris. Rinse, place in a deep pot, and add water to cover by 1 inch (2.5 cm). Add the quartered onion and the garlic and place over medium heat. Bring to a boil, reduce the heat to low, and simmer, partially covered, until the beans are soft, about 2 hours, adding more hot water if needed. Season with salt and cook until thick, about 40 minutes. Stir occasionally, adding only enough water to keep the beans from sticking.

Put the chiles in a bowl and add boiling water to cover. Let soak for 15 minutes, then drain and place in a blender with the tequila. Blend until almost smooth.

In a heavy frying pan over medium-high heat, warm the lard or oil until it starts to smoke. Add the chopped onion, reduce the heat to medium-low, and fry until the onion is translucent, about 3 minutes. Add the chile mixture and cook until reduced, about 2 minutes. Add the onion-chile mixture to the beans and cook until the consistency of thick cream with only some beans remaining whole. Taste and add more salt, if needed.

Stir 1 cup (5 oz/155 g) of the cheese into the beans. Spoon the beans onto a large platter, sprinkle with the remaining cheese, and garnish with *totopos.* Serve with additional *totopos* and the salsa.

serves 8–10

Nopales

The new growth of various species of the prickly pear cactus, or nopal *(Opuntia ficus-indica),* is used as a food source throughout the world. But in Mexico it is the historic symbol of the beginning of the Aztec empire.

According to legend, one of the seven tribes of the Chichimecas, nomadic Indians from the north, was instructed by their tribal god to settle wherever an eagle, with a snake trapped in its talons, was seen perched on a nopal. The sighting occurred at Tenochtitlán, one of two small islands in Lake Texcoco, site of the present-day Mexico City. The probable date was A.D. 1325, and the people who settled there became known as the Aztecs. In the almost two hundred intervening years before Hernán Cortés arrived, the Aztecs conquered most of what is now Mexico, and today the nopal, their symbol, is depicted on the Mexican flag.

These historic roots, combined with the abundance of the nopal and its culinary attributes—a gentle crunchy texture with a sorrel-sour flavor—make this versatile cactus a common ingredient in Mexican cooking. One of my favorite ways to prepare it comes from Mexico's smallest state, Tlaxcala. Outside the entrance to the Maya ruins at Cacaxtla, local vendors partially slice the tender paddles, or *nopales,* to resemble the fingers on a hand, brush them with a little oil and lime juice, and grill them over glowing coals. When they are tender and browned, the *nopales* are chopped and wrapped together with a tasty salsa in a blue-corn tortilla.

Look for the egg-shaped *tuna,* or prickly pear, the fruit of the nopal cactus. It ranges in color from dead white, through all the spectrum of greens and reds, to the exotic magenta *tuna,* which is prized for its tropical-sweet watermelonlike flavor. I especially like *tunas* chopped and mixed with other tropical fruits such as pineapple and macerated with juice and silver tequila for a light dessert. At Christmastime, vendors in Oaxaca sell an *horchata,* or rice drink, that is lifted out of the ordinary by the addition of the puréed *tuna.*

Tlaxcala

Ensalada de Nopalitos con Chile

cactus salad with chile

Nopales, *or the paddles of the opuntia cactus, are a favorite vegetable in Mexico. I am always amazed when I watch the women in the market hold four or five of the prickly* nopales *in one hand and, with a knife in the other, deftly slice them into pieces. Tlaxcala, the smallest of Mexico's states, seems to have even more ways of preparing the cactus than anywhere else in the country: in soups or stews; combined with beans, rice, eggs, or meats; and even grilled whole. It is most commonly found in colorful, crunchy salads.*

When the paddles are boiled, they exude a rather slimy substance, much as okra does. Cooking the cactus in an unlined copper pot, dropping copper coins into the water, or adding the husks of tomatillos or a little baking soda can reduce this condition. Immediately rinsing the cooked cactus in cold water also works well. While canned nopales *are widely available now, they lack the crisp vitality of the freshly prepared ones.*

NOPALES

7 fresh nopales, *the smallest available*

1 thick slice white onion

2 cloves garlic, peeled but left whole

10 tomatillo husks or 1 teaspoon baking soda (sodium bicarbonate)

1 teaspoon sea salt

SALAD

1 small white onion, sliced into very thin rings

1 teaspoon dried oregano, preferably Mexican

juice of 1 lime or 1 tablespoon mild vinegar, or to taste

1 teaspoon Worcestershire sauce

about ¼ cup (2 fl oz/60 ml) olive oil

sea salt to taste

3 árbol chiles, toasted (page 247) and crumbled

1 cup (1½ oz/45 g) chopped fresh cilantro (fresh coriander)

1 large, ripe tomato or 4 plum (Roma) tomatoes, finely diced

1 avocado, preferably Haas, pitted, peeled, and sliced

1 cup (5 oz/155 g) crumbled queso fresco

To prepare the *nopales,* use a sharp paring knife or vegetable peeler to scrape off the stickers and their "bumps." Cut off the base end and trim the outer edge. Cut into strips ¼ inch (6 mm) wide, then into pieces about 1 inch (2.5 cm) long.

Bring a large saucepan three-fourths full of water to a boil. Add the cactus strips, onion slice, garlic, tomatillo husks or baking soda, and salt. Reduce the heat to medium and cook at a slow boil until tender but still green, 5–10 minutes, depending on the age of the paddles. Drain and quickly place under running cold water to remove the slimy residue and stop the cooking. Remove the onion, the garlic, and the husks, if used, and discard. Shake the cactus strips to remove as much moisture as possible and put in a bowl while they are still warm.

To make the salad, add the onion, oregano, lime juice or vinegar, and Worcestershire sauce to the bowl holding the cactus strips. Then add just enough of the olive oil to bind the ingredients. Season with salt and gently mix in the chiles. Allow the salad to stand for at least 10 minutes. (The salad can be prepared several hours in advance and refrigerated. Bring to room temperature before serving.)

Just before serving, add the cilantro and tomato and toss to combine. Spoon onto a serving platter or individual plates, and top with the avocado slices and crumbled cheese.

serves 6

Guanajuato

Salsa Verde

fresh tomatillo salsa

This is my favorite, the rustic green salsa that is always on the table, in one version or another, wherever Mexican food is served. This fresh salsa is not a good keeper, so it must be served as soon as it is made.

1 lb (500 g) tomatillos, husked and rinsed

3 tablespoons roughly chopped white onion

3 serrano chiles, coarsely chopped

2 cloves garlic, coarsely chopped

½ teaspoon sea salt

¼ cup (⅓ oz/10 g) finely chopped fresh cilantro (fresh coriander)

In a saucepan over medium heat, combine the tomatillos with water to cover and bring to a gentle boil. Cook, uncovered, until soft but not soggy, 8–10 minutes. Drain and transfer to a blender or food processor. Add the onion, chiles, garlic, and salt and process until a rather smooth purée forms that still has some rough texture.

Pour into a bowl, stir in the cilantro, and serve.

makes about 2 cups (16 fl oz/500 ml)

Jalisco

Salsa de Chile Seco

pasilla and árbol chile salsa

The first time that I tried this pungent salsa was during a charreada, *or rodeo, at a dinner cooked by Consuelo Ibarra López and her daughter.*

4 árbol chiles

2 pasilla chiles

2 cloves garlic, unpeeled

6 ripe plum (Roma) tomatoes, roughly chopped

juice of ½ lime

about ½ teaspoon sea salt

Toast the chiles (page 247), then seed. Roast the garlic (page 248), then peel. In a saucepan over medium heat, combine the chiles with water to cover and bring to a simmer. Cook for 5 minutes, remove from the heat, and let soak for about 10 minutes. The chiles should be very soft.

Put the garlic, tomatoes, and lime juice in a blender or food processor and blend only until broken up. Drain the chiles, tear into small pieces, and add to the tomato mixture. Add the salt and process to a slightly rough-textured consistency. If the mixture is too thick, add a few tablespoons of water. Transfer to a bowl and serve. (The salsa will keep for 1 day, covered, in the refrigerator.)

makes about 2 cups (16 fl oz/500 ml)

México, D.F.

Salsa de Mango y Pepino

tropical salsa

This sprightly mixture of mango, cucumber, and orange comes from members of the Junior League in Mexico City, who have included it in their cookbook, a project to raise funds for the city's homeless children.

2 mangoes

1 orange

½ cucumber, peeled, halved, seeded, and cut into ½-inch (12-mm) cubes

juice of 1 lime

2 serrano chiles, finely chopped

sea salt to taste

Peel and pit the mangoes, cutting the flesh into ½-inch (12-mm) dice (page 249). Place the diced mangoes in a nonmetallic bowl. Remove the zest from half of the orange in long, thin strips, cut into ½-inch (12-mm) pieces, and add to the bowl. Then place the orange upright on a cutting board and cut down along the sides, removing all the white pith and membrane. Cut along either side of each segment to free it from the membrane, then cut the segments into ½-inch (12-mm) cubes. Remove any seeds and add the orange cubes to the mangoes.

Add the cucumber, lime juice, and chiles. Toss well, season with salt, and toss again, then serve. (The salsa will keep for 1–2 hours, covered, in the refrigerator.)

makes about 3 cups (24 fl oz/750 ml)

Puebla

Quiche de Calabacitas

zucchini quiche

The French may not have occupied Mexico for long—indeed, no longer than three years—but their culinary influence remains evident, especially in the central part of the country. This highly flavorful quiche, with its rich sauce of poblano chiles, pairs well with grilled meats or can easily stand on its own as a light main course. Well-cured Spanish Manchego cheese, made from sheep's milk, adds an especially distinctive flavor to the filling.

empanada dough (page 232) or your favorite flaky pie or tart dough

FILLING

⅓ cup (3 oz/90 g) unsalted butter

3 poblano chiles, roasted, seeded, and deveined (page 247), then cut lengthwise into narrow strips

1 white onion, finely chopped

2¼ lb (1.1 kg) small zucchini (courgettes), sliced ¼ inch (6 mm) thick

½ cup (4 fl oz/125 ml) water

3 teaspoons chicken bouillon granules

¼ lb (125 g) regular or low-fat cream cheese, at room temperature

3 eggs

½ cup (4 fl oz/125 ml) heavy (double) cream

½ teaspoon freshly grated nutmeg

¼ teaspoon sea salt

freshly ground pepper to taste

½ lb (250 g) Manchego, white cheddar, or Monterey jack cheese, shredded

Prepare the dough as directed, seal in plastic wrap, and refrigerate until ready to use.

Preheat an oven to 350°F (180°C). Butter a 9-inch (23-cm) quiche dish or a tart pan with a removable bottom. Position a rack in the lower third of the oven.

To make the filling, in a frying pan over medium heat, melt the butter. Add the chile strips and onion and sauté until softened, about 3 minutes. Remove them with a slotted spoon and set aside. Put the zucchini slices in the still-hot pan along with the water and 1½ teaspoons of the bouillon granules and cook until the zucchini is just tender, about 5 minutes. Drain and let cool.

In a blender or food processor, combine half of the onions and chile strips, the remaining 1½ teaspoons bouillon granules, and the cream cheese, eggs, cream, nutmeg, salt, and pepper. Process until puréed.

On a lightly floured work surface, roll out the dough into an 11-inch (28-cm) round about ⅛ inch (3 mm) thick. Drape the round over the rolling pin, transfer it to the prepared pan, and ease it into the pan. Trim off the edges even with the rim. Arrange the zucchini and the remaining onions and chile strips in the lined pan, then top with half of the shredded cheese and all of the cream cheese mixture. Top with the remaining shredded cheese.

Bake until a knife inserted into the center comes out clean and the top is brown, 45–60 minutes. Remove from the oven and let firm up for several minutes. If using a tart pan, remove the sides and slide the quiche onto a plate. Serve hot or at room temperature.

serves 6–8

Coahuila

Elote Asado

grilled corn on the cob

Grilled corn is one of Mexico's favorite street foods. Sometimes the chewy corn is lavished with thick cream, and other times with mayonnaise, but inevitably there are limes and ground chiles for flavor accents. The field corn eaten in Mexico has a starchy texture and is not at all sweet. To better duplicate the flavor, look for corn that is not marketed as ultra- or supersweet.

6 ears corn, unshucked

1 cup (8 fl oz/250 ml) crema *(page 248)*

1 cup (5 oz/155 g) crumbled queso añejo *or (4 oz/125 g) grated Parmesan cheese*

2 limes, quartered

½ cup (1½ oz/45 g) ground pequín or other hot ground chile

½ cup (4 oz/125 g) sea salt

Carefully pull the husks back from the corn, remove the silk, and pull the husks back in place. Soak the ears in cold water to cover for 30 minutes.

Meanwhile, prepare a fire in a grill.

Remove the corn from the water and place it directly on the grill rack over medium-hot coals. Grill, turning frequently, for about 20 minutes. If the husk is very burned but the corn is not yet tender, wrap in aluminum foil and continue roasting until done. Transfer the corn to a platter.

Put the *crema,* cheese, and limes in separate small bowls. Place the chile and salt in shakers or small bowls. Let everyone shuck their own corn. They then rub it with lime that has been dusted with chile, spread it with *crema,* sprinkle on the cheese, and season with salt—or proceed in any order that appeals.

serves 6

La Noche de Rábanos

On December 23, tourists from Mexico and all over the world join thousands of Oaxacan residents to celebrate La Noche de Rábanos—"the Night of the Radishes"—a community festival that has been held annually in the *zócalo,* or town square, since 1897.

Truck farmers and craftsmen join forces to create a visual feast of color and design, carving gigantic, misshapen radishes into scenes of incredible beauty that are displayed in stalls encircling the plaza. Crowds start gathering early in the day to watch the immense radishes assembled into detailed traditional, historical, or biblical scenes. After the judging, a seemingly endless queue of spectators parades by to view the unique artwork. The line is so long that it encircles the nearby cathedral and winds its way through the festive crowd that doesn't disperse until the night sky gives the first hints of dawn.

As long ago as 1563, the Spanish viceroy offered the local people seeds from the Old World and land in which to plant them. On the day before Christmas Eve, these farmers would gather in the *zócalo* to sell their produce, setting up stands that would remain until midnight mass the following night. To attract more customers, they made little figures from radishes, decorating them with small cauliflower leaves and tiny flowers made of onions. Out of this simple vigil market tradition evolved today's elaborate celebration.

Tlaxcala

Frijoles Refritos

well-fried beans

These homey frijoles refritos *are not beans that have been fried twice, but soupy pot beans that are coarsely mashed and then fried until dry. For an attractive presentation, it is common to form the beans into a long roll before garnishing them. If using canned beans, rinse them and substitute 1 cup (8 fl oz/250 ml) water for the bean broth.*

½ cup (4 oz/125 g) flavorful lard (page 249) or (4 fl oz/125 ml) safflower or canola oil, or more if needed

½ white onion, finely chopped

4 cups (28 oz/875 g) Pot Beans (page 201) with 2 cups (16 fl oz/500 ml) bean broth

3 avocado leaves, toasted (page 246) and finely crumbled (optional)

sea salt to taste

GARNISH

⅔ cup (3 oz/90 g) crumbled queso fresco

totopos *(page 251)*

6 small romaine (cos) lettuce leaves

8 radishes, with leaves attached

In a large, heavy frying pan over medium heat, warm the ½ cup (4 oz/125 g) lard or (4 fl oz/125 ml) oil. Add the onion and sauté, stirring frequently, until soft and golden, about 5 minutes.

Pour in 1 cup (7 oz/220 g) of the beans with 1 cup (8 fl oz/250 ml) of the broth, smashing the beans down with the back of a large wooden spoon. Continue until the remaining beans and broth have been mashed to a coarse purée. Stir in the avocado leaves, if using, raise the heat to medium-high, and cook, stirring occasionally, until the purée begins to dry out, 10–15 minutes, adding more lard or oil if needed. Season with salt. If desired, form the beans into a roll: fry them until they draw away from the edges of the pan, and then lift one edge of the pan and tip the solidified mass of beans over on itself.

Transfer the beans to a platter or individual plates and garnish with the cheese. The *totopos* can be stuck in the mound of beans, as a decoration and as a way to scoop them up. Add the lettuce leaves and red radishes on the side for color contrast.

serves 4–6

Campeche

Salsa de Chiltomate

roasted habanero chile and tomato salsa

In the three states that make up the Yucatán peninsula—Campeche, Quintana Roo, and Yucatán—the habanero is the chile most frequently used in salsas. Alongside a bowl of the biting-hot pure habanero salsa, though, will probably also be this much milder version.

Charring deepens the distinctive fruit-sweet and tangy flavor of the habanero, and even the tomato tastes sweeter when roasted. In nearby Mérida, the locals often just "walk" the chile through the tomatoes to impart enough heat to enliven this rustic salsa, but for added fire the habanero is simmered in the sauce. Chiles dulces, *similar to small bell peppers, are a surprising addition to many dishes from Campeche and Yucatán, including this warm salsa, which is traditionally used to top* huevos Motuleños, *black beans and fried eggs on a tostada, or to give a zing to virtually any type of bean dish.*

4 ripe tomatoes, roasted (page 250)

1 small green bell pepper (capsicum), roasted, seeded, and deveined (page 246)

3 tablespoons safflower or canola oil

1 white onion, chopped

1 habanero chile, roasted (page 247) and slit partially on all 4 sides

1 teaspoon sea salt, or to taste

In a blender or food processor, combine the tomatoes with all their juices and the bell pepper and coarsely purée. In a saucepan over medium heat, warm the oil. Add the onion and sauté until golden, about 3 minutes. Stir in the tomato mixture and fry until the sauce changes color, about 3 minutes. Add the chile and simmer over medium-low heat for about 15 minutes to blend the flavors.

Just before serving, remove and discard the habanero chile and stir in the salt. Serve hot. (The salsa will keep for 4 days, covered, in the refrigerator. Reheat before serving.)

makes about 2 cups (16 fl oz/500 ml)

Jalisco

Calabacitas Rellenas de Requesón

ricotta-stuffed zucchini

Mexican cooks love to stuff vegetables, especially chiles and different types of squashes. Typical are these dugouts of zucchini filled with a surprising contrast of textures and tastes. Miguel Ramirez Hernández, the owner of a popular restaurant in Guadalajara, combines the rather bland requesón, *made the same way as ricotta, with brazenly dark green* rajas, *or chile strips, and tops it all with a colorful yogurt dressing. He has also prepared this dish for me with a stuffing of ground pork, bacon, deviled ham, onions, and tomato, so use your imagination.*

Almost every meal in this part of Jalisco is composed of meat, but dairy products are plentiful. Special cases in the markets offer a variety of fresh and aged cheeses, as well as small plastic sacks of requesón. *After days of eating nothing but meat, I especially welcome vegetable dishes like this one.*

SAUCE

2 ripe tomatoes or 1½ cups (9 oz/280 g) drained canned chopped tomatoes

¼ white onion

1 clove garlic, unpeeled

2 tablespoons safflower or canola oil

½ teaspoon dried oregano, preferably Mexican

⅛ teaspoon ground allspice

1 cup (8 oz/250 g) plain yogurt

sea salt to taste

ZUCCHINI

6 small zucchini (courgettes), trimmed

sea salt to taste

2 tablespoons safflower or canola oil

½ white onion, finely chopped

1 clove garlic, finely chopped

1 poblano chile, roasted, seeded, and deveined (page 247), then cut into narrow strips 1 inch (2.5 cm) long

1 cup (8 oz/250 g) ricotta cheese

GARNISH

6 lettuce leaves, finely chopped

3 tablespoons finely chopped fresh cilantro (fresh coriander)

To make the sauce, if using ripe tomatoes, roast them (page 250), then peel and seed. Roast the onion (page 249) and the garlic (page 248). Put the tomatoes, onion, and garlic into a blender or food processor and purée briefly, leaving some texture. In a saucepan over medium-high heat, warm the oil. Add the tomato mixture and cook, stirring occasionally, until the sauce thickens, 4–5 minutes. Stir in the oregano and allspice and remove from the heat. Add the yogurt, stirring well, and season with salt. Set aside to cool.

To prepare the zucchini, cut each one in half lengthwise. Place the halves in a saucepan with water to cover, add salt, and bring to a slow boil over medium heat. Cook just until tender, about 10 minutes. Drain and place under running cold water to stop the cooking. Using a spoon or melon baller, remove the pulp down the middle of each half, leaving a thick shell.

In a frying pan over medium-high heat, warm the oil. Add the onion, garlic, and chile strips and sauté, stirring often, until softened, about 5 minutes. Transfer to a bowl and let cool. Add the ricotta cheese, mix well, and season with salt.

Place a bed of chopped lettuce on each serving plate. Fill each zucchini with several spoonfuls of the ricotta mixture. Place 2 zucchini halves on each plate, spoon on the sauce, and sprinkle with cilantro. Serve at room temperature.

serves 6

México, D.F.

Ensalada de Lechugas con Jícama y Mango

green salad with jicama and mango

The colorful medley of ingredients in this easy-to-make salad is stunning. The mango, the spectacular color of a summer sunset, offers a sweet contrast to the crisp, ivory white of the jicama, the flecks of the reddish tinted onion, and the many hues of the greens and avocado.

1 mango

1 head red oak-leaf lettuce, leaves separated

1 head butter (Boston) lettuce, leaves separated

½ red (Spanish) onion, finely diced

½ jicama, cut into thin strips ¼ inch (6 mm) wide by 2 inches (5 cm) long

DRESSING

1 cup (8 fl oz/250 ml) safflower or canola oil

½ cup (4 fl oz/125 ml) olive oil

2½ tablespoons cider vinegar

1 cup (1½ oz/45 g) chopped fresh flat-leaf (Italian) parsley

½ cup (½ oz/15 g) fresh cilantro (fresh coriander) leaves, chopped

1 clove garlic, chopped

1 shallot, chopped

1½ teaspoons honey

1½ teaspoons sea salt, or to taste

¼ teaspoon freshly ground pepper

small pinch of ground cloves

1 avocado, preferably Haas, pitted, peeled, and sliced

Peel and pit the mango, cutting the flesh into ¼-inch (6-mm) cubes (page 249). Place the mango cubes in a large salad bowl. Tear the lettuce leaves into bite-sized pieces and add to the salad bowl along with the onion and jicama.

To make the dressing, in a blender, combine the oils and vinegar. Add the parsley, cilantro, garlic, shallot, honey, salt, pepper, and cloves. Blend until smooth. Pour just enough dressing over the salad to moisten it, then toss to coat evenly. Garnish with the avocado slices and serve.

serves 6

Jalisco

Ensalada de Espinaca

spinach salad

This spinach salad is tossed with a delicous rose-colored dressing made from the dried flower calyxes of jamaica, *or hibiscus flowers. Look for the flowers in health-food stores.*

1 cup (8 fl oz/250 ml) water
½ cup (1½ oz/45 g) dried jamaica *flowers*
2 teaspoons sugar, or to taste
½ teaspoon sea salt, or to taste
½ teaspoon freshly ground pepper
¼ cup (2 fl oz/60 ml) extra-virgin olive oil
¼ cup (3 oz/90 g) dark honey
1 cup (8 oz/250 g) amaranth seeds
8 slices lean bacon
4 cups (4 oz/125 g) baby spinach leaves
½ small jicama, peeled and julienned

In a saucepan over medium heat, bring the water to a boil with the *jamaica* and maintain a slow boil for 3–5 minutes, stirring frequently. Pour through a medium-mesh sieve into a small bowl. You should have ¼ cup (2 fl oz/60 ml). Whisk in the sugar, salt, and pepper, then whisk in the olive oil in a slow, steady stream. If the *jamaica* liquid is allowed to sit before mixing, it will thicken, but when mixed with the oil, it will return to the correct consistency.

Warm the honey in a frying pan over medium heat until the edges just start to bubble. Add the amaranth seeds and stir until they start to stick together, 40–60 seconds. Immediately pour onto a sheet of waxed paper and let cool. If they are still sticking together, rub between your palms to break them apart. Place the bacon in a cold frying pan and fry over medium-low heat until crisp, 6–8 minutes. Drain on absorbent paper and coarsely crumble.

Put the spinach in a bowl with the bacon, stir the dressing well, and add just enough to moisten the leaves. Toss and adjust the seasoning. Divide among individual plates, top with the jicama strips and amaranth seeds, and serve.

serves 4

Los Mercados Populares

The first time I went to a market in Mexico, it changed the course of my life. In retrospect, Pochutla's narrow, multileveled market is rather ordinary. Located in the second-largest town in Oaxaca, only a few miles from the coast, it has a comparatively meager selection of chiles, fruits, herbs, and vegetables, but to me it was the start of a wondrous adventure that is still continuing today.

I wandered by open bags of wine-colored *jamaica,* the dried hibiscus flowers that make such a refreshing drink, as well as bins of bulging tamarind pods with plastic bags of the sticky sweet-and-sour paste stacked nearby. Tiny tomatoes the size of marbles caught my eye, and I found out that they were *miltomates,* the wild tomatoes that the locals use to make an especially flavorful sauce. Exotic fruits were everywhere, especially the *guanábana* (soursop), a lumpy, warty green fruit with perfumed white flesh, and the *zapote negro,* which to me looked like a nearly rotten fat avocado. I learned that both make delicate sweet *nieves* (sorbets), but I like the *zapote negro* best just mixed with a little lime and orange juice, as demonstrated by the vendor.

Interspersed in the crowd, handsome women who had come up from the Isthmus of Tehuantepec were dressed in vividly colored velvets, satins, and lace; billowing skirts; and heavy gold jewelry. On their heads they carried rush baskets of tiny dried shrimp (prawns), slabs of dried and smoked fish, and all sorts of fresh ocean fish and other sea creatures. An especially stately woman had a most unusual hairpiece: four docile iguanas covered the whole top of her head. Across the street from the market was a cluster of equally colorful men and women, gypsies selling bundles of dried avocado leaves for flavoring black beans, as well as a tangle of dubious jewels.

I stopped to regain my energy at one of the several *fondas* with signs featuring *comida corrida,* the daily lunch special. If I recall correctly, it was at that meal that I first tasted *caldo de nopales con camarón,* a tomato-based broth swimming with tiny pink shrimp and squares of green cactus.

From that day on, I was hooked—I knew there is no better place than a market to experience the fundamental vitality of Mexico.

State of México

Salsa Verde con Aguacate

avocado salsa

If you are fortunate enough to have a molcajete, *this sweet but tart salsa can be made in it. Serve with chips or tacos, or to accompany grilled meats, fish, or chicken.*

3 serrano chiles, coarsely chopped

½ white onion, cut into small chunks

½ cup (4 fl oz/125 ml) water

½ lb (250 g) tomatillos (10–12), husked, rinsed, and coarsely chopped

¾ cup (1½ oz/45 g) chopped fresh cilantro (fresh coriander), plus whole leaves for garnish

1 teaspoon dark brown sugar

2 avocados, preferably Haas, pitted

sea salt to taste

In a blender, combine the chiles, onion, and water. Process until partially smooth. Add the tomatillos, chopped cilantro, and brown sugar and blend until the mixture is roughly textured.

Scoop the avocado into a bowl and coarsely mash with a fork. It should be chunky. Stir in the chile sauce and season with salt. Lightly garnish with cilantro leaves and serve. (The salsa will keep for 3 hours, covered, in the refrigerator.)

makes about 3 cups (24 fl oz/750 ml)

Jalisco

Salsa de Chile de Arbol

árbol chile salsa

Fiercely hot, this table salsa from Guadalajara made with the skinny, shiny, deep red árbol chile is one to be used in moderation.

4 cloves garlic, unpeeled

12 tomatillos, husked and rinsed, or 2 cups (12 oz/375 g) drained canned tomatillos

3 or 4 árbol chiles

¼ teaspoon sea salt, or to taste

¼ cup (1¼ oz/45 g) minced white onion

Roast the garlic (page 248) and the fresh tomatillos, if using (page 250). Toast the chiles (page 247).

Remove the charred peel from the roasted garlic cloves. In a blender or food processor, purée the garlic and tomatillos. Add the chiles one at a time and continue to process, stopping when your heat tolerance is reached and adding a little water as needed to form a slightly thick sauce. Add the salt.

Stir in the onion just before serving. (The salsa will keep for 2 days, covered, in the refrigerator.)

makes about 2 cups (16 fl oz/500 ml)

Yucatán

Curtido de Cebolla Roja

pickled red onions

These hot, tangy onions are essential with Grilled Pork Ribs (page 142), as they are with many other Yucatecan dishes.

2 small red (Spanish) onions, thinly sliced

⅓ cup (3 fl oz/80 ml) fresh lime juice

2 cloves garlic, slightly smashed

1 teaspoon sea salt

¼ teaspoon freshly ground pepper

⅛ teaspoon dried oregano, preferably Mexican

1 habanero chile, roasted (page 247)

Place the onion slices in a heatproof bowl and add boiling water to cover. Let soak for 2–3 minutes. Drain well, put into a small bowl, and toss with the lime juice, garlic, salt, pepper, and oregano. Bury the chile in the bottom of the onions. Let marinate for 1 hour, stirring occasionally, so that all of the slices come into contact with the chile.

Before serving, retrieve the habanero chile and place it on top of the onion slices. Remember, the habanero is the hottest of all chiles and only folks trying to prove how macho they are should dare to try a bite. (The onions will keep for 2 weeks, covered, in the refrigerator.)

makes about 2 cups (7 oz/220 g)

Jalisco

Chimichurri Salsa

spicy parsley and garlic salsa

I always thought of chimichurri *as the typical partner to the traditional beef dishes of Argentina. There, it commonly contains a hefty amount of black pepper instead of the dried chiles that more and more often I have found in small bowls of this tasty parsley sauce on the tables of Mexico's restaurants. Recently, I was at Asadero, a pleasant restaurant in Guadalajara, where the owner, Miguel Ramirez Hernández, served this version over tiny crisp-fried fish that were first topped with ceviche—an unusual but delectable combination.*

Chimichurri *has a biting taste that goes equally well with simple grilled meat dishes such as Marinated Steak with Herbs (page 155) or even with a beef stew or soup such as Potato and Meatball Soup (page 88).*

4 cups (4 oz/125 g) fresh flat-leaf (Italian) parsley leaves (about 2 large bunches)

6 cloves garlic

¾ cup (6 fl oz/180 ml) olive oil

½ cup (4 fl oz/125 ml) pineapple vinegar (page 250) or other mild white vinegar

2 teaspoons fresh oregano leaves, chopped, or ½ teaspoon dried oregano, preferably Mexican

½ árbol chile, crumbled, or ½ teaspoon red pepper flakes

sea salt to taste

♛ In a blender or food processor, briefly blend the parsley, garlic, olive oil, and vinegar. Add the oregano and árbol chile or red pepper flakes. Process to a smooth purée.

♛ Pour the salsa into a bowl and season with salt. Serve at room temperature. (The salsa can be made several days in advance. Store, covered, in the refrigerator. Bring to room temperature before serving.)

makes about 1½ cups (12 fl oz/375 ml)

Michoacán

Frijoles con Nopales de Doña Lola

pinto beans with cactus

Many years ago, when Mexican food expert Diana Kennedy was relearning to drive, Doña Lola, an acquaintance, accompanied her on the long, sinuous mountain road from her home in Michoacán to Mexico City, an experience that can make or break a friendship. It must have been positive, as she then shared this recipe with Diana, and Diana, in turn, shared it with me. There is no substitute for the flavor of fresh epazote. If you have to use the dry, it helps to put it in a metal tea ball or wrap it in a square of cheesecloth (muslin).

2 tablespoons safflower or canola oil

⅓ cup (2 oz/60 g) finely chopped white onion

3 serrano chiles

½ lb (250 g) ripe tomatoes, simmered in water until tender and drained, or 1 can (14½ oz/455 g) diced tomatoes, undrained

2 cups (12 oz/375 g) diced cooked nopales *(see Cactus Salad with Chile, page 177) or well-rinsed canned* nopales

2 large fresh epazote sprigs

sea salt to taste

3 cups (21 oz/655 g) Pot Beans (page 201) made with pinto beans, plus ½ cup (4 fl oz/125 ml) bean broth

1 corn tortilla, homemade (page 251) or purchased (optional)

In a frying pan over medium heat, warm the oil. Add the onion and chiles and sauté until the onion is translucent, about 3 minutes. Transfer the chiles to a blender, add the tomatoes, and blend to a slightly textured purée. Stir into the pan holding the onion and cook over medium-high heat, stirring often, until the sauce is reduced, about 5 minutes.

Add the *nopales,* epazote, and salt. Reduce the heat to medium and, when the mixture starts to boil, stir in the beans and their broth and simmer for about 5 minutes to heat through.

Scoop the beans onto a warmed serving dish on top of a tortilla, if desired, and serve immediately.

serves 4–6

Epazote

A bowl of black beans is incomplete without the unforgettable pungency imparted by a few sprigs of epazote, an herb that grows profusely in the wet, warm soil of southern Mexico and is unknowingly regarded in some places outside the country as a troublesome weed.

The distinct flavor of epazote makes it one of the most important herbs used by Mexican cooks in central and southern Mexico. A simple quesadilla comes to life when a leaf is tucked on top of the melting cheese, a rather bland pork stew gains character with addition of the herb, and squash and corn dishes are complemented by its earthy flavor. Epazote should be added at the end of the cooking process and used sparingly, as the flavor is intense. Although related to spinach, Swiss chard, and beets, epazote has such an assertive quality that the leaves are made into a strong tea to deter ants and rid the body of intestinal parasites. It is also used to reduce the gastric distress some people experience after eating beans.

Luckily, epazote is easy to grow from seed, as it is seldom found fresh outside of Mexico. It is sold in dry form, packaged in little cellophane sacks that usually contain more woody stems than leaves, but is only marginally satisfactory. I grow my epazote outdoors in large pots and, during the growing season, pluck off a sprig or two whenever I need it.

México, D.F.

Ensalada de Verano

summer salad

I find that more and more of the women I know in Mexico City are serving salads for comida, *with perhaps some tasty* antojitos *and a bowl of soup. Especially in the summer months, Margarita Salinas likes to combine tart tomatillos with tangy* chiles chipotles en adobo *for an unusual salad. It is an ideal dish to start a meal, followed by a soup such as Golden Squash Blossom Cream Soup (page 82).*

1 lb (500 g) tomatillos, husked, rinsed, and chopped into ½-inch (12-mm) pieces

½ white onion, finely chopped

3 tablespoons finely chopped fresh cilantro (fresh coriander)

DRESSING

¼ cup (2 fl oz/60 ml) olive oil

1 or 2 chiles chipotles en adobo, *finely chopped*

1 teaspoon brown sugar

sea salt to taste

1 cup (5 oz/155 g) crumbled queso añejo

totopos *(page 251)*

In a bowl, toss together the tomatillos, onion, and cilantro.

To make the dressing, pour the olive oil into a small bowl, add 1 of the chiles, the brown sugar, and the salt, and whisk vigorously until well blended. Taste and add the other chile, if desired. Remember, the dressing will not taste as potent after it is mixed with the tomatillos.

Spoon on enough of the dressing to coat the tomatillos thoroughly. Arrange on a platter and sprinkle with the cheese. The *totopos* can be served around the salad or in a separate bowl.

serves 6

Michoacán

Papas Cambray al Mojo de Ajo

tiny garlic potatoes

Beans, yes, rice, yes, but potatoes are not what most outsiders expect to eat in Mexico. Tiny new potatoes, though, often accompany saucy dishes and are a tasty side to grilled fish and meat. The first time I ever tried these potatoes cooked with garlic was at Rancho San Cayetano, a small inn outside of Zitácuaro, Michoacán, which serves very delectable meals. Try them with Marinated Steak with Herbs (page 155).

6 cloves garlic

1 cup (8 fl oz/250 ml) olive oil

2 teaspoons sea salt

1 teaspoon freshly ground pepper

2 lb (1 kg) very small new potatoes (about 1 inch/2.5 cm in diameter)

Preheat an oven to 250°F (120°C).

Using a mortar and a pestle, crush the garlic and oil until a thin paste forms. Mix in the salt and pepper. Spread the potatoes on a baking sheet and brush them on all sides with some of the garlic oil.

Bake the potatoes, basting them occasionally with the remaining garlic oil, until tender, 30–45 minutes. The timing will depend on the size of the potatoes. Spoon the potatoes into a bowl and serve.

serves 6–8

In the marketplaces, boys weave through the crowd selling handfuls of purple garlic.

México, D.F.

Aspic de Camarón y Chile Poblano

shrimp and poblano chile aspic

Not many people think of gelatins as a Mexican food, but they are very popular. When I think of gelatins, Mexico City's great cook María Dolores Torres Yzábal comes immediately to mind, as there is seldom a meal that I have shared at her home when we have not had one, either as a first course or as a dessert. This aspic can also be prepared in individual molds.

4¼ cups (34 fl oz/1.1 l) water

2 lime slices

1 clove garlic, smashed

1 teaspoon peppercorns

1 bay leaf

20 shrimp (prawns) in the shell

1 package (2¼ teaspoons) unflavored gelatin

2 tablespoons bottled chili sauce

2 tablespoons finely chopped fresh cilantro (fresh coriander)

1 tablespoon finely chopped fresh chives

1 teaspoon fresh lime juice

¼ teaspoon sea salt, or to taste

4 poblano chiles, roasted, seeded, and deveined (page 247), then finely diced

1 red bell pepper (capsicum), roasted, seeded, and deveined (page 246), then finely diced

½ cup (4 oz/125 g) plain yogurt

¼ cup (2 fl oz/60 ml) crema *(page 248)*

In a large saucepan, combine 4 cups (32 fl oz/1 l) of the water with the lime slices, garlic, peppercorns, and bay leaf and bring to a boil. Reduce the heat so that it maintains a slow boil and allow the liquid to reduce for 5–10 minutes, to make a strong liquor. Drop in the shrimp and cook until they turn pink and just begin to curl, about 2 minutes. Drain the shrimp, reserving the liquid, and place them under running cold water to stop the cooking. Peel the shrimp and set aside. Strain the broth. Measure out 1 cup (8 fl oz/250 ml) broth and keep hot.

Place the remaining ¼ cup (2 fl oz/60 ml) water in a bowl and sprinkle the gelatin over the surface. Allow to soften for about 3 minutes. Then stir in the hot shrimp broth. (If the broth has cooled, first bring it back to the boiling point.) Add the chili sauce, cilantro, chives, lime juice, and ¼ teaspoon salt and stir gently to combine.

Select a 1-qt (1-l) bowl or mold, the deeper the better. Rinse with cold water, shaking out any excess. Spoon a thin layer of the aspic into the bottom, cover, and refrigerate until it has the consistency of raw egg whites. Stir the chiles and half of the bell pepper into the remaining aspic and set aside at room temperature.

When the refrigerated aspic has started to set, after about 20 minutes, dip the peeled shrimp in the remaining liquid aspic and arrange in one layer in the bowl or mold. Return to the refrigerator until completely set, about 20 minutes longer. Then pour the rest of the aspic over the shrimp, cover, and refrigerate until set, at least 2–3 hours. The aspic can remain in the mold for up to 1 day.

Just before serving, put the yogurt and *crema* in a small bowl and stir in the remaining bell pepper and salt to taste. Loosen the aspic by thrusting a spatula in around the edge of the mold, and very quickly dip the mold in and out of a bowl of hot water. (If the mold is glass, it may need to stay in the water for up to 10 seconds.) Invert onto a cold serving plate. Accompany with the yogurt sauce.

serves 4–6

Hidalgo

Salsa Borracha

drunken pasilla chile salsa

This very simple rustic sauce is served with the regional barbacoa *of lamb in the states of Hidalgo, Tlaxcala, Puebla, and México. It is traditionally thinned with* pulque, *a mildly alcoholic fermented—but not distilled—beverage made from the sap of the maguey. The meat itself is wrapped and cooked in the membranes of the maguey's swordlike leaves and presented on a platter accompanied with the sauce, lots of corn tortillas, and a bowl of aromatic and tasty broth loaded with chickpeas (garbanzo beans) and vegetables. Every Sunday the roadside* barbacoa *stands are filled with families that get together for this special treat.* Salsa borracha *is also a spirited table sauce to serve with tacos of grilled steak.*

5 pasilla chiles, lightly toasted (page 247)
3 cloves garlic, coarsely chopped
1 thin slice white onion, coarsely chopped
¾ cup (6 fl oz/180 ml) fresh orange juice
¼ cup (2 fl oz/60 ml) beer or tequila blanco
½ teaspoon sea salt

In a bowl, combine the toasted chiles with very hot water to cover and let soak until soft and pliable, about 15 minutes. Drain the chiles and tear into pieces. Place in a blender or food processor along with the garlic, onion, orange juice, and beer or tequila. Purée until smooth.

Pour the salsa into a small serving bowl and season with the salt. The salsa can be made up to a week in advance, as it improves with age. Store, covered, in the refrigerator.

makes about 1½ cups (12 fl oz/375 ml)

Camotes

I was introduced to Mexico's use of the sweet potato in a most musical fashion. Sitting one evening in the courtyard of my hotel in Mexico City, I was startled by a melancholy wail that dominated all other street sounds. I decided to investigate and found it coming from a small cart being pushed down a nearby street. As I watched, the mournful cry emitted by the steam escaping from the metal drum on the cart attracted several neighborhood residents, and I soon learned that what the vendor was selling was one of Mexico's comfort foods, steamed sweet potatoes.

The creamy-textured, light-colored sweet potato, or *camote,* a member of the morning glory family, is native to Mexico. Nowadays it is seldom eaten except in this manner as a snack food or is made into various sweets. From what we know of the Maya diet, before the coming of the Spaniards, sweet potatoes were frequently steamed in their skins and eaten with wild honey, and were used as an extender for corn in tortillas, tamales, and beverages when grain supplies ran low.

Zacatecas

Camotes al Horno

baked sweet potatoes

The tasty tubers were once a significant part of the pre-Hispanic diet but now are more apt to be found made into candies, such as the famous camotes *of Puebla, or they are steam-baked and sold by vendors for a nourishing morning or evening snack. In Zacatecas, it can get very cold, and the eerie sound of the steam escaping from the vendors' carts is a signal to come get a warming* camote.

4 sweet potatoes, well scrubbed

¾ cup (5 oz/155 g) firmly packed brown sugar or chopped piloncillo *(page 249)*

⅓ cup (3 fl oz/80 ml) fresh lime juice

⅓ cup (3 fl oz/80 ml) fresh orange juice

1½ teaspoons ground cinnamon

½ teaspoon ground allspice

¼ cup (2 oz/60 g) unsalted butter (optional)

1 teaspoon sea salt, or to taste

½ teaspoon freshly ground pepper

Preheat an oven to 400°F (200°C).

Poke a few holes in the top of each sweet potato and place the potatoes on a baking sheet. Bake until soft to the touch, about 45 minutes. The timing will depend on the size of the sweet potatoes.

Just before the sweet potatoes are ready, in a saucepan, stir together the brown sugar or *piloncillo,* lime and orange juices, cinnamon, and allspice. Place over low heat and cook, stirring, until the sugar dissolves and the mixture is syrupy, about 3 minutes.

When the sweet potatoes are done, remove them from the oven and let cool slightly so they can be handled. Slit vertically and lightly mash the flesh inside with a fork, adding an equal amount of the butter to each one, if desired.

Place the potatoes in a serving dish. Pour an equal amount of the syrup into each opening, season with salt and pepper, and squish the syrup into the flesh, letting it puddle in the dish. Serve immediately.

serves 4

Guerrero

Ensalada de Berros

watercress salad with mushrooms

Salads are a recent addition to Mexican cuisine and, with restaurants in Mexico City and resort areas leading the way, are becoming extremely popular. Items such as extra-virgin olive oil and balsamic vinegar from Italy are standard in city supermarkets. I have a vivid memory of eating a version similar to this recipe one day in a restaurant high on the cliffside overlooking Zihuatanejo's Playa La Ropa.

2 bunches watercress, about ½ lb (250 g) total, tough stems removed

8 fresh white mushrooms, brushed clean, stems removed, and thinly sliced

6 slices lean bacon, cut into 1-inch (2.5-cm) pieces

2 tablespoons balsamic vinegar

2 tablespoons extra-virgin olive oil

1 tablespoon corn or canola oil

½ teaspoon Dijon mustard

½ teaspoon sea salt

⅛ teaspoon freshly ground pepper

3 tablespoons sesame seeds, toasted

1 tomato, thinly sliced

Tear the watercress into small sprigs and place in a salad bowl. Add the mushrooms and toss lightly to combine. Set aside.

In a frying pan over medium heat, fry the bacon until crisp, 3–5 minutes. Using a slotted spoon, transfer the bacon to absorbent paper to drain. Reserve 1 tablespoon of the bacon fat.

In a small bowl, whisk together the vinegar, oils, reserved bacon fat, mustard, salt, and pepper. Taste and adjust the seasoning.

When ready to serve, sprinkle the bacon and sesame seeds over the watercress and mushrooms. Toss the salad with just enough of the dressing to coat the leaves and mushrooms. Scatter the tomato slices over the top and serve immediately.

serves 4

Durango

Frijoles de la Olla

pot beans

Nearly all Mexican bean dishes start with frijoles de la olla, *and these indispensable beans—still usually cooked in the large clay* ollas *(pots) that gave them their name—are ubiquitous in Mexico. Black beans in the south, pinto beans in the north and throughout central Mexico, and all shades in between are found simmering away on the back of the stove. They are especially essential in Durango, where the sparse terrain is primarily used for grazing, and meat, beans, tortillas, and salsa compose the primary diet.*

When buying beans, look for so-called new crop beans, that is, beans that have not sat on the shelf for more than a season, as the older the beans are, the longer they need to cook. In Mexico, cooks seldom soak their beans before cooking them, considering it an unnecessary step. Some authorities advise, however, that soaking reduces gas-causing sugars. If this is a concern, after bringing the beans and water to a boil, remove the pot from the heat and let stand for 1–2 hours. Drain off the water, replace with the same amount of cold water, and continue with the cooking process, which now may take less time.

A bowl of these beans can be a healthy and tasty light meal by itself, served perhaps with a green salad and a stack of hot tortillas. Or the beans can be used in other dishes.

2½ cups (18 oz/560 g) dried beans (see note)

2 tablespoons safflower or canola oil, flavorful lard (page 249), or rendered bacon fat

1 white onion, finely chopped

1 clove garlic, minced

2 fresh epazote sprigs, especially if cooking black beans (optional)

about 1 rounded teaspoon sea salt, or to taste

½ cup (2½ oz/75 g) crumbled queso fresco *(optional)*

Pick over the beans and discard any broken beans or small rocks or other debris. Rinse well, place in a large pot, and add water to cover by several inches. Bring to a boil, then reduce the heat until the water is barely simmering.

Meanwhile, in a small frying pan over medium heat, warm the oil, lard, or bacon fat. Add the onion and sauté until dark yellow, about 4 minutes. Stir in the garlic and cook for 1 minute longer. Add the onion and garlic to the beans, reduce the heat to medium-low, and continue to cook, partially covered, until the beans are just tender, about 2 hours. The timing will depend on the age of the beans. Stir the beans from time to time and, if necessary, pour in enough hot water to keep the water level at 1 inch (2.5 cm) above the beans.

Add the epazote, if using, and salt and continue to cook until the beans are quite soft, about 40 minutes longer. Again, the timing may vary. (If time allows, let the beans cool in the broth. The earthy flavor will intensify if the beans are stored, covered, in the refrigerator for at least overnight, then slowly reheated. They will keep for up to 4 days.)

If serving the beans as they are, ladle the broth and beans into warmed bowls and garnish with the crumbled cheese, if desired.

makes about 8 cups (3½ lb/1.75 kg); serves 4 as a main course

POSTRES, DULCES, Y BEBIDAS

Nuns of the early religious orders perfected recipes for many of Mexico's best-loved sweets.

Preceding pages: Various fruit-flavored *gelatinas* shimmer like cool jewels in a Mexico City shop. **Above top:** Pyramids of mangoes and other fresh fruits regularly tempt market shoppers. **Above:** Wooden *molinillos* are traditionally dipped into cups of hot chocolate and rolled between the palms to whip up impressive clouds of voluminous foam. **Right:** An exhaustive list of ice cream flavors at one market includes such unusual and inviting flavors as avocado, tamarind, and *guanábana*.

EARLY IN LIFE, I came to adore the smell of good things baking. I delighted in being behind the scenes in a bakery owned by the parents of my closest friend, and whenever I am in Mexico and walk by a *panadería,* my natural instinct is to go in, bypass the shelves of baked goods, and head to the back room.

One of my favorites is the cavernous baking areas of La Flor de Puebla, among Puebla's oldest bakeries, where the third-generation maestro works alongside his son and others to produce the high-quality baked goods for which they are famous. The last time I was there, the men were singing while they rhythmically pounded, rolled, and shaped the mounds of dough into sixty thousand loaves of *pan de muertos,* their daily quota for this festive egg bread that is always included in the offerings to the dead on All Souls' Day. Others were busy making all of the other varieties expected by their customers, and the large wood-fired oven was repeatedly filled and emptied to keep up with the pace.

Puebla was the hub of Spain's trade routes across Mexico, the stopping place on the trek between Veracruz, Mexico City, and Acapulco. Not surprisingly, it became a major commercial center, and by the eighteenth century, Poblanos grew or purchased much of the country's wheat and dominated the flour industry. The Spanish had always loved their *pan dulce,* and during the short French occupation of Mexico (1864–67), other breads and pastries became equally important. Skilled bakers from Europe lived in Puebla, and with flour, butter, and other needed ingredients close at hand, their bakeries soon were renowned throughout the country.

In smaller towns, the baking is done in homes, identified by a discreet sign over the door. To buy your daily breads and pastries, you walk through the living room (giving greetings to any elderly or children gathered there) into the eating area, where the baked goods are usually sold. The adjacent courtyard doubles as the bakery, with a brick wood-burning oven in an enclosed space nearby.

Mexico is known the world over for its sweet tooth. Puebla has a whole street dedicated to small *dulcerías* (candy stores), and in Morelia, the capital of Michoacán state, the Mercado de Dulces has some thirty shops displaying their sticky delights. In both places, it was the nuns of the early religious orders who perfected the many recipes for sweets and confections that have been handed down from one generation of Mexican cooks to the next: the jellied fruit *ates* and the flat *morelianas,* caramel-like disks of burnt milk and sugar, of Morelia; the famous *camotes* of Puebla made of sweet potatoes; the *alegrías* of Tlaxcala fashioned from amaranth seeds; and the fudgelike *panocha* of Sinaloa. Every region has its specialties, which are stacked in orderly confusion among the more common nut brittles, crystallized fruits, coconut-stuffed limes, and countless other sweets.

In Jalapa, I went with a friend in search of yet another sweet. After ringing the bell on the side door of a certain convent he knew, a panel opened and our order was spoken into darkness. Before long, on a rotating shelf behind the panel, a reclusive nun silently exchanged our payment with a small carton of exquisitely formed marzipan fruits and

Above: During a fiesta at Tlacotálpam, a Navy band plays for a delighted audience of residents and visitors, encouraging them to dance in the crowded plaza. **Right:** A juicy-fleshed mango, cut in the shape of a spiky flower, beckons from a street vendor's stand. **Far right top:** According to a Oaxacan tradition, if you make a wish after eating a crisp, golden *buñuelo* and then immediately smash your plate, your wish will come true. **Far right:** *Panaderías* all over Mexico fill their shelves with the sweets and treats typically found in their region, such as these cream-filled pastry horns from Oaxaca.

vegetables: pomegranates bursting with seeds, leafy green cabbages, and speckled bananas. They rivaled, in miniature, the variety and color of the produce of the market.

The influence of the nuns is found again in the characteristic use of eggs in desserts. Just as in Spain, the yolks are made into flans, custards, and puddings. One of the sweetest is *huevos reales,* or "royal eggs," in which egg yolks are mixed with baking powder and butter, baked, and then cooked again in sugar syrup and sherry. Egg whites are whipped into all sorts of light-as-air creations, from floating islands to meringues. The highlight of my dessert research was seeing perfect meringues being baked, contrary to all the rules, over coals outside in humid Yucatán.

With the exception of several classic cakes—including the moist and rich *pastel tres leches,* a cake soaked with a mixture of three types of milk (cream and both evaporated and condensed milk); the syrup-soaked *antes;* and the elaborate emperor's cake—pies and cakes are seldom seen on a Mexican table. Instead, the beloved cheesecakes, flans, and rice and bread puddings end most meals. Fruits are popular, especially the omnipresent canned peaches, as are unusual flavors of gelatins, ices, and ice creams.

A profusion of beverages exists to wash down all the savories and sweets of Mexico, and they are everywhere. Some street vendors squeeze oranges on demand on busy corners, while others have giant glass jars of vividly tinted *aguas frescas,* refreshing beverages of water mixed with fruits, flowers, and even rice or seeds. In the center of Oaxaca's Mercado Benito Juárez, several stalls have huge earthenware pots of such drinks. The usual milky-white rice *horchata* is colored pink with puréed cactus fruit, and the last time I was there, it was also mixed with chopped nuts. The exotic *guanábana* fruit, when blended, still has a multitude of large slippery seeds, so it is served with a small bowl on the side in which to discard them. Drinks like these are so popular that benches, two deep, clog the aisles, every inch of them taken up by people sipping their hard-won refreshments, while other customers wait patiently to be served.

Every market has its juice bar. Do you want fresh beet or carrot juice, mango or papaya juice, or perhaps just orange juice enlivened with energy-giving alfalfa? Or try a nutritious *licuado* with all sorts of fruits blended with milk. Eggs in a wire basket sit nearby, waiting to be added to drinks, transforming them into quick and complete liquid breakfasts.

A cup of rustic *atole* or chocolate is the traditional accompaniment to tamales. Both are drinks of the ancient tribes of Mexico, made and served today in virtually the same manner as in the past. *Atole,* a gruel-like *masa,* is usually smooth textured, almost like a hot wheat cereal, only made with corn. (This popular pre-Columbian beverage may also be rice- or fresh corn-based, but these versions

Far left top: A statue of Beatriz Hernández, founder of Guadalajara, gazes down on one of the city's many plazas. **Far left bottom:** Boxes of plump berries glisten in the sun at the Zitácuaro market, in Michoacán. **Above top:** A row of pitchers displays a rainbow of lime, strawberry, mango, pineapple, and tamarind *aguas frescas*. **Above:** A vendor wheels his sweetly perfumed wares through Oaxaca's plazas and along its narrow streets. **Left:** The stone tower of the Iglesia de la Tercera Orden rises above one of Mérida's historical streets.

are rarer.) Although it may be flavored with different fruits or nuts, probably the most popular version is *champurrado,* made with chocolate and usually scented with cinnamon. The texture may seem a little odd for a drink, but I have always found it a warming and comforting beverage.

I will never forget one particularly dark, cold night in Teloloapan, high in Guerrero. It was close to midnight, and my friend, a local, stopped his car by the narrow entrance to the market. Only a few bare bulbs lit our way as we zigzagged past closed stalls until deep in the market we reached his goal, a vendor who stayed open to sell her delicious handmade tamales and *atole* to latecomers. We sampled bubbling hot *atole* of purple wild cherries,

one made with pungent epazote, and another silky smooth with beans. But my favorite was her *chileatole,* made from fresh corn and piercingly hot chile. It was the perfect way to end a wonderful day in Mexico.

Left: The calyxes of *jamaica* (hibiscus) flowers are turned into a refreshing, brilliantly hued beverage called *agua de jamaica,* regularly drunk by locals. **Above:** A baker slides a sheet full of treats into the wood-fired oven at the Santa María *panadería* in Valle de Bravo. **Above right:** *Canela,* or true cinnamon bark, imported from Sri Lanka, is found in nearly every marketplace and is an indispensable addition to dishes sweet and savory. **Right:** Trays of freshly baked, ridged *conchas* and light, flaky *hojaldras* are displayed to customers who line up, tongs in hand, to choose sweet pastries to savor with their morning coffee.

Guanajuato

Pay de Queso y Nuez con Cajeta

pecan cheesecake with caramel

Most of the small restaurantes *and* fondas, *conveniently located on almost every block of every city, include cheesecake among their dessert treats as an alternative to the more familiar Mexican flan and rice pudding. This version is embellished with a topping of nuts, usually the native pecan, and* cajeta. *The latter, thick goat's milk caramel syrup, is a specialty of Celaya, a small town in Guanajuato where virtually every household makes and sells the confection. The name* cajeta *refers to the little wooden* cajetes, *or thin oval boxes, in which it is traditionally sold. Making* cajeta *does take time, and fortunately it is now available in jars in Hispanic markets. Homemade has a much better flavor, however.*

CAJETA

4 cups (32 fl oz/1 l) goat's milk

1 cup (8 oz/250 g) sugar

½ cup (4 fl oz/125 ml) cow's milk

¼ teaspoon baking soda (bicarbonate of soda)

1 tablespoon vanilla extract (essence), rum, or brandy

½ cup (2 oz/60 g) pecans, toasted and finely chopped, plus chopped pecans for garnish

pinch of sea salt

CRUST

1½ cups (4½ oz/140 g) finely crushed vanilla wafers

¼ cup (2 oz/60 g) unsalted butter, melted

FILLING

1½ lb (750 g) cream cheese, at room temperature

¾ cup (6 oz/185 g) sugar

1 teaspoon vanilla extract (essence)

3 eggs

TOPPING

2 cups (16 fl oz/500 ml) sour cream

¼ cup (2 oz/60 g) sugar

2 teaspoons vanilla extract (essence)

25–30 pecan halves

To make the *cajeta,* in a large, heavy saucepan, bring the goat's milk to a simmer over medium heat. Add the sugar and stir until completely dissolved. In a small bowl, stir together the cow's milk and baking soda. Ladle in a small amount of the hot goat's milk, stirring constantly. Remove the pan from the heat and whisk the soda mixture into the hot goat's milk. Return the pan to the stove, stir well with a wooden spoon, and continue to simmer over medium heat, stirring frequently, until the mixture begins to thicken, about 30 minutes. As the mixture darkens, reduce the heat to low and stir constantly until the *cajeta* becomes a dark caramel color and coats the back of the spoon, another 20 minutes or so. Pour the *cajeta* into a bowl and let cool, then stir in the vanilla or liquor. Pour half of the *cajeta* into another bowl, stir in the ½ cup (2 oz/60 g) chopped nuts and salt, and set aside. Refrigerate the remaining *cajeta.*

Preheat an oven to 350°F (180°C).

To make the crust, in a bowl, mix together the crushed vanilla wafers and butter until the crumbs are evenly moistened. Transfer to a 9-inch (23-cm) springform pan. Pat the crumb mixture evenly onto the bottom and 1 inch (2.5 cm) up the sides of the pan. Refrigerate for 30 minutes.

To make the filling, in a bowl, using an electric mixer, beat the cream cheese until creamy. Add the sugar and vanilla and beat until blended. Add the eggs one at a time and beat just until smooth, scraping down the sides and along the bottom of the bowl so the ingredients are thoroughly mixed.

Drizzle the pecan *cajeta* evenly over the prepared crust. Pour the cheese filling over the *cajeta.* Bake until the cheesecake is firm, 50–60 minutes. Remove from the oven and immediately place in the refrigerator on a kitchen towel. Chill for 15 minutes. Raise the oven temperature to 450°F (230°C).

To make the topping, mix the sour cream, sugar, and vanilla together in a bowl. Pour over the top of the cheesecake and bake for 10 minutes. Transfer to a wire rack to cool.

Place a circle of pecan halves around the entire outer edge of the cheesecake, or create your own design. Cover and refrigerate until well chilled, for at least 24 hours or up to 3 days.

To serve, release the sides of the springform pan, leaving the cake in the bottom, and place the cake on a serving plate. Heat the remaining *cajeta* to lukewarm. Drizzle some of it around the plate. Slice the cake, place the slices on individual plates, drizzle each serving with more *cajeta,* and garnish with the remaining chopped nuts.

serves 12

Oaxaca

Agua de Jamaica

hibiscus water

The vivid, wine-colored drink made from the dried red calyxes that surround the yellow petals of the Hibiscus sabdariffa, *a smaller version of the showier ornamental, is one of Mexico's most beloved thirst quenchers. High in vitamin C, the flower, known as* jamaica *in Spanish, is now sold packaged as a tea or as a diuretic on the health-food shelves of well-stocked food markets, or it can be found in Hispanic grocery stores. This particular version is the recipe of Emilia Arroya and her daughter, Aurora.*

6 cups (48 fl oz/1.5 l) water

2 cups (6 oz/185 g) dried jamaica *flowers*

zest of 1 orange (optional)

½ cup (4 oz/125 g) sugar or (6 oz/185 g) honey, or as needed

2 tablespoons fresh lime juice

still water, sparkling water, or fresh orange juice

ice cubes

lime slices

In a saucepan, combine the water, the *jamaica*, and the orange zest, if using. Bring to a simmer over medium heat and simmer for 5 minutes. Pour into a heatproof glass bowl, stir in the sugar or honey, and let cool for 10 minutes.

Strain the mixture through a fine-mesh sieve into a glass or plastic container and add the lime juice. Taste for sweetness, adding more sugar or honey if necessary. Cover and refrigerate for up to 3 days.

To serve, dilute to taste with still water, sparkling water, or orange juice. Pour over ice cubes in tall glasses and garnish with lime slices.

makes about 6 cups (48 fl oz/1.5 l) concentrate; serves 10–12

Street vendors hawk vividly tinted aguas frescas made from fruits, flowers, seeds, and even rice.

Veracruz

Horchata de Coco

coconut-rice cooler

I find the flavors of horchata, *a cooling rice drink, among the most refreshing of Mexico's many* aguas frescas. *It is made with a base of ground rice or melon seeds and is often flavored with cinnamon and almonds. This version adds the abundant coconuts of Veracruz for a different taste. I have simplified the recipe by using canned coconut milk in place of extracting the milk from the meat of a fresh coconut.*

2⅔ cups (19 oz/590 g) uncooked rice, pulverized in a spice grinder

½ cup (1 oz/30 g) crumbled true cinnamon bark, plus 4-inch (10-cm) pieces for garnish (optional)

4 cups (32 fl oz/1 l) hot water

15 blanched almonds, lightly toasted and finely ground

1 can (13½ fl oz/420 ml) coconut milk

1 cup (8 oz/250 g) sugar

1 cup (8 fl oz/250 ml) cold water

zest of 1 lime, cut into long, wide strips

ice cubes

light rum (optional)

6–8 fresh mint sprigs (optional)

One day in advance, combine the rice, crumbled cinnamon, and hot water in a bowl. Cool, cover, and set aside. Refrigerate if the weather is hot.

The next day, stir the nuts and coconut milk into the soaked rice. Working in batches, add the rice mixture to a blender and process until quite smooth. Each batch will take about 5 minutes. Strain through a medium-mesh sieve and pour into a pitcher.

In a saucepan over low heat, combine the sugar, cold water, and lime zest. Cook, stirring, until the sugar is just dissolved. Let cool, then remove the lime zest. Pour the cooled syrup into the pitcher and mix well. If the drink is too thick for your taste, add more water. Cover and refrigerate until chilled.

Stir well and pour over ice cubes in tall glasses. If desired, add a splash of light rum to each glass before adding the *horchata*. Garnish, if desired, with a mint sprig and a piece of cinnamon bark.

serves 6–8

Jalisco

Mangos Flameados

mangoes flambéed with tequila

In this simple recipe, Paula Mendoza Ramos, longtime family cook for the Romo de la Peña family, combines the voluptuously sweet mango with the slightly tart flavor of white tequila.

6 ripe mangoes, about 3 lb (1.5 kg) total weight
3 tablespoons dark brown sugar
3 tablespoons unsalted butter, cut into small pieces
finely shredded zest of 1 lime
finely shredded zest of ½ orange
1 tablespoon fresh lime juice
1 tablespoon fresh orange juice
¼ cup (2 fl oz/60 ml) tequila blanco
1 qt (1 l) coconut or French vanilla ice cream
½ cup (2 oz/60 g) shredded unsweetened coconut, toasted (page 246)

Preheat an oven to 400°F (200°C). Lightly butter an attractive shallow baking dish measuring about 9 inches (23 cm) by 13 inches (33 cm).

Peel and pit each mango (page 249), cutting the flesh into slices. Arrange the slices, slightly overlapping them, in the prepared dish. Sprinkle with the brown sugar and dot with the butter. Scatter the lime and orange zests over the top, then drizzle with the lime and orange juices.

Bake, uncovered, until the mango slices begin to brown, about 20 minutes. Though best served immediately, the mangoes can be kept warm for about 30 minutes.

When ready to serve, sprinkle the tequila over the mangoes and carefully ignite with a long match. Jiggle the pan for a moment until the flames die out, then divide among individual plates. Add a scoop of ice cream to each plate and garnish with a sprinkle of toasted coconut.

serves 6

Oaxaca

Flan de Coco

coconut flan

Just as it is in Spain, flan is Mexico's preeminent dessert. Here, though, it is more apt to be made with canned milk rather than fresh milk, as until recently refrigeration was a luxury that few could afford. Iliana de la Vega serves this coconut version in her delightful restaurant, El Naranjo in Oaxaca, where she specializes in the traditional dishes of the region with a modern twist. Her coconut flan, however, is a classic rendition that she makes from fresh coconut, using both the milk and the flesh. I have simplified the task by using a combination of canned coconut milk along with evaporated and condensed milk.

Coconuts, though not indigenous to Mexico, grow freely in all of the coastal regions, and the beaches of Oaxaca are no exception. Young boys with machetes stand alongside piles of the shiny green nuts and are quick to lop off the top of one and serve you the milk in the rest of the shell, either plain or mixed with rum for a coco loco.

The rich character of the flan is best enjoyed after a not-too-fussy main dish such as Marinated Steak with Herbs (page 155). I also delight in the contrast of textures and flavors when the flan follows Ancho Chiles Stuffed with Chicken Picadillo (page 157).

1½ cups (12 oz/375 g) sugar

¼ cup (2 fl oz/60 ml) water

10 eggs

2 cans (12 fl oz/375 ml each) evaporated milk

1 can (13½ fl oz/420 ml) coconut milk

1 can (14 fl oz/440 ml) sweetened condensed milk

¾ cup (3 oz/90 g) sweetened shredded dried coconut

♛ Preheat an oven to 350°F (180°C).

♛ In a small, heavy saucepan over medium-high heat, stir together the sugar and water and heat until the mixture becomes a clear syrup. Do not stir again until it begins to caramelize, then only gently swirl the pan until the syrup turns amber. Continue cooking for a few more minutes until the color deepens. Remove from the heat and immediately pour the syrup into the bottom of a 2½-qt (2.5-l) flan dish or other ovenproof glass or ceramic baking dish, quickly tilting and turning the dish so the syrup adheres partway up the sides. Set aside.

♛ In a large bowl, beat the eggs until blended. Mix in the evaporated milk, coconut milk, and condensed milk, then stir in the shredded coconut. Pour into the prepared dish.

♛ Place the filled flan dish in a baking pan and carefully pour very hot water into the baking pan to reach halfway up the sides of the dish. Carefully place the flan in the oven and bake until a toothpick inserted into the middle comes out clean, about 1½ hours. Remove from the oven and let the flan cool in the water bath. Remove from the water bath, cover, and refrigerate until ready to serve.

♛ To unmold, run a knife around the edges of the mold to loosen the flan. Invert a deep serving dish over the top, and invert the flan and dish together. The flan should drop. If it resists unmolding, place the bottom of the flan dish in hot water for just a few seconds and try turning it out again. Serve at once.

serves 10–12

Veracruz

Pan de Elote

corn cake

When a rich, fancy dessert is just not right, this rustic, moist corn bread is usually perfect with an after-dinner coffee. I've tasted many versions, but my favorites are from Veracruz or nearby Puebla.

- *½ cup (4 oz/125 g) unsalted butter, at room temperature, plus 2 tablespoons*
- *½ cup (4 oz/125 g) sugar, plus extra for garnish (optional)*
- *1 cup (6 oz/185 g) fresh corn kernels*
- *4 eggs*
- *1 tablespoon all-purpose (plain) flour*
- *1 teaspoon baking powder*
- *1 teaspoon salt*
- *1 tablespoon corn oil*

Preheat an oven to 350°F (180°C).

In a bowl, using an electric mixer, beat together the ½ cup (4 oz/125 g) butter and the ½ cup (4 oz/125 g) sugar until creamy. Put the corn kernels in a food processor and process until ground, with some texture remaining. Add the ground corn to the butter mixture and beat until well mixed. Beat in the eggs one at a time, beating well after each addition. Add the flour, baking powder, and salt and beat until just combined.

Put the 2 tablespoons butter and the oil in a 9-inch (23-cm) ovenproof frying pan or quiche dish and heat in the oven until the butter is melted. Add the creamed corn mixture and bake until set and a toothpick inserted into the middle comes out clean, about 20 minutes. There should be no liquid visible when the pan is shaken or tilted. Remove from the oven and sprinkle with sugar, if desired.

Cut the cake into wedges and serve directly from the pan.

serves 8

Puebla

Ponche Caliente

hot punch

The Christmas season is a time when hot punch is a welcome treat. This version from Ana María Gutiérrez López has the exotic flavors that I associate with the cuisine of Puebla. I like to use full-flavored English breakfast tea or a pure Darjeeling.

- *5 cups (40 fl oz/1.25 l) water*
- *3 tea bags (see note)*
- *1 cup (8 oz/250 g) sugar*
- *2 oranges, sliced*
- *1½ cups (9 oz/280 g) pitted prunes*
- *½ vanilla bean*
- *3-inch (7.5-cm) piece true cinnamon bark*
- *2 cups (16 fl oz/500 ml) dry red wine*
- *½ cup (4 fl oz/125 ml) dark rum*
- *juice of 2 limes*

In a large nonaluminum pot over high heat, bring 4 cups (32 fl oz/1 l) of the water to a rolling boil. Add the tea, remove from the heat, and let steep for just 4 minutes. Remove the tea bags.

In a saucepan, dissolve the sugar in the remaining 1 cup (8 fl oz/250 ml) water, stirring over low heat until just dissolved. Add the orange slices, prunes, vanilla bean, and cinnamon and bring to a boil.

Pour the flavored syrup into the tea and add the wine, rum, and lime juice. Stir well and remove the vanilla bean (rinse, dry, and save for another use). Taste the punch and add more sugar, lime juice, or even more wine to your liking. Ladle into glass cups directly from the pot and serve at once.

serves 6

Day and night, Veracruzans and visitors fill the lively cafés of the centuries-old Zócalo.

Vainilla

In the distant past, before Mexico's recorded history, the native vine of the vanilla orchid rambled through the tropical trees of the humid rain forests of southeastern Mexico. The region, now Veracruz, was home to the Totonacs, who learned to cultivate the long, ripe pods of the plant and to cure them to develop their aroma. In later years, these *vainilla* "beans" were especially prized as a tribute paid to the ruling Aztec nobles and used to flavor a chocolate beverage drunk exclusively by them.

According to Totonac legend, a time existed when there was no vanilla. The ruler of the ancient city of El Tajín deemed that his beautiful daughter, "Light of the Morning Star," serve the goddess of agriculture, and every day the princess brought offerings to the temple of the goddess, which had been built by her father. One day, a neighboring young prince caught sight of the young maiden performing her duty and immediately fell in love. As she passed by, he leapt from behind a tree, took her in his arms, and ran with her up the slopes of a mountain. Although startled at first, the princess soon returned his ardor and willingly joined him in flight.

Growing tired, the couple was captured by the pursuing priests who had been guarding the temple, and they were instantly beheaded. From the spot where their blood spilled, an emerald green vine sprang up and, with clinging tendrils, began to intertwine the branches of the nearby trees. Delicate yellow flowers bloomed, then before the priests' eyes, the orchids turned into slender green beans from which later came such a splendid aroma that the Totonacs made this vanilla a divine offering to their gods and to the world.

Although vanilla, the transmuted blood of the princess and her prince, is now grown in other tropical countries, to me Mexican vanilla is the most deeply flavored and richly scented. The plant itself is a climber, reaching 45 feet (15 meters) or more in height as it ascends trees or other convenient supports. Along with the pods, or beans, which are cured before use, the robust vines bear beautiful orchids. Today, the main commercial use for vanilla in Mexico is as one of the secret ingredients in Coca-Cola; only a small amount is bottled as vanilla extract for flavoring ice creams and cakes.

Puebla

Jericalla

classic custard

Whenever I visit Ana María López Landa, who has lived in Puebla for all of her eighty-eight years, I almost always find her in the kitchen. This rich custard, named after the small city of Jerico in Colombia, is also popular in Mexico, whether in the markets or at the dinner parties where Sra. Landa presides.

3 cups (24 fl oz/750 ml) milk
¾ cup (6 oz/185 g) sugar
2-inch (5-cm) piece true cinnamon bark
½ vanilla bean, split lengthwise
3 egg yolks

In a saucepan over medium heat, stir together the milk, sugar, and cinnamon. Using the tip of a small knife, scrape the seeds from the vanilla bean into the milk. Bring to a slow boil, stirring until the sugar is dissolved, then reduce the heat to low and simmer gently until the mixture is thick enough just to coat the back of a spoon, about 20 minutes. Strain the milk mixture and let cool slightly.

Preheat an oven to 325°F (165°C).

In a bowl, beat the egg yolks until blended. Add ⅓ cup (3 fl oz/80 ml) of the hot milk, stirring constantly, then pour the egg mixture into the rest of the milk mixture, again stirring constantly. Divide the mixture evenly among 6–8 flameproof dishes or ramekins. Place the custard dishes on a rack in a baking pan, making sure they do not touch, and pour hot water into the pan to a depth of 1 inch (2.5 cm). Bake until a toothpick inserted in the middle of a custard comes out clean, about 1 hour.

Remove the custard dishes from the water bath, arrange on a baking sheet, turn the oven to broil (grill), and slip under the broiler (griller) until the tops are browned. Let the custards cool, then cover and refrigerate for several hours until chilled.

Serve cold in the dishes, or run a knife blade around the edge of each dish to loosen the custard and then unmold onto dessert plates.

serves 6–8

Puebla

Mamón del Emperador

emperor's cake

This extravagant fruit-studded cake from my friend Mónica Mastretta typifies the European influence on Mexican cuisine and culture in the late 1800s.

CAKE

1 cup (8 oz/250 g) unsalted butter

¾ cup (6 oz/185 g) granulated sugar

8 eggs, at room temperature, separated

¾ cup (4 oz/125 g) plus 1 tablespoon sifted all-purpose (plain) flour

½ teaspoon baking powder

pinch of sea salt

SYRUP

1 cup (8 fl oz/250 ml) water

3 cups (1½ lb/750 g) granulated sugar

CUSTARD

8 egg yolks

1 tablespoon cornstarch (cornflour), sifted

1 tablespoon ground cinnamon

½ teaspoon sea salt

finely shredded zest of 1 lemon

1 tablespoon unsalted butter

2 tablespoons Cognac

FILLING

½ cup (3 oz/90 g) each crystallized figs, orange, and citron, finely chopped

⅓ cup (2 oz/60 g) crystallized lime, finely chopped

½ cup (4 fl oz/125 ml) Cognac

ICING

4 egg whites, at room temperature

2½ cups (20 fl oz/625 ml) heavy (double) cream, chilled in the freezer for 30 minutes

1 cup (4 oz/125 g) confectioners' (icing) sugar, sifted

ASSEMBLY

½ cup (4 fl oz/125 ml) Cognac

3 crystallized figs, cut into thin strips

1 crystallized orange, cut into thin strips

2 crystallized limes, cut into thin strips

¼ cup (1 oz/30 g) pine nuts, lightly toasted

10 almonds, lightly toasted

Position a rack in the lower third of an oven. Preheat to 350°F (180°C). Line two 8-inch (20-cm) round cake pans with waxed paper, then butter and flour, tapping out the excess flour.

To make the cake, in a bowl, beat the butter until creamy. Gradually add the sugar and beat until the mixture has lightened in color. Beat in the yolks one at a time. In a bowl, stir together the flour, baking powder, and salt. Gradually add the flour mixture to the yolk mixture, stirring until just combined.

In a bowl, beat the whites until soft peaks form. Fold one-third of the whites into the yolk mixture. Fold in the remaining whites in 2 additions. Divide the batter between the pans. Bake until a toothpick inserted into each cake comes out clean, about 35 minutes. Let cool in the pans on a rack for 10 minutes, then unmold each cake and discard the paper.

To make the syrup, in a heavy saucepan, combine the water and sugar, bring to a boil, and cook without stirring until the mixture reaches the hard-ball stage, 260°F (125°C) on a candy thermometer.

To make the custard, in a bowl, whisk the yolks for about 2 minutes. Slowly pour in the syrup and beat until thickened, about 2 minutes. Stir in the cornstarch, cinnamon, salt, lemon zest, and butter. Place in a large double boiler over simmering water and stir until the mixture coats the back of a spoon, no more than 15 minutes. Remove from the heat and stir in the Cognac. Place plastic wrap directly on the surface and refrigerate for 2 hours.

To make the filling, combine the fruits and Cognac in a bowl and mix well; let stand for 1 hour.

To make the icing, in a bowl, beat the egg whites until soft peaks form. In another bowl, beat the cream until soft peaks form. Gradually add the sugar and beat until stiff peaks form. Fold one-third of the beaten whites into the whipped cream. Gently fold in the remaining whites. Cover and refrigerate.

To assemble, slice each cake layer in half horizontally. Drain the filling. Place 1 cake layer on a platter and sprinkle with one-third of the Cognac. Spread one-third of the custard on top, followed by one-third of the fruit filling. Top with another cake layer, half of the remaining Cognac, half of the remaining custard, then half of the remaining fruit filling. Top with another cake layer and the remaining Cognac, custard, fruit filling, and cake layer. Frost the cake and garnish with the fruit strips and nuts. Refrigerate for at least 2 hours before serving.

serves 10–14

Coahuila

Higos al Horno con Queso de Cabra

baked figs with goat cheese

I am lucky to have a spot in my garden where enough figs ripen once a year to make this traditional recipe from northern Mexico, where figs are bountiful. The simple dessert is a nice ending to a meal featuring Shrimp with Orange and Tequila (page 125).

Intensely sweet tree-ripened figs are often difficult to find in supermarkets. Look for them at their seasonal peak, in summer, at farmers' markets.

12 ripe Mission figs

¼ cup (2 oz/60 g) firmly packed dark brown sugar

⅓ cup (1½ oz/45 g) walnut halves

¼ cup (2 oz/60 g) unsalted butter, cut into small cubes

¾ cup (4 oz/125 g) crumbled fresh goat cheese

Preheat an oven to 350°F (180°C). Butter a shallow baking dish in which the figs will fit snugly once they are cut.

Snip the stems from the figs and quarter them from the stem end down to, but not quite through, the bottoms. Spread the figs open and place, cut side up, in the prepared baking dish. Sprinkle evenly with the brown sugar, scatter the walnuts on top, and dot with the butter.

Cover and bake until the figs are heated through, about 20 minutes. Spoon some of the crumbled goat cheese onto each fig and, if desired, lightly toast the cheese in a broiler (griller) or very hot oven for just a few minutes.

Serve the figs warm or at room temperature on individual plates with some of the syrup that forms during baking spooned over the tops.

serves 4

Puebla

Tamales Canarios

sweet canary yellow tamales

Although I know that these pale yellow tamales made with rice flour and egg yolks are found in other parts of central Mexico, I have eaten them only in the state of Puebla. On one of my first stays in Cholula, a small city in the shadow of the snow-covered peaks of the volcanoes Popocatépetl (Smoking Mountain) and Iztaccíhuatl (Sleeping Woman), a friend took me for a morning snack at a small fonda *near the market. The specialty was little sweet tamales that we had with hot chocolate. They were exceptional, but try as we would, the cook would not share the recipe with us. Later, though, I was given a recipe by Ana María Gutiérrez López from Puebla, who not only had been making them for festive occasions all of her adult life, but also remembered them from her childhood.*

DOUGH

1 cup (8 oz/250 g) unsalted butter, at room temperature

¾ cup (6 oz/185 g) sugar

5 eggs

1½ cups (7½ oz/235 g) rice flour

½ cup (4 fl oz/125 ml) milk

2 tablespoons brandy

FILLING

2 cups (16 fl oz/500 ml) milk

3 egg yolks, lightly beaten

½ cup (4 oz/125 g) sugar

⅛ teaspoon ground cinnamon

2 tablespoons cornstarch (cornflour) dissolved in ¼ cup (2 fl oz/60 ml) water

½ cup (3 oz/90 g) raisins

½ cup (2 oz/60 g) chopped pecans

50 corn husks

1 tablespoon unsalted butter, melted

♛ To make the dough, combine the butter and sugar in a bowl and beat with an electric mixer until creamy. Add the eggs one at a time, beating well after each addition. Fold in the rice flour and stir in the milk and brandy. The batter should be very creamy.

♛ To make the filling, in a saucepan, bring the milk to a simmer over medium heat. In a bowl, whisk together the egg yolks, sugar, and cinnamon. Slowly stir half of the milk into the yolk mixture, then pour into the saucepan. Simmer, stirring gently, until lightly thickened, 8–10 minutes. Stir in the cornstarch mixture. Cook over medium heat, stirring constantly, until thick, about 5 minutes. Let cool.

♛ Meanwhile, rinse the corn husks and soak in very hot water until pliable, about 15 minutes. Drain the corn husks and pat dry. Put 4 or 5 torn husks in the bottom of a steamer basket or rack.

♛ Lay out 40 of the best corn husks and brush a thin layer of melted butter over the surface of each one. Thickly spread 1 rounded tablespoon of the dough down the center of the husk. Put a teaspoon of the filling in the middle and press in a few raisins and some chopped nuts. Fold the sides of the husks over the filling and turn up the pointed end. If desired, tie the tamales with narrow strips of soaked husks. Arrange the tamales horizontally in the lined steamer basket or rack. When all of the tamales are in the basket, fill the bottom of a large pot with water to a depth of at least 2 inches (5 cm). Bring to a low boil. Put the steamer basket over the water, cover the tamales with more husks and a kitchen towel, and then cover the pot with a tight lid.

♛ Steam, without uncovering, for 40 minutes. Carefully remove a tamale from the pot and unwrap it to see if the dough pulls away from the corn husk. If it does, it is ready to eat. Serve the tamales hot, letting each person unwrap his or her own tamales.

makes 40 small tamales

México, D.F.

Budín de Arroz con Coco

coconut rice pudding

Here, rice pudding, the soothing, most traditional of Mexican desserts, is glorified with the addition of coconut and a voluptuous chocolate sauce.

PUDDING

3 cups (24 fl oz/750 ml) milk

1 cup (8 fl oz/250 ml) canned coconut milk

1 cup (4 oz/125 g) sweetened shredded dried coconut, plus 2 tablespoons for garnish

½ cup (3½ oz/105 g) medium-grain white rice

2 egg yolks

1 tablespoon sugar

1 teaspoon vanilla extract (essence)

SAUCE

½ cup (4 fl oz/125 ml) heavy (double) cream

2 tablespoons sugar

½ vanilla bean, split lengthwise

1½ teaspoons espresso coffee granules

3 oz (90 g) high-quality bittersweet chocolate, finely chopped

1 tablespoon unsalted butter

To make the pudding, in a heavy saucepan over medium heat, combine the milk, coconut milk, 1 cup (4 oz/125 g) coconut, and rice. Bring to a slow boil, reduce the heat to very low, and simmer uncovered, stirring frequently, until the rice is very tender and all of the liquid is absorbed, about 1 hour.

In a small bowl, whisk together the yolks, sugar, and vanilla. Whisk in ½ cup (4 fl oz/125 ml) of the rice. Stir this mixture back into the rice. The pudding can be served warm, at room temperature, or cold, but wait to make the sauce until just before serving.

To make the sauce, stir the cream and sugar together in a heavy saucepan. Scrape the seeds from the vanilla bean into the cream. Bring to a rolling boil over medium heat, remove from the heat, and stir in the coffee granules and chocolate. Stir until melted, about 1 minute. Whisk until shiny and smooth, then whisk in the butter.

Spoon the pudding into goblets and top with the sauce and shredded coconut. Serve immediately.

serves 4

Chocolate

No matter the time of year, the first morning of every visit to Oaxaca, I always go to the closest market to have my cup of hot, foamy chocolate. Of course, the ritual would not be complete without ordering the airy *pan de yema,* a bread similar to brioche that is made for dunking and for dipping up the thick foam.

My friend Abigail Mendoza, a vivacious young Zapotec Indian, tells me that before a young woman is accepted in marriage, the prospective mother-in-law inspects the amount of foam that the bride-to-be can beat from the hot liquid with a *molinillo*—a special carved stick encircled with wooden rings. It should be thick enough to be eaten with a special flat wooden utensil and to stand without collapsing for at least an hour. Abigail's foam stands taller and lasts longer than the foam on the top of the chocolate made by any of the other women in her village, including most of the mothers of the eligible men, so she has her choice of husbands. For now, Abigail has decided to maintain her independence.

Chocolate in Mexico primarily refers to the beverage made from roasted cacao beans, sugar, and often almonds. Don't look for desserts of chocolate cake or ice cream, as they are an introduced rarity. One other important use is a savory one: to add a depth of flavor to certain moles.

Oaxaca

Plátano al Horno con Rompope y Crema

baked plantain with mexican eggnog and cream

Plantains still sizzling from the hot coals in the wood-burning adobe horno, *or "oven," topped with rich eggnoglike* rompope *and drizzled with tangy* crema, *are the delightful dessert specialty of Dos Jorges, one of Oaxaca's best seafood restaurants. Plantains are similar in appearance to large bananas, but unlike bananas are always cooked before eating. Select fully ripe, blackened plantains for this recipe.*

The rompope *recipe makes enough for other uses and is wonderful served over fruit, ice cream, or puddings. Ready-made* rompope *can be purchased in Hispanic grocery stores but lacks the richness of the homemade.*

ROMPOPE

2 cups (16 fl oz/500 ml) milk

½ cup (4 oz/125 g) sugar

1½-inch (4-cm) piece true cinnamon bark

⅛ teaspoon baking soda (bicarbonate of soda)

6 egg yolks

ice cubes or crushed ice

¼ cup (2 fl oz/60 ml) brandy

2 black-ripe plantains (see note)

2 tablespoons unsalted butter, cut into small pieces

1 cup (8 fl oz/250 ml) crema *(page 248)*

To make the *rompope,* in a saucepan over medium heat, stir together the milk, sugar, cinnamon bark, and baking soda. When it begins to boil, reduce the heat and simmer for about 20 minutes. Set aside to cool, then strain and discard the cinnamon bark.

Place the egg yolks in a bowl and whisk or beat with an electric mixer until thick and lemon yellow, about 5 minutes. Continuing to beat, slowly pour the cool milk mixture into the yolks. Return to the saucepan and cook over low heat, stirring constantly, until the mixture thickens and lightly coats the back of a wooden spoon. Remove from the heat and stop the cooking by pouring the *rompope* into a metal bowl set into a large bowl of ice cubes or crushed ice. Stir until cooled. Gradually stir in the brandy. You should have about 2 cups (16 fl oz/500 ml). (The *rompope* can be stored, tightly covered, in the refrigerator for several weeks.)

Preheat an oven to 425°F (220°C).

Lightly oil a baking dish. Cut the plantains in half lengthwise through the peels and lay the halves, cut sides up, in a single layer in the prepared dish. Dot with the butter.

Bake until the plantains turn a dark golden brown, about 10 minutes.

Remove from the oven and transfer to a serving platter. Spoon the *rompope* over the plantains, letting it puddle around them. Reserve any extra *rompope* for another use (see note). Drizzle on the *crema* and serve very hot.

serves 4

México, D.F.

Rosca de Almendra

almond ring

This is one of many desserts I have shared at the Mexico City table of María Dolores Torres Yzábal. I occasionally spoon on a colorful raspberry sauce.

CAKE

5 egg whites, at room temperature

pinch of sea salt

¾ cup (6 oz/185 g) granulated sugar

3 cups (16½ oz/515 g) blanched almonds, finely ground

3 tablespoons unsalted butter, melted and cooled

¼ teaspoon almond extract (essence)

SAUCE

2 cups fresh or thawed frozen raspberries

½ cup (3½ oz/105 g) superfine (caster) sugar

1 tablespoon fresh lemon juice

¼ cup (2 fl oz/60 ml) amaretto liqueur

Preheat an oven to 350°F (180°C). Lightly oil or butter a 4-cup (32–fl oz/1-l) ring mold.

To make the cake, in a bowl, using an electric mixer, beat together the egg whites and salt until soft peaks form. Gradually add the granulated sugar and continue to beat until stiff peaks form. Fold in the ground almonds, melted butter, and almond extract. Gently pour the mixture into the prepared mold.

Bake the cake until it is golden and a toothpick inserted into the middle comes out clean, about 30 minutes. Let cool in the mold on a rack for 10 minutes, then run a knife blade around the edges to loosen the cake and turn out onto a serving plate. Let cool completely.

To make the sauce, set aside some whole berries. In a blender or food processor, purée the remaining berries until broken up. Add the superfine sugar, lemon juice, and amaretto and continue to process until smooth. Strain through a fine-mesh sieve.

Slice the ring and place the slices on individual plates. Top with the sauce, garnish with the reserved whole berries, and serve.

serves 8–10

Veracruz

Rosca de Reyes

three kings ring cake

For children in Mexico, the morning of January 6 is as eagerly awaited as Christmas. The day commemorates the arrival in Bethlehem of the three kings who welcomed the baby Jesus with gifts of gold, myrrh, and frankincense, so Mexican children traditionally receive small gifts as part of the celebration. On the same day, friends and family share in eating a magnificently decorated ring-shaped cake in which is hidden a tiny porcelain doll that symbolizes the Christ child. The suspense comes with the cutting of the cake and serving of the portions, as the person who receives the doll in his or her slice now has an obligation to organize a tamale party on February 2, El Día de la Candelaria, or Candlemas Day.

A few of the ingredients for decorating the cake may take ingenuity to search out. If they are not available, use your imagination and substitute other items. Acitrón *is the candied fruit of the biznaga cactus and is sold in Hispanic markets. Serve this festive cake with Hot Chocolate (page 239).*

DOUGH

½ cup (4 fl oz/125 ml) warm water (110°F/43°C)

5 teaspoons (2 packages) active dry yeast

½ cup (4 oz/125 g) unsalted butter, melted and cooled

½ cup (4 oz/125 g) sugar

4 egg yolks, lightly beaten with 2 tablespoons water, plus 2 whole eggs, well beaten

1 tablespoon finely grated orange zest

1 tablespoon finely grated lime zest

½ teaspoon orange flower water (optional)

1 teaspoon sea salt

4–5 cups (20–25 oz/625–780 g) all-purpose (plain) flour, preferably unbleached

1 cup (6 oz/185 g) crystallized fruits, chopped

½ cup finely chopped pecans

2 tiny porcelain or ovenproof plastic dolls

TOPPING

2 whole eggs

1 tablespoon heavy (double) cream

6 sun-dried or crystallized figs, cut into strips (optional)

1 candied orange cut in strips (optional)

1 crystallized acitrón *(see note), cut into strips (optional)*

strips of other crystallized fruits (optional)

⅓ cup (3 oz/90 g) sugar

To make the dough, pour the warm water into a large bowl, sprinkle on the yeast, and let stand until foamy, about 5 minutes. Stir in the butter, sugar, diluted egg yolks, whole eggs, grated orange and lime zests, orange flower water (if using), and salt.

Add 3 cups (15 oz/470 g) of the flour and beat vigorously for 3 minutes with a wooden spoon or on low speed with an electric stand mixer fitted with the dough hook. Gradually add more of the remaining flour, ¼ cup (1½ oz/45 g) at a time, and beat until the dough forms a slightly sticky ball and begins to pull away from the sides of the bowl.

Turn the dough out onto a floured work surface and knead, adding more flour as needed, until smooth and elastic, about 10 minutes. You will know it has had enough kneading when blisters start to form on the surface. Shape the dough into a ball.

Oil or butter a large bowl. Roll the dough in the bowl so the surface is coated. Cover with a damp, tightly woven kitchen towel and let the dough rest in a warm place until doubled in bulk, about 1½ hours.

Grease 2 baking sheets with oil or butter. Turn the dough out onto a lightly floured surface and divide into 2 equal portions. Sprinkle each piece with half of the crystallized fruits and pecans, then knead them in until they are evenly distributed throughout the dough. Push a doll into each piece of dough. One at a time, using your palms, roll each piece into a log about 24 inches (60 cm) long and 2 inches (5 cm) in diameter. Form each log into a ring, pinching the ends together, and place a ring on each baking sheet. To keep each ring's shape, place a well-oiled ovenproof bowl or soufflé dish in the center. Cover lightly with a kitchen towel and let rise until almost doubled in size, 45–60 minutes.

Preheat an oven to 375°F (190°C).

To make the topping, in a bowl, whisk together the eggs and cream. Brush the tops of the rings with the egg mixture. If desired, decorate with strips of all the crystallized and candied fruits interspersed with bands of sprinkled sugar. Bake until the surface is golden, about 25 minutes. Do not overbake. Transfer the cakes to racks to cool completely.

makes 2 large ring cakes; serves 16

Yucatán

Empanadas con Piña

pineapple turnovers

These pineapple-filled empanadas, which can be baked or fried, are similar to those sold on the streets of Mérida. I have tried many recipes for the dough, and this one is still my favorite.

DOUGH

6 oz (185 g) low-fat cream cheese, at room temperature

1 cup (8 oz/250 g) unsalted butter, at room temperature

2 cups (10 oz/315 g) unbleached all-purpose (plain) flour

½ teaspoon sea salt

FILLING

½ cup (4 fl oz/125 ml) pineapple juice

2 tablespoons cornstarch (cornflour)

3 tablespoons sugar

½ cup (2 oz/60 g) chopped pecans

½ cup (2 oz/60 g) unsweetened shredded fresh or dried coconut

¼ cup (1½ oz/45 g) raisins

1 egg, lightly beaten with 1 teaspoon water, if baking

sugar and ground cinnamon

safflower or canola oil, if frying

If baking the empanadas, preheat an oven to 375°F (190°C). Lightly grease a baking sheet.

To make the dough, in a bowl, mix together the cream cheese and butter until well blended, using a spoon, an electric mixer, or your hands. Add the flour and salt and mix well. Turn the dough out onto a lightly floured work surface and gently knead for about 1 minute, then form into a ball. Wrap with plastic wrap and refrigerate for at least 15 minutes.

To make the filling, whisk the pineapple juice and cornstarch together in a saucepan. Heat over medium heat, stirring until the cornstarch is dissolved. Add the sugar and bring the mixture to a boil, continuing to stir. Reduce the heat to low and simmer, stirring occasionally, until the mixture is quite thick, 3–5 minutes. Remove from the heat and stir in the pecans, coconut, and raisins. Let cool.

On a lightly floured surface, roll out the dough until slightly less than ¼ inch (6 mm) thick. Divide the dough in half and roll again to no more than ⅛ inch (3 mm) thick. Depending on whether you are making empanadas or bite-sized *empanaditas,* cut out rounds 3 inches (7.5 cm) in diameter or 1½–2 inches (4–5 cm) in diameter. Gather up any scraps of dough, reroll, and cut into more rounds.

Place about 1 teaspoon filling, or less for the *empanaditas,* in the center of each round. Fold one side over the filling, seal tightly with your fingers, and then crimp the edges with the tines of a fork.

If baking, brush the tops with the beaten egg, sprinkle with sugar and cinnamon, and place on the baking sheet. Bake for 12 minutes. Check to see if the turnovers are browning evenly; if they are not, rotate the pan 180 degrees. Continue to bake until golden brown, 4–5 minutes more. Serve immediately.

Alternatively, to fry the turnovers, omit the egg wash. Pour oil to a depth of ½ inch (12 mm) into a frying pan and place over medium-high heat until very hot but not smoking. Add the turnovers a few at a time and fry until they turn a crusty golden brown, 2–3 minutes per side. Transfer to absorbent paper to drain. Keep warm in a low oven. Sprinkle with sugar and cinnamon while still hot and serve.

makes 15–20 empanadas or 30 empanaditas;
serves 10–12

México, D.F.

Nieve de Hierba Buena

mint ice

Over the years I keep returning to one of Mexico City's most delightful dining spots, El Estoril Restaurant. Among its signature dishes is an unusual mint ice. This lovely green granita with its finely crushed ice crystals makes a refreshing ending to a meal. My simplified version omits the use of an ice-cream maker and instead freezes the ice in a shallow baking pan.

6 cups (6 oz/185 g) fresh spearmint leaves, plus 4–6 leaves

4 cups (32 fl oz/1 l) water

2 cups (1 lb/500 g) sugar

1 tablespoon fresh lemon juice

¼ teaspoon ground cinnamon

3 drops green food coloring (optional)

In a blender or food processor, combine the 6 cups (6 oz/185 g) spearmint leaves and 2 cups (16 fl oz/500 ml) of the water and process until completely smooth. Pour through a fine-mesh sieve into a bowl. Add the remaining 2 cups (16 fl oz/500 ml) water along with the sugar, lemon juice, cinnamon, and green food coloring if a deeper shade of green is preferred. Stir until the sugar is dissolved.

Pour into a shallow baking pan (even a pie pan will do), cover tightly with plastic wrap, and place in the freezer until solid, about 2 hours, stirring and breaking up the ice with a fork every 30 minutes.

When ready to serve, scoop out modest portions into chilled crystal glasses or shallow bowls. Garnish each serving with a mint leaf.

serves 4–6

Papaya Fría con Lima

chilled papaya with lime

When driving along southern Mexico's dusty roads, you often see skinny, stalklike plants, fifteen to twenty feet (5–6.5 m) tall, crowned with a cluster of giant leaves. Sheltered under the leaves are what look like overgrown pears or small watermelons in muted shades of sunset yellow, orange, and pink. What they are, however, are sublimely sweet papayas. The flesh is so delicious that it needs nothing more than a squirt of tart lime juice.

There are many different varieties of papayas from tropical countries other than Mexico. All are usually harvested while still green but will ripen well at room temperature. When I was in the Solomon Islands, I saw the women just barely slit the skin of the fruit from top to bottom on both sides and then balance the fruit upside down on the top of a glass for a day or so while it ripened. They told me it helps to sweeten the papaya.

1 firm, but ripe papaya, about 2 lb (1 kg)
1 lime, cut into 8 wedges

When the papaya is completely ripe, refrigerate it for at least 4–6 hours, but no longer than 2 days. Cut the fruit in half vertically and scrape the glistening gray-black seeds into a small bowl. Cut the fruit into slices ½ inch (12 mm) thick and remove the skin with a small, sharp knife.

Arrange the papaya slices overlapping on individual dessert plates or a decorative platter. Serve with the lime wedges and a sprinkling of the peppery papaya seeds.

serves 4

Baja California Norte

Margaritas

margaritas

There are as many tales about who first concocted that most popular tequila drink, the margarita, as there are variations on making one. Since the drinking of mezcal *and tequila with citrus juice has been around for centuries, and a lick of salt is a traditional accompaniment, only a slight modification was necessary to change this most Mexican of flavors into one of today's favorite cocktails.*

Unfortunately, most of the premixed margaritas use cheap tequila and lots of "smushed" ice, resulting in a drink that is a far cry from the real thing. This recipe will cost a bit more to make, but the resulting bright, tangy flavor is well worth it. You can experiment with different tequilas, types of orange liqueurs, and shaking the ingredients versus blending them with the ice.

3 fl oz (90 ml) tequila blanco
1 oz (30 ml) Cointreau or triple sec
1 oz (30 ml) fresh lime juice
1 cup (8 fl oz/250 ml) coarsely cracked ice
coarse sea salt
several lime wedges

In a cocktail shaker or a jar with a lid, combine the tequila, Cointreau or triple sec, lime juice, and ice. Shake 12–15 times. Remember, the more you shake, the more the ice will diffuse into the drink.

Spread salt on a flat, small plate. Moisten the rims of two 6-fl oz (180-ml) glasses, preferably long-stemmed, with the lime wedges and invert onto the plate of salt, then shake off any excess. Strain the margarita mixture into the glasses and serve at once.

serves 2

Maguey

It was an inky black night, as the story is told. No moon or stars were visible. Suddenly, a great bolt of lightning severed the sky, striking deep into the heart of a towering maguey plant and setting it ablaze. As the villagers drew near, they were astonished to see an aromatic nectar appear from within the swordlike leaves. They drank of it with fear and reverence, accepting the beverage, now known as pulque, as a gift from the gods.

Mexico's native peoples have always utilized every part of the one hundred or more species of the plant they named maguey, also called agave, the scientific name of the genus, but it is the juice obtained from the giant pineapple-shaped heart *(piña)* that has made it famous. Pulque, a mildly intoxicating beverage, came first and was favored by the Aztec nobles. *Mezcal,* a much more potent drink, followed, created when the Spanish introduced the process of distilling, first roasting the *piñas* in underground pits to produce a distinctive sweet-smoky flavor.

Mezcal is still a highly prized libation in Mexico's more rural areas. In some Oaxacan villages, making this popular beverage is the livelihood of nearly every family. Each home "factory," called a *palenque,* includes a deep roasting pit and a circular area where the cooked hearts are crushed with a large stone wheel pulled round and round by a horse. Wooden vats hold the mash while it ferments, and a small, primitive copper still is used to distill the rustic drink. Some of this Oaxacan *mezcal* is now produced for export.

Tequila, the best known of the maguey spirits, is just another type of *mezcal,* although it is a very special one. It is distilled only from the smaller blue agave that grows in Jalisco and a handful of other states.

Unlike *mezcal,* tequila production is big business. I have visited most of the distilleries that produce my favorites, from the beautiful and historical buildings of the Herradura estate, with their state-of-the art equipment, to the tiny, little-known Tequila Catador Alteño distillery. The last time I traveled through this hilly countryside, I was rewarded not only with sips of Catador Alteño's delightfully herbaceous tequila, but also with plates of gutsy *carnitas.* We listened delightedly to a group of mariachis and watched, astonished, as a visitor's horse imbibed a bottle of beer.

México, D.F.

Polvorones de Cacahuate

peanut clouds

To add a new dimension to these classic Mexican cookies, my friend Laura Caraza Campos adds finely ground peanuts.

1 cup (5 oz/155 g) raw peanuts, skins removed and coarsely chopped

½ cup (4 oz/125 g) unsalted butter, at room temperature

½ cup (4 oz/125 g) vegetable shortening, at room temperature

½ cup (2 oz/60 g) confectioners' (icing) sugar, plus 1 cup (4 oz/125 g), sifted

1 tablespoon dark rum

2 cups (10 oz/315 g) all-purpose (plain) flour, preferably unbleached

¼ teaspoon sea salt

In a spice grinder or food processor, finely chop the peanuts. Be careful not to overprocess to a paste. In a bowl, using an electric mixer, beat together the butter and vegetable shortening until creamy. Add the ½ cup (2 oz/60 g) sugar and the rum and continue beating until the mixture is light and fluffy.

Place most of the flour and the salt in a sifter and sift into the bowl containing the butter-sugar mixture. Stir until well blended. Add the ground nuts and the remaining flour and mix well. Cover and refrigerate for at least 1 hour or as long as overnight.

Position a rack in the upper third of an oven and preheat to 325°F (165°C).

Using your hands, roll small pieces of the dough into ¾-inch (2-cm) balls. Place on an ungreased baking sheet, spacing them about 1 inch (2.5 cm) apart. Bake the cookies until light gold, about 15 minutes. If they are not browning evenly, rotate the pan halfway through the baking. Remove from the oven.

Spread the sifted confectioners' sugar in a shallow plate. While the cookies are still hot, roll them in the sugar, coating evenly, then set on a rack to cool completely. When cooled, roll again in the sugar.

Serve the cookies, or store them between layers of parchment (baking) paper in a tightly covered container at room temperature for up to several weeks.

makes about 36 cookies

Michoacán

Chocolate

hot chocolate

In Mexico, hot chocolate is traditionally made with water, but the practice of using milk is now widely accepted. Tablets made from chocolate ground together with sugar, cinnamon, and often almonds are put in a special clay pot filled with hot water or milk. The cook rapidly twirls a molinillo, *a wooden stick encircled with intricately carved rings at its base, back and forth between his or her palms to create a thick layer of foam on the chocolate, and then the chocolate is poured into individual drinking bowls or cups. Packages of the chocolate tablets can be purchased in well-stocked food stores and in Hispanic markets.*

4 cups (32 fl oz/1 l) milk or water

2 chocolate tablets, about ¼ lb (125 g) total, broken into small pieces

1 vanilla bean (optional)

In a saucepan over low heat, warm 1 cup (8 fl oz/250 ml) of the milk or water. Add the chocolate tablets and stir with a wooden spoon until melted. Add the remaining 3 cups (24 fl oz/750 ml) milk or water and the vanilla bean, if using, and let simmer for several minutes.

Remove the pan from the heat. Lift out the vanilla bean and save for another use. Using a whisk or rotary beater, beat the chocolate milk vigorously until a thick layer of foam covers the surface. Pour into mugs or cups, distributing the foam evenly. Serve immediately.

serves 4

A day is not complete without a cup of foamy chocolate, especially if tamales are served.

México, D.F.

Gelatina de Anís con Frutas Frescas y Nueces

anise gelatin with fruits and nuts

Austin chef Roberto Santibañez first described this recipe to me. Over fifty years ago, his aunt Moraima Leandro and his grandmother Adoración attended a fancy wedding in Mexico City where each table had a dramatic centerpiece of transparent gelatin laden with fresh flowers and fruits. It was designed for looks, not eating. Inspired, they developed their own version at home, as wonderful to eat as to admire. Roberto has now modified their recipe for me. I, in turn, hope others will use it as a springboard for creating their own spectacular desserts. Use edible flowers or other fruits, as long as they are not, like pineapple, high in acidity, or use molds of different shapes. The possibilities are endless; the only rule is to keep the proportions of fruit to liquid the same. There should be a little more than three pounds (1.5 kg) of cut fruit.

1 cup (8 oz/250 g) sugar

3 cups (24 fl oz/750 ml) water

3 tablespoons plus 1 teaspoon (4 packages) unflavored gelatin

1 cup (8 fl oz/250 ml) anisette liqueur, preferably sweetened

1 large or 2 small ripe mangoes, generous 1 lb (500 g)

1 small ripe papaya, 1 lb (500 g), halved, seeded, peeled, and cut into ½-inch (12-mm) cubes (about 10 oz/315 g)

¼ cantaloupe, 1 lb (500 g), seeded, peeled, and cut into ½-inch (12-mm) cubes (10 oz/315 g)

1 lb (500 g) green apples, peeled, cored, and cut into ½-inch (12-mm) cubes

8 strawberries, stemmed and quartered (6 oz/185 g)

¼ lb (125 g) seedless green grapes

¼ lb (125 g) seedless red or black grapes

10 large pitted prunes, each cut into 3 or 4 pieces (¼ lb/125 g)

30 small pecan halves (1–2 oz/30–60 g)

♛ Lightly chill a 9½-inch (24-cm) cake pan or a 7-cup (56–fl oz/1.75-l) mold.

♛ In a small nonaluminum saucepan, combine the sugar and 2 cups (16 fl oz/500 ml) of the water and bring to a boil, stirring to dissolve the sugar.

♛ Meanwhile, sprinkle the gelatin over the remaining 1 cup (8 fl oz/250 ml) water in a small bowl and let stand until softened, about 3 minutes. Stir the softened gelatin into the sugar water and heat together for 30 seconds, or until the mixture is clear. Set aside and let cool, then stir in the anisette liqueur.

♛ Meanwhile, prepare the fruits: Peel and pit the mango(es) (page 249), cutting the flesh into ½-inch (12-mm) cubes. You should have about 10 oz (315 g) cubes. Place the mango, papaya, cantaloupe, and apple cubes; quartered strawberries; grapes; prunes; and pecans in a bowl. Mix well.

♛ Transfer the mixture to the prepared mold. Pour the cooled liquid gelatin over the fruits. The mold should be totally full. Cover and refrigerate until the gelatin is firmly set, 2–3 hours. Chill a serving platter at the same time.

♛ Dip the mold in hot water for just a few seconds, then cover with an inverted serving platter. Invert the mold and platter together and shake back and forth—not up and down. The gelatin should drop out easily.

♛ Cut the gelatin into thick slices and serve at once on chilled dessert plates.

---

serves 8–10

Gelatinas

One of the constant delights of walking the streets of any Mexican city or village is the easy access to quick, refreshing treats. I may opt for a glass of freshly squeezed orange juice, a paper cone filled with crisp pieces of jicama sprinkled with ground chile and lime juice, or a plastic cup filled with shimmering layers of rainbow-hued gelatins. My favorite of the *gelatinas* is a plum-flavored one embellished with a layer of *rompope,* a thick eggnog laced with brandy (page 228). It is usually hidden among the others in the very center of a portable multishelved cagelike structure, requiring dexterity on the part of the vendor to locate my choice.

But in Mexico gelatin is much more than just a street snack. The windows of the historic pastry shops in central Mexico City feature towering creations that are the dream of every young child to have at his or her birthday party instead of a cake. I am often served molded salads of vegetables and seafood at friends' homes, and hostesses at elegant dinner parties always try to serve the most unusual gelatin desserts in an effort to outdo their friends. Of those I have enjoyed the most, one was flavored with Kahlúa and served with a dollop of whipped cream, one was chock-full of fresh fruits with a hint of anisette, and another was thickened with puréed almonds and bits of brandy-soaked prunes.

Baja California Norte

Agua Fresca de Uva y Melón

green grape and melon cooler

Refreshing fruit waters such as this one add a colorful accent to any meal and are appreciated as thirst quenchers on a warm day.

2 lb (1 kg) seedless green grapes

1 very ripe honeydew melon, halved, seeded, peeled, and cut into chunks

juice of 1 lime

2 cups (16 fl oz/500 ml) still water

¼–½ cup (2–4 oz/60–125 g) sugar

2 cups (16 fl oz/500 ml) cold sparkling water or still water

ice cubes

2 limes, quartered

In a blender, combine half of the grapes, melon, and lime juice with 1 cup (8 fl oz/250 ml) of the still water. Purée until smooth and pour into a bowl. Add the remaining grapes, melon, lime juice, and still water to the blender and purée until smooth. Add to the bowl. Add the sugar to taste and mix well.

Pour the fruit mixture through a medium-mesh sieve into a pitcher. Add the sparkling or still water and the ice cubes. Serve in tall glasses, with a lime quarter placed on the rim of each glass.

serves 8

Guerrero

Micheladas

iced spicy beer

Beer over ice may seem odd but is actually a perfect hot-weather drink. My first sip was at Restaurante Machis in Iguala, a small town in Guerrero.

¼ cup (2 oz/60 g) sea salt

2 lime slices

ice cubes

¼ cup (2 fl oz/60 ml) fresh lime juice

dash of Worcestershire sauce

dash of habanero chile sauce or other hot sauce

1 bottle (12 fl oz/375 ml) Mexican beer such as Superior or Bohemia

Spread the salt on a small flat plate. Rub the rim of a tall glass with a lime slice and turn the glass rim in the salt, so that the salt clings to the edges. Fill the glass with ice cubes and add the lime juice and the Worcestershire and habanero sauces.

Pour in the beer, garnish with the remaining lime slice, and serve.

serves 1

Michoacán

Sangrita

"little blood" tequila chaser

In most restaurants, tequila arrives with a bowl of cut limes, salt, and a small glass filled with a red picante *chaser. When the* sangrita *is housemade, rather than a bottled preparation, it adds a fresh flavor that I enjoy.*

2 árbol chiles, toasted (page 247) and seeded

1½ cups (12 fl oz/375 ml) fresh orange juice

½ cup (4 fl oz/125 ml) tomato juice

2 tablespoons fresh lime juice

2 tablespoons finely chopped white onion

1 teaspoon sea salt

2 cups (16 fl oz/500 ml) tequila blanco *or* tequila reposado

In a bowl, soak the chiles in very hot water to cover until soft, about 15 minutes. Drain, tear into small pieces, and place in a blender. Add the orange, tomato, and lime juices, the onion, and the salt and purée until smooth. Pass through a fine-mesh sieve placed over a glass container, pressing down with the back of a spoon. Cover and refrigerate for at least 1 hour. The *sangrita* will keep for about 1 week.

When ready to serve, pour the *sangrita* into tiny glasses (2–3 fl oz/60–80 ml) and set each alongside another small glass filled with good-quality tequila.

serves 8

Guanajuato

Flan de Kahlúa y Ron

kahlúa and rum flan

Flan, one of Mexico's favorite desserts, traces its origins to the Spanish conquest, as do so many of the country's sweets. This version, contemporized by the addition of Kahlúa and rum, is an especially good ending to a meal featuring Chicken in a Clay Pot (page 128).

8 cups (64 fl oz/2 l) milk
1⅔ cups (13 oz/405 g) sugar
2-inch (5-cm) piece true cinnamon bark
¼ cup (2 fl oz/60 ml) water
6 whole eggs, plus 4 egg yolks
2 tablespoons Kahlúa or other coffee liqueur
1 tablespoon dark rum
1 teaspoon vanilla extract (essence)
ground cinnamon (optional)

In a large saucepan over medium-low heat, bring the milk, 1 cup (8 oz/250 g) of the sugar, and the cinnamon bark to a boil, stirring to dissolve the sugar. Reduce the heat to low. Simmer uncovered, stirring frequently, until the milk is reduced to about 4 cups (32 fl oz/1 l), about 45 minutes. (In order to judge accurately when the milk has reduced sufficiently, pour half of the milk into the pan before you add the remainder, to see where the final level should be.) Let the reduced milk cool slightly.

Place the remaining ⅔ cup (5 oz/155 g) sugar and the water in a small, heavy saucepan over medium-high heat and bring to a boil. Continue to boil without stirring until the syrup begins to color, about 15 minutes. Reduce the heat to a simmer, then swirl the pan until the syrup is a deep amber, about 1 minute. Immediately pour the caramel into a 2½-qt (2.5-l) soufflé dish or charlotte mold, or into individual molds, tilting to distribute the caramel evenly over the bottom. Some of the syrup may run up the sides of the mold, but try to keep most of it on the bottom. Set aside.

Preheat an oven to 350°F (180°C).

In a large bowl, beat the whole eggs, egg yolks, Kahlúa, rum, and vanilla until blended. Slowly beat in the reduced milk mixture. Pour the mixture through a fine-mesh sieve into the prepared mold(s). Place the mold(s) in a baking pan and pour in hot water to reach three-fourths up the side of the mold(s). Cover loosely with aluminum foil.

Bake until just set and a knife inserted in the middle comes out clean, 40–50 minutes. Remove the baking pan from the oven and let the flan cool in the water. (The flan can be covered and refrigerated for up to 2 days before serving.)

To unmold, run a knife around the edge of the mold(s) to loosen the custard. Invert a deep serving plate or individual plate over the top, and invert the flan and dish together. The flan should drop from the mold. If it resists unmolding, dip the mold(s) in hot water for just a few seconds, then invert. The flan should drop out easily. Sprinkle with ground cinnamon, if desired, and serve at once.

serves 6–8

Yucatán

Caballeros Pobres

poor gentlemen's dessert

The ne'er-do-well Spaniards who followed in the wake of the conquest had palates for grand cuisine but not the purses to afford it. Dishes like this one, served by Raul Rosada Lixa at his Yucatecan restaurant, were the resulting compromise.

¾ cup (6 oz/185 g) sugar

1½ cups (12 fl oz/375 ml) water

2 pieces true cinnamon bark, each 3 inches (7.5 cm) long

6 whole cloves

6 allspice berries

½ teaspoon aniseeds

1 cup (6 oz/185 g) raisins

1 cup (4 oz/125 g) sliced (flaked) almonds

4 eggs, separated

pinch of salt

2 tablespoons unsalted butter

1 teaspoon safflower or canola oil

12 baguette slices, each ¾ inch (2 cm) thick, crusts removed

Put the sugar in a 1-qt (1-l) saucepan and stir in the water. Add the cinnamon bark, cloves, allspice, and aniseeds. Bring to a simmer over medium heat, stirring gently, until the sugar is dissolved. Cover and continue to simmer for 2 minutes longer. Strain, add the raisins and almonds to the syrup, and let cool.

In a bowl, whisk together the egg whites and salt until fluffy. Lightly whisk the egg yolks in a small bowl just until blended, then fold into the whites.

In a frying pan over low heat, melt the butter with the oil. Raise the heat to medium and, working in batches, dip the bread slices in the egg batter, then place in the hot oil. Fry, turning once, until slightly crisp, 5–6 minutes total. Transfer to absorbent paper to drain. Arrange the slices in a serving dish and pour the syrup over the top. Let stand for 15–20 minutes. Serve warm or at room temperature.

serves 6

GLOSARIO

The following entries cover key Mexican ingredients and basic recipes called for throughout the book. Look for Mexican ingredients in Hispanic markets, specialty-food stores, and well-stocked supermarkets. For information on items not found below, please refer to the index.

ACHIOTE PASTE

This seasoning paste made from the hard, brick-red seeds of the annatto, a tropical tree, contributes a mild flowery flavor and a deep yellow-orange color to foods. It is a typical ingredient in the Yucatán peninsula.

ACITRÓN

The name suggests kinship with citrus fruit, but mildly sweet *acitrón* is actually a crystallized form of the biznaga cactus. It is sold in small rectangular bars and will keep, well wrapped, for several months in a cool, dry place. The most acceptable substitute is candied pineapple.

AMARANTH SEEDS

These nutritious, protein-rich seeds, native to Mexico and used in rituals since Aztec times, are occasionally featured in contemporary cooking. *Alegría* (Spanish for "joy"), a popular sweet in central Mexico, is made from popped seeds combined with sugar syrup.

AVOCADO LEAVES

The long, leathery leaves of the avocado tree act as a seasoning in south-central Mexico. They may be used fresh or dried, and added whole or crumbled to contribute an aniselike taste to savory dishes.

TO TOAST AVOCADO LEAVES, heat a heavy frying pan or griddle over medium heat. Place the leaves on the griddle, press down on them with a spatula, and cook them briefly, turning once, just until they color lightly and give off their fragrance.

BANANA LEAVES

The large, pliable leaves of the banana tree are used to wrap tamales for steaming and seafood, poultry, or meat for steaming, grilling, or roasting. They protect the food while contributing a mild grassy flavor. Before using the leaves, soften them by steaming or passing over a flame.

BELL PEPPERS

Mild-tasting bell peppers (also known as capsicums), used in Yucatecan cooking, are often roasted to enhance their sweet flavor and to make them tender. To roast bell peppers, see instructions for roasting fresh chiles (page 247).

CHAYOTE

A pear-shaped member of the squash family, the chayote, also known as the vegetable pear, choko, mirliton, or christophene, has a mild, cucumber-like flavor. Indigenous to Mexico, it comes in varieties with skin ranging from a smooth-textured ivory to a prickly dark green.

CHEESE

Several types of cheese predominate in Mexican cooking. Melting cheeses include the pale, slightly tangy *asadero;* the flavorful, quite rare *queso Chihuahua;* and *quesillo de Oaxaca,* which resembles string cheese. Fresh cheeses, or *quesos frescos,* are soft, tangy, lightly salted cow's milk cheeses that are crumbled or sliced for adding to dishes. They are labeled *queso fresco* or *queso ranchero.* When *queso fresco* is aged, it becomes *queso añejo,* a tangy, dry cheese, more authentically called *queso cotijo,* which is grated as a garnish for tacos, enchiladas, and other everyday dishes. Mexican Manchego resembles the Spanish cheese of the same name but is made from cow's rather than sheep's milk. Spanish Manchego may be substituted for the Mexican variety, which is often hard to find outside Mexico.

CHICHARRONES

Known in English as fried pork rinds, these are the crisp cracklings made from sheets of air-dried pork skin with just a paper-thin layer of fat. In Mexican markets, they are sold in huge sheets. The more widely available snack variety, sold as bite-sized pieces, may be used in most recipes.

CHOCOLATE

Mexican chocolate, a mixture of cacao beans, almonds, sugar, and often cinnamon and vanilla, is formed into disks, or tablets, usually weighing 3 ounces (90 g). It has a grainier texture than typical cooking chocolate and is not suitable for baking or candy.

CILANTRO

Introduced by Spanish explorers, this native herb of the Mediterranean and Asia has become a signature seasoning of Mexico. The fresh green leaves resemble those of Italian (flat-leaf) parsley, but their pungent, aniselike aroma and bright, astringent taste are distinctive. Also known as fresh coriander and Chinese parsley.

CINNAMON BARK, TRUE

Canela, the type of cinnamon favored by Mexican cooks for savory and sweet dishes, is true cinnamon, the flaky, aromatic bark of a laurel tree native to Sri Lanka. The long coils of bark are worth bringing home from Mexico if you are limited to using cinnamon sticks or ground cinnamon. These more aggressive-flavored forms of cinnamon are derived from cassia, the bark of another Southeast Asian variety of laurel. If you can find only the stronger flavored products, reduce the amount used.

COCONUT, SHREDDED

The rich, chewy white flesh of this fruit of a tropical palm tree is used in sweet and savory recipes. Toasting gives it an even richer, nutlike flavor.

TO TOAST SHREDDED COCONUT, preheat an oven to 350°F (180°C). Evenly spread the coconut in a thin layer in a baking dish and toast, stirring frequently, until golden brown, 7–10 minutes.

CHILES

Chiles, whether dried or fresh, have distinctive flavors and degrees of heat, so they cannot be used interchangeably. Look for fresh chiles with smooth, shiny skins and no breaks or cracks. Dried chiles should be relatively supple and without discolored patches of skin.

FRESH CHILES

ANAHEIM ~ Familiar long green, mild to moderately spicy chile found in most markets. Similar to New Mexican variety of chile.

GÜERO ~ A pale yellow to light green chile. Several varieties may be used, including the Fresno, yellow banana, and Hungarian wax, which vary in degree of heat. Most are rather sweet with a pungent punch.

HABANERO ~ Renowned as the hottest of all chiles, this 2-inch (5-cm) lantern-shaped variety from Yucatán combines its intense heat with flavors recalling tomatoes and tropical fruits. Available in unripe green and ripened yellow, orange, and red forms.

JALAPEÑO ~ The most popular and widely available fresh variety, this tapered chile, 2–3 inches (5–7.5 cm) in length, has thick flesh and varies in degree of hotness. It is found in green and sweeter ripened red forms. Available pickled *(en escabeche)* as well.

POBLANO ~ Named for the state of Puebla, this broad-shouldered, tapered, moderately hot chile is 5 inches (13 cm) long and a polished deep green.

SERRANO ~ Slender chiles measuring 1–2 inches (2.5–5 cm) long and very hot, with a brightly acidic flavor. Available in both green and ripened red forms.

TO ROAST FRESH CHILES, use long-handled tongs to hold them over a gas-stove burner until their skins are evenly blistered and charred, about 5 minutes; or roast directly over a very hot charcoal or gas grill. Alternatively, roast under a preheated broiler (griller), turning occasionally, until evenly blackened and blistered, 6–8 minutes. Transfer to a paper or heavy-duty plastic bag or a damp kitchen towel and leave for 5 minutes before peeling.

TO PEEL AND SEED ROASTED CHILES, use your fingertips to peel away the blackened and blistered skins. If any areas resist, use a knife or rinse under running cold water. Don't worry if charred bits remain. Slit the chiles open and use your fingertips, a small spoon, or the tip of a small, sharp knife to remove the seeds and white veins.

DRIED CHILES

ANCHO ~ Dried form of the poblano, 4½ inches (11.5 cm) long, with wide shoulders, wrinkled, deep reddish brown skin, and a mild, bittersweet flavor reminiscent of chocolate and a slight aroma of prunes.

ÁRBOL ~ Smooth-skinned, bright reddish orange chile about 3 inches (7.5 cm) long, narrow in shape, and fiery hot.

CASCABEL ~ "Rattle" chile, describing the sound made by its seeds when the medium-hot globe-shaped chile is shaken. It is about 1½ inches (4 cm) long, with brownish red, smooth skin.

CHIPOTLE ~ The smoke-dried form of the ripened jalapeño, rich in flavor and very hot. Sold in its dried form, it is typically a leathery tan, although some varieties are a deep burgundy. It is available packed in a vinegar-tomato sauce *(chiles chipotles en adobo)* and is lightly pickled *(en escabeche).*

GUAJILLO ~ Moderately hot, this burgundy chile is about 5 inches (13 cm) long, tapered, and with rather brittle, smooth skin and a sharp, uncomplicated flavor.

MORITA ~ A smoke-dried chile about 1 inch (2.5 cm) long, the morita resembles the chipotle except for its almost bluish red color.

MULATO ~ Looks like the ancho but has dark, almost-black skin and a distinctive full, sweet flavor.

PASILLA ~ Skinny, wrinkled, raisin-black chile, about 6 inches (15 cm) long, with a sharp, fairly hot flavor.

TO SEED DRY CHILES, clean them with a damp cloth, then slit them lengthwise and use a small, sharp knife to remove the seeds.

TO TOAST DRIED CHILES, clean them with a damp cloth, then heat a *comal,* heavy frying pan, or griddle over medium heat. Add the whole or seeded chiles, press down firmly for a few seconds with a spatula, turn the chiles, and press down for just a few seconds more before removing. The chiles should change color only slightly and start to give off their aroma.

CAUTION

The oils naturally present in chiles can cause a painful burning sensation. When handling chiles, be very careful not to touch your eyes or other sensitive areas. After handling them, wash your hands thoroughly with warm, soapy water. If you have particularly sensitive skin, wear latex kitchen gloves or slip plastic bags over your hands before working with chiles.

CORN HUSKS

Dried corn husks are the most typical wrapper for Mexican tamales, imprinting the dough with their own ridged pattern and subtly scenting it during steaming. Outside Mexico, the husks are sold stacked and packaged in plastic.

CREMA

Although *crema* translates simply as "cream," in Mexico it usually refers to a thick, rich, slightly soured variety found commercially in grocery stores. In its place, you can use the more widely available French crème fraîche, which is similar in consistency. An adequate substitute may be made by thinning commercial sour cream slightly with whole milk or half-and-half (half cream).

TO MAKE *CREMA,* in a small nonaluminum bowl, stir together 1 cup (8 fl oz/250 ml) heavy cream (do not use an ultrapasteurized product) and 1 tablespoon buttermilk or good-quality plain yogurt with active cultures. Cover with plastic wrap, poke a few holes in the plastic, and leave at warm room temperature (about 85°F/30°C) until well thickened, 8–24 hours. Stir, cover with fresh plastic wrap, and refrigerate until firm and well chilled, about 6 hours. If the *crema* becomes too thick, thin with a little whole milk or half-and-half (half cream).

GARLIC

In Mexican kitchens, whole unpeeled cloves of garlic are often roasted to deepen their flavor.

TO ROAST GARLIC CLOVES, separate them from their head and remove any loose papery pieces of skin but leave them unpeeled. Heat a griddle or frying pan over medium heat. Add the garlic cloves and roast, turning them frequently, until they soften and their skins blacken, about 10 minutes. Let cool before peeling.

HOMINY, WHITE, CANNED. See *pozole,* page 250.

JAMAICA

The deep-red dried calyxes of the hibiscus flower *(Hibiscus sabdariffa), jamaica* is infused and iced as a refreshing beverage of the same name. The beverage is highly acidic and should be stored in a glass or plastic container.

JICAMA

Sold year-round, this large, brown-skinned indigenous Mexican tuber, also known as yam bean, has a refreshingly crisp, mild white flesh that is most often eaten raw. Before serving, thickly peel away the skin and the fibrous layer beneath it.

CHORIZO

Although the word applies to well-seasoned links of fresh pork sausage in both Mexico and Spain, the chorizo of the New World is the spicier and more fragrant of the two. Avoid prepackaged, plastic-wrapped varieties sold in the refrigerated case of markets. If you can't find chorizo, substitute fresh Polish kielbasa or a similarly spiced, fresh country sausage or, preferably, make your own chorizo at home.

Ask the butcher to trim away any stringy tendons from the pork and any fat before grinding. Or grind the meat and fat at home, cutting into small cubes and partially freezing before chopping in a food processor or, preferably, passing through a meat grinder.

1 lb (500 g) boneless lean pork shoulder, coarsely ground (minced)

6 oz (185 g) pork fat, coarsely ground (minced)

5 cloves garlic, coarsely chopped

5 ancho chiles, toasted (page 247) and seeded

1 tablespoon sweet paprika

2 teaspoons dried oregano, preferably Mexican

1 rounded teaspoon sea salt

½ teaspoon ground cinnamon

½ teaspoon freshly ground pepper

¼ teaspoon ground cloves

¼ teaspoon ground coriander

4–5 tablespoons (2–2½ fl oz/60–75 ml) cider vinegar

♛ Put the pork, fat, and garlic in a large bowl and mix thoroughly with your hands.

♛ Grind the chiles in a spice grinder and put them in a small bowl. Add the paprika, oregano, salt, cinnamon, pepper, cloves, and coriander and mix well. Sprinkle the spice mixture over the meat and work it in well with your hands.

♛ Splash on the vinegar a tablespoon at a time. Stop after 4 tablespoons (2 fl oz/60 ml), fry a nugget of the mixture, and taste it before adding more vinegar. Adjust the seasoning with salt or spices at the same time.

♛ Transfer the chorizo to a sieve placed over a bowl, cover tightly with plastic wrap, and refrigerate to cure for several days, remixing and squeezing out any extra liquid every day. (The chorizo will keep for up to 1 week in the refrigerator; any extra can be frozen for up to 3 months.)

makes 1⅓ pounds (21 oz/655 g)

LARD

Rendered pork fat *(manteca)* lends a rich taste to such classic dishes as refried beans and the *masa* used to make tamales. When cooking, do not use the processed white commercial variety, which lacks authentic flavor. Instead, look for a butcher shop that renders its own. Or render it yourself, using pork fat from a reputable butcher. Ask the butcher to grind it for you, or chop it finely at home in a food processor before rendering.

TO RENDER FAT INTO LARD, preheat an oven to 300°F (150°C). Spread 1–2 lb (500 g–1 kg) ground (minced) or chopped pork fat in a large roasting pan. Roast until most of the fat has melted, leaving behind light golden scraps of connective tissue, 30–45 minutes. If the lard itself begins to color, reduce the temperature a bit. Remove from the oven and let cool slightly, then pour through a sieve into sealable containers. When cooled completely, seal the containers. It will keep refrigerated for several months and frozen for up to 1 year.

LIMA AGRIA

Translating as "bitter lime"or "sour lime," this highly aromatic variety, with its distinctive protruding navel, is found primarily in Yucatán. Unripe regular limes, such as the Persian, or Meyer lemons may be substituted.

MAGGI SEASONING

This widely available commercial brand of liquid vegetable extract has a taste reminiscent of concentrated beef bouillon. It is used in Mexico as a flavor enhancement for sauces and other savory dishes.

MANGO

Native to India, the mango thrives in Mexico's tropical climate, and its many varieties are enjoyed as a refreshing breakfast food, dessert, or snack. To avoid any mess when preparing the fruit for use in a recipe, cut and peel it in the following manner.

TO PREPARE A MANGO, place it horizontally on a cutting board and make a slice slightly off-center, cutting off the flesh from one side of the flat pit in a single piece. Repeat on the other side. Hold each slice, cut side up, and score the flesh lengthwise to make slices. Then, if desired, score crosswise in a lattice pattern, creating cubes of the dimension called for in a particular recipe. Do not cut through the peel. Press against the skin side of the peel to invert the slice, then slice the flesh from the peel. Place in a nonmetallic bowl. Cut the remaining skin from around the pit, and cut away any flesh.

MASA

Kernels of dried field corn are treated with a solution of calcium hydroxide (powdered lime) and water to loosen and remove their tough outer skins and then are ground and mixed with water to make *masa,* literally "dough," for preparing tortillas (page 251), tamales, or other foods. Fresh-ground *masa* comes in 5- or 10-lb (2.5- or 5-kg) plastic bags. Use what you need and divide the rest into smaller amounts and freeze. Use freshly made or frozen *masa* within a day of purchase or thawing.

MASA HARINA

Flour ground from dried corn, used for making tortillas, tamales, or other dishes. Two basic types are available, the fine-ground *masa harina* for tortillas and the coarser-ground *masa harina* for tamales.

NUTS

Almonds, pine nuts, and other nuts are used whole, in pieces, or ground in a wide variety of Mexican dishes. They are often toasted to develop their flavor.

TO TOAST NUTS, spread in a single layer in a dry frying pan over medium heat and cook, stirring continuously, until they begin to turn golden. Transfer to a heat-resistant dish to cool. The nuts will continue to darken slightly from residual heat as they cool.

ONIONS, WHITE

Most Mexican cooks use the common white-skinned onion, which has a clear, pungent flavor that is enriched and sweetened by roasting.

TO ROAST AN ONION, first cut it as directed in individual recipes, or leave whole. Prepare a fire in a charcoal or gas grill or line a griddle or heavy cast-iron frying pan with heavy-duty aluminum foil, shiny side up (to prevent sticking) and place over medium heat. Add the onion and roast, turning occasionally, until blackened in spots and softened. Roast green (spring) onions whole.

ORANGE JUICE, FRESH BITTER

The aromatic bitter oranges of Yucatán are seldom found outside their region of origin. When a recipe calls for their juice, look for similar Seville oranges, which also have a thick, wrinkled peel, or approximate the juice with a mixture of 1 part regular orange juice, 2 parts lime juice, and 1 part grapefruit juice. To intensify the flavor, add a bit of finely grated grapefruit zest.

OREGANO, MEXICAN, DRIED

Of the thirteen varieties of the herb known and used as oregano in Mexico, two of the most common are the long-leaved *Poliomentha longiflora* from northern Mexico and *Lippia graveolens* or *L. geminata* from the verbena family. The latter, the one labeled Mexican oregano in Hispanic markets, has a more pronounced flavor than the more common Mediterranean varieties.

PILONCILLO

This unrefined sugar commonly comes in hard cones that are grated or chopped before use. The most common ones weigh ¾ ounce (20 g), while the larger ones weigh about 9 ounces (280 g). In southern Mexico, the unrefined sugar is often made into thin, round cakes or into bricks. The darker the sugar, the more pronounced the molasses flavor. Well-wrapped *piloncillo* will keep indefinitely. Dark brown sugar may be substituted.

PLANTAIN

Closely related to the banana, the large plantain, or *plátano,* is starchier and firmer. It is always cooked before eating. Fresh plantains have almost uniformly black skins when ripe and will yield to gentle finger pressure. Some recipes may call for the firmer texture of an underripe plantain that has only lightly spotted or yellow-green skin.

POZOLE

The Mexican term for hominy, *pozole* (posole in English) is made commercially by first boiling dried field corn with calcium hydroxide (powdered lime) to dissolve its tough hull. The resulting grain is simmered until tender to make a foundation for robust soups of the same name, usually containing pork and chile, or to add to the tripe stew known as menudo. In Mexican markets, *pozole* is also sold freshly cooked or frozen. Canned white hominy may be used, although it lacks the rich aroma and chewier texture of the other forms.

PUMPKIN SEEDS

Mexican cooks have long ground the hulled seeds of various pumpkins and other hard-shelled winter squashes for use as thickening agents in sauces. The whole hulled seeds may also be eaten as a snack or used as an ingredient in confections and baked goods. Brief toasting helps develop their flavor and texture.

TO TOAST PUMPKIN SEEDS, spread them in a dry frying pan over medium heat and cook, stirring continuously, until they just begin to darken. Transfer to a heat-resistant dish to cool; the seeds will continue to darken slightly from residual heat.

SQUASH BLOSSOMS

With their delicate flavor and vivid color, the yellow blossoms of native Mexican squashes may be stuffed or rolled or chopped and used as fillings. Harvest them from your own garden or buy them at farmers' markets. The blossoms should be freshly picked early in the morning, just before they open. Most gardeners take only the male flowers, leaving the rest to develop into future squash.

SQUID

Caught off both the Pacific and the Caribbean coasts of Mexico, this soft-bodied shellfish has a mild, sweet flavor and a slightly chewy texture that is at its best when quickly cooked or slowly simmered. Fresh squid will have a mild, delicate taste and a light gray color.

TO CLEAN SQUID, pull the head and tentacles from the body pouch, then discard the clinging innards. Just below the eyes, cut off the tentacles and reserve them, discarding the eye portion. Squeeze the cut end of the tentacles to expel the hard, round beak; discard. Pull out and discard the long, transparent quill from inside the body pouch. Rinse the pouch and tentacles thoroughly under running cold water and peel the gray membrane from the pouch. Cut up or leave squid bodies whole as directed in individual recipes.

TAMARIND

The sweet-sour pulp from the seedpods of this tree native to India is popular as a flavoring. The long, brown seedpods resemble fava (broad) bean pods in shape. Tamarind paste and concentrate are also available.

TEQUILA

There are two basic categories of tequila: 100 percent blue agave, made entirely from the juice of the agave plant, bottled in Mexico, and the less expensive *mixto,* which may be blended with up to 40 percent grain alcohol and other additives. Check the label: any tequila that does not indicate it is 100 percent blue agave is a *mixto.* Within these two categories are four basic types. *Blanco,* or silver, a 100 percent blue agave tequila, is a high-quality clear beverage that must be bottled within 60 days of distillation. It has a fresh agave taste and distinctive aroma and is the choice of many connoisseurs. *Reposado* (rested) tequila, a 100 percent blue agave aged two months to one year, is a smoother drink than its blanco kin and is the favorite of most tequila drinkers. *Añejo* (aged) tequilas, 100 percent blue agave aged for at least one year and for up to five years, are the most subtle and expensive of the four types, and are usually sipped straight from snifters like a brandy. Finally, gold or *joven* (young) tequilas are made from 51 percent blue agave mixed with 49 percent other alcohols and aged less than two months to become a *mixto.* Cheaper to produce, it is probably the best seller outside of Mexico for mixed drinks.

TOMATILLOS

Resembling small, unripened green tomatoes, these fruits are actually members of the gooseberry family. They have a bracing, astringent flavor and tomato-like texture that is often featured in fresh and cooked salsas and in stews. The fruits are found fresh and are also available canned. Fresh tomatillos come encased in their parchmentlike calyx, which must be removed.

TO ROAST A TOMATILLO, line a heavy frying pan or griddle with heavy-duty aluminum foil to catch the fruit's juices and heat over medium heat. Roast the tomatillo, turning occasionally, until its skin is blistered and begins to blacken and its interior softens and begins to ooze. Carefully trim off only the most blackened parts of the skin before using the tomatillo.

TOMATOES

Since pre-Columbian times, tomatoes have been an essential ingredient in Mexican cuisine. Cooks rely on vine-ripened, sweet, deep red tomatoes and frequently roast them just until their skins are blackened to develop their flavor and make their flesh a bit more tender. To roast, see directions for tomatillos, above.

VINEGAR, PINEAPPLE

Pineapple is a common source for a mild commercial vinegar favored in Mexico. If you cannot find it, use equal amounts of apple cider vinegar, water, and rice vinegar.

TORTILLAS

Many markets sell good corn and flour tortillas, which are usually best to use in dishes where the tortillas are to be fried or cooked. To accompany a meal, nothing compares with homemade tortillas. The only specialized equipment you need is a tortilla press. The most common type is made of metal and has two round plates hinged at one side, so a small ball of *masa* can be flattened between them. To reheat tortillas, wrap stacks of 5 tortillas each in aluminum foil and warm in a 275°F (135°C) oven for 5–10 minutes. To reheat fewer, put the tortillas back on a *comal* or griddle and reheat for several seconds on each side. For making the crisp corn chips called *totopos,* use the thinnest corn tortillas you can find. If you prefer not to fry them, place them in a single layer on a baking sheet, top with a wire rack to prevent curling, and toast in a 300°F (150°C) oven for about 30 minutes.

CORN TORTILLAS

1 pound (500 g) freshly prepared tortilla masa *or 1¾ cups (9 oz/280 g)* masa harina *for tortillas*

1 teaspoon sea salt, or to taste

1 cup (8 fl oz/250 ml) plus 2 tablespoons warm water, if using masa harina

♛ If using fresh *masa,* put in a bowl and knead with the salt, adding a little warm water, if needed, to make a soft dough. If using *masa harina,* put in a bowl, add the warm water, and mix with your hands. Allow the dough to rest 5 minutes, then add the salt and knead for 1 minute. Shape into golf ball–sized balls, then cover with a damp kitchen towel or plastic wrap.

♛ Heat a large griddle, cast-iron frying pan, or *comal* over medium heat.

♛ Put 2 sheets of heavy plastic cut from a plastic storage bag inside the tortilla press. Put a *masa* ball between the sheets and gently press down the top plate of the press. Open the press and peel off the top sheet of plastic. Invert the tortilla onto one hand and remove the remaining plastic.

♛ Slide the tortilla off your hand—do not flip it—onto the hot griddle. Cook until the underside is freckled, about 30 seconds. Flip over and cook for another 20–30 seconds, then flip back to the first side for just a second. Transfer to a plate. As the tortillas are cooked, stack them on top of one another and cover with a kitchen towel to keep warm.

makes about 10 tortillas, each 5 inches (13 cm) in diameter

FLOUR TORTILLAS

3 cups (15 oz/470 g) unbleached all-purpose (plain) flour

1 teaspoon baking powder

½ cup (4 oz/125 g) flavorful lard (page 249) or vegetable shortening, at room temperature, cut into small pieces

1½ teaspoons sea salt

¾ cup (6 fl oz/180 ml) lukewarm water

♛ In a bowl, stir together the flour and the baking powder. Add the lard or shortening and rub in with your fingers until the mixture is the consistency of coarse meal. Dissolve the salt in the ¾ cup (6 fl oz/180 ml) water, then work it into the flour mixture, adding more water only if needed to dampen the flour. Mix well, form the dough into a ball, and knead in the bowl for several minutes. Cover with plastic wrap. Let rest for 30 minutes at room temperature.

♛ One at a time, break off pieces of the dough and roll into balls 1½ inches (4 cm) in diameter. Keep the unworked dough covered with plastic wrap. Preheat a griddle, large, heavy frying pan, or *comal* over medium heat. Place a ball on a lightly floured work surface and flatten it into a small round. Roll out, always working from the center and rotating the round until it forms a paper-thin tortilla about 7 inches (18 cm) in diameter.

♛ Lay the tortilla on the hot griddle or pan and cook, turning once, for about 30 seconds on each side. The tortilla should puff slightly and be flecked with brown. Wrap in a kitchen towel to keep warm or wrap in aluminum foil and keep warm in a low oven.

makes 18 tortillas, each 7 inches (18 cm) in diameter

TOSTADAS AND TOTOPOS

8 purchased thin corn tortillas, 4–6 inches (10–15 cm) in diameter

corn or peanut oil for frying

sea salt (optional)

♛ For *totopos*—chips, strips, or squares—stack the tortillas in 2 equal piles. Cut each pile into 4–6 triangular wedges, strips ¼ inch (6 mm) wide by 1 inch (2.5 cm) long, or small squares. Leave whole for tostadas. Spread in a single layer, cover with a heavy kitchen towel or wire rack to prevent curling, and let dry for at least several hours.

♛ Pour oil to a depth of 1 inch (2.5 cm) into a heavy frying pan and heat to 375°F (190°C) on a deep-frying thermometer. Add the whole tortillas one at a time and lift out as soon as their color deepens. Drain on absorbent paper. To make *totopos,* add the smaller pieces a few at a time and fry, tossing them, until light gold. Do not let them darken, or they will be bitter. Lift out and drain as for tostadas. Salt the *totopos,* if you like, while still hot.

♛ Cover with a dry kitchen towel and keep warm for up to 30 minutes in a 200°F (95°C) oven. Store for up to 1 day, in an airtight plastic bag. Recrisp, if necessary, for a few minutes in a 200°F (95°C) oven.

makes 8 tostadas or 3 cups (3 oz/90 g) totopos

INDEX

ACKNOWLEDGMENTS

Marilyn Tausend offers her warmest appreciation, as always, to her husband, Fredric, and to her many friends in Mexico who contributed to this book, especially Ana Elena Martinez, Ricardo Muñoz Zurita, María Dolores Torres Yzábal, and Diana Kennedy. Special thanks go to Kathie Vezzani and Susan Goldberg for their testing skills, and to Chris Keff, Jodi Olson, Claire Archibald, and Lupe Peach for their valued expertise.

Noel Barnhurst wishes to thank his photography assistant, Noriko Akiyama; Suzanne Cushman for her help with props; and Cokes-Diko in Santa Rosa. George Dolese wishes to thank Leslie Busch, food stylist, and Elisabet der Nederlanden, food styling assistant, as well as Iguana Ameramex and Artemisia for use of their props. Special thanks go to El Plato Design for generously providing the props shown on the cover.

Steven Rothfeld wishes to thank Andrea Fenton for falling back in time with him on the journey through Yucatán and for helping him communicate with all the kind souls along the way. Her knowledge of the area, her patience, and her exquisite taste made the experience an unforgettable one. Thanks also go to Marisela Castro of the Villas La Hacienda in Yucatán, Luis Fernando Sosa of the Casa Vieja hotel in Mexico City, and Alberto Chiarpei of Playa del Carmen.

Ignacio Urquiza wishes to give special thanks to Laura and to his sons, Ignacio, Sebastián, and Alonso, for their companionship during his travels. Thanks also go to assistants Rene and Rosi; to friend and partner Antonio Galvez for generously opening his home in Morelia; and to Marilyn Tausend.

Weldon Owen would like to thank Sandra Eisert, Linda Bouchard, Kathryn Meehan, Desne Border, and Ken DellaPenta. For assistance with the cover photography, we also thank Marie-Pierre Colle, Lucy Muñiz de Gevins, and the wonderful staff at Costa Careyes in Jalisco, Mexico. Thanks also go to our scenic photographers for their wonderful images of Mexico (t = top, c = center, b = bottom, br = bottom right): Via **Tony Stone Agency: Robert Frerck** 6–7; **Ted Wood** 12–13; **Steven Rothfeld** 1, 4–5, 26t, 30b, 70t, 106–107, 110t, 113c, 113b, 115t, 115b, 163b, 209br; all other scenic photography by **Ignacio Urquiza**.

TIME LIFE INC.
President and CEO: Jim Nelson

TIME-LIFE TRADE PUBLISHING
Vice President and Publisher: Neil Levin
Senior Director of Acquisitions and Editorial Resources: Jennifer Pearce
Director of Design: Kate L. McConnell
Project Manager: Jennifer L. Ward

WILLIAMS-SONOMA INC.
Founder and Vice-Chairman: Chuck Williams
Book Buyer: Cecilia Michaelis

WELDON OWEN INC.
Chief Executive Officer: John Owen
President: Terry Newell
Chief Operating Officer: Larry Partington
Vice President International Sales: Stuart Laurence
Creative Director: Gaye Allen
Associate Publisher: Hannah Rahill
Art Director: Jamie Leighton
Managing Editor: Judith Dunham
Copyeditor: Sharon Silva
Consulting Editor: Norman Kolpas
Production Director: Stephanie Sherman
Production Manager: Chris Hemesath
Editorial Assistant: Dana Goldberg
Prop and Style Director: George Dolese
Calligraphy: Jane Dill

THE SAVORING SERIES
conceived and produced by Weldon Owen Inc.
814 Montgomery Street, San Francisco, CA 94133
Telephone: 415-291-0100, Fax: 415-291-8841

In collaboration with Williams-Sonoma Inc.
3250 Van Ness Avenue, San Francisco, CA 94109

Separations by Colourscan Overseas Co. Pte. Ltd.
Printed in Singapore by Tien Wah Press (Pte.) Ltd.

pp 4–5: South of Cancún, the town of Tulúm offers visitors an intriguing mix of well-preserved ornate Maya architecture and palm-fringed beaches fronting the inviting waters of the Caribbean. **pp 6–7:** At Christmastime in Oaxaca, vendors line the *zócalo* near the city's towering cathedral. **pp 8–9:** In preparation for wedding festivities to be held the following day, two *señoras* in the Oaxacan town of Teotitlán del Valle tend a cauldron of slowly simmering *carnitas*. **pp 12–13:** Palenque, rising up from the foothills of the Chiapas highlands, is the most important archaeological site in the northern Maya region.

A WELDON OWEN PRODUCTION

First printed 2001
10 9 8 7 6 5 4 3 2 1

Library of Congress
Cataloging-in-Publication Data

Tausend, Marilyn.
Savoring Mexico: recipes and reflections on Mexican cooking/recipes and text, Marilyn Tausend; general editor, Chuck Williams; recipe photography, Noel Barnhurst; travel photography, Steven Rothfeld, Ignacio Urquiza; illustrations, Marlene McLoughlin.
p. cm -- (The Savoring series)
ISBN 0-7370-2049-0
1. Cookery, Mexican. I. Williams, Chuck, II. Title. III. Series.
TX716.M4 T38 2001
641.5972--dc21 00-061527
CIP